Lecture Notes in Computer Scie

T0238401

Commenced Publication in 1973
Founding and Former Series Editors:
Gerhard Goos, Juris Hartmanis, and Jan van Leeuwen

Editorial Board

Yuri Gurevich   Bertrand Meyer (Eds.)

Tests and Proofs

First International Conference, TAP 2007
Zurich, Switzerland, February 12-13, 2007
Revised Papers

 Springer

Volume Editors

Yuri Gurevich
Microsoft Research
Redmond, WA 98052, USA
E-mail: gurevich@microsoft.com

Bertrand Meyer
ETH Zurich
8092 Zurich, Switzerland
E-mail: Bertrand.Meyer@inf.ethz.ch

Library of Congress Control Number: 2007931908

CR Subject Classification (1998): D.2.4-5, F.3, D.4, C.4, K.4.4, C.2

LNCS Sublibrary: SL 2 – Programming and Software Engineering

ISSN	0302-9743
ISBN-10	3-540-73769-3 Springer Berlin Heidelberg New York
ISBN-13	978-3-540-73769-8 Springer Berlin Heidelberg New York

Springer is a part of Springer Science+Business Media

springer.com

© Springer-Verlag Berlin Heidelberg 2007
Printed in Germany

Typesetting: Camera-ready by author, data conversion by Scientific Publishing Services, Chennai, India
Printed on acid-free paper   SPIN: 12095476   06/3180   5 4 3 2 1 0

Preface

To prove the correctness of a program is to demonstrate, through impeccable mathematical techniques, that it has no bugs. To test a program is to run it with the expectation of discovering bugs.

These two paths to software reliability seem to diverge from the very start: if you have proved your program correct, it is fruitless to comb it for bugs; and if you are testing it, that surely must be a sign that you have given up on any hope to prove its correctness.

Accordingly, proofs and tests have, since the onset of software engineering research, been pursued by distinct communities using different kinds of techniques and tools. Dijkstra's famous pronouncement that tests can only show the presence of errors — in retrospect, perhaps one of the best advertisements one can imagine for testing, as if "only" finding bugs were not already a momentous achievement! — didn't help make testing popular with provers, or proofs attractive to testers.

And yet the development of both approaches leads to the discovery of common issues and to the realization that each may need the other. The emergence of model checking was one of the first signs that apparent contradiction may yield to complementarity; in the past few years an increasing number of research efforts have encountered the need for combining proofs and tests, dropping earlier dogmatic views of incompatibility and taking instead the best of what each of these software engineering domains has to offer.

TAP — Tests And Proofs — results from an effort to present and discuss some of the most interesting of today's research projects at the convergence of proofs and tests. The first event of its kind, TAP 2007 was held at ETH Zurich on February, 12–13 2007. The conference demonstrated that this is indeed a vibrant topic with exciting developments and the potential for much further growth and cross-fertilization between the ideas pursued by many groups.

We hope that you will agree that TAP 2007 advanced the understanding of two equally promising approaches to software quality, and that you will find in the results, collected in this volume, a source of insight inspiration, and new challenges.

The success of TAP was the result of contributions by many people. We are particularly grateful to the authors who submitted excellent papers; to the keynote speakers, Yuri Gurevich, Jonathan Ostroff and Yannis Smaragdakis; to the Program Committee members and outside referees who made it possible to conduct an effective process leading to a selection of high-quality papers.

The conference was sponsored by IFIP; we are particularly grateful to the support of IFIP Working Group WG2.3 on Programming Methodology (through its Chairperson, Pamela Zave, and all the other members who supported the idea of IFIP sponsorship) as well as TC2 (the Technical Committee on Programming, especially its Chair Robert Meersman and its then secretary Judith Bishop). ETH Zurich provided excellent facilities and impeccable organization.

The financial support of Microsoft Research was particularly useful and is gratefully acknowledged.

The organization, including the preparation of these proceedings, was made possible by the work of the Organizing Committee: Ilinca Ciupa, Manuel Oriol, Andreas Leitner, Claudia Günthart, and Lisa Liu without whom the conference could not have taken place.

Yuri Gurevich
Bertrand Meyer

Organization

Committees

Conference Chair

Bertrand Meyer, ETH Zurich, Switzerland and Eiffel Software, California, USA

Program Chair

Yuri Gurevich, Microsoft Research

Program Committee

Chandrasekhar Boyapati, University of Michigan, USA
Ed Clarke, Carnegie Mellon University, USA
Michael Ernst, MIT CSAIL, USA
Kokichi Futatsugi, JAIST, Japan
Tom Henzinger, EPFL, Switzerland
Daniel Kroening, ETH Zurich, Switzerland
Gary T. Leavens, Iowa State University, USA
Bertrand Meyer, ETH Zurich, Switzerland
Peter Müller, ETH Zurich, Switzerland
Huaikou Miao, Shanghai University, China
Jeff Offutt, George Mason University, USA
Jonathan Ostroff, York University, Canada
Benjamin Pierce, University of Pennsylvania, USA
Wolfram Schulte, Microsoft Research, USA
Yannis Smaragdakis, University of Oregon, USA
Tao Xie, North Carolina State University, USA
T.H. Tse, University of Hong kong, China

External Referees

Gerard Basler
Nicolas Blanc
Arindam Chakrabarti
Yuri Chebiriak
Adam Darvas
Weiqiang Kong
Masaki Nakamura
Martin Nordio
Kazuhiro Ogata
Joseph Ruskiewicz
Faraz Torshizi
Jianwen Xiang

Organizing Committee

Lisa (Ling) Liu, ETH Zurich, Switzerland
Ilinca Ciupa, ETH Zurich, Switzerland
Andreas Leitner, ETH Zurich, Switzerland
Claudia Günthart, ETH Zurich, Switzerland
Manuel Oriol, ETH Zurich, Switzerland

Sponsors

ETH Zurich
IFIP
Microsoft Research

Table of Contents

Combining Static and Dynamic Reasoning for Bug Detection

Yannis Smaragdakis[1] and Christoph Csallner[2]

[1] Department of Computer Science
University of Oregon, Eugene, OR 97403-1202, USA
`yannis@cs.uoregon.edu`
[2] College of Computing
Georgia Institute of Technology, Atlanta, GA 30332, USA
`csallner@gatech.edu`

Abstract. Many static and dynamic analyses have been developed to improve program quality. Several of them are well known and widely used in practice. It is not entirely clear, however, how to put these analyses together to achieve their combined benefits. This paper reports on our experiences with building a sequence of increasingly more powerful combinations of static and dynamic analyses for bug finding in the tools JCrasher, Check 'n' Crash, and DSD-Crasher. We contrast the power and accuracy of the tools using the same example program as input to all three.

At the same time, the paper discusses the philosophy behind all three tools. Specifically, we argue that trying to detect program errors (rather than to certify programs for correctness) is well integrated in the development process and a promising approach for both static and dynamic analyses. The emphasis on finding program errors influences many aspects of analysis tools, including the criteria used to evaluate them and the vocabulary of discourse.

1 Introduction

Programming is hard. As an intellectual task, it attempts to approximate real-world entities and conditions as abstract concepts. Since computers are unforgiving interpreters of our specifications, and since in software we can build up complexity with no physical boundaries, it is easy to end up with artifacts that are very hard to comprehend and reason about. Even moderate size programs routinely surpass in detail and rigor the most complex laws, constitutions, and agreements in the "real world". Not only can individual program modules be complex, but the interactions among modules can be hardly known. Most programmers work with only a partial understanding of the parts of the program that their own code interacts with. Faced with this complexity, programmers need all the help they can get. In industrial practice, testing has become significantly more intense and structured in the past decade. Additionally, numerous static analyses attempt to automatically certify properties of a program, or detect errors in it.

B. Meyer and Y. Gurevich (Eds.): TAP 2007, LNCS 4454, pp. 1–16, 2007.
© Springer-Verlag Berlin Heidelberg 2007

In the past few years, we have introduced three program analysis tools for finding program defects (bugs) in Java applications. *JCrasher* [3] is a simple, mostly dynamic analysis that generates JUnit test cases. Despite its simplicity it can find bugs that would require complex static analysis efforts. *Check 'n' Crash* [4] uses JCrasher as a post-processing step to the powerful static analysis tool ESC/Java. As a result, Check 'n' Crash is more precise than ESC/Java alone and generates better targeted test cases than JCrasher alone. *DSD-Crasher* [5] adds a reverse engineering step to Check 'n' Crash to rediscover the program's intended behavior. This enables DSD-Crasher to suppress false positives with respect to the program's informal specification. This property is more useful for bug-finding than for proving correctness, as we argue later.

In this paper, we report on our experience with these tools and present their comparative merits through a simple example. At the same time, we discuss in detail our philosophy in building them. All three tools are explicitly geared towards finding program errors and not towards certifying program correctness. Viewed differently, program analyses (regardless of the artificial static/dynamic distinction) can never accurately classify with full confidence all programs as either correct or incorrect. Our claim is that analyses that choose to be confident in their incorrectness classification (*sound for incorrectness*) are gaining ground over analyses that choose to be confident in their correctness classification (*sound for correctness*). We discuss this point next in more detail.

2   Bug Finding Musings

There are several dichotomies in program analysis. Clearly, analyses are often classified as *static* or *dynamic*. Additionally, analyses are often classified as *sound* or *complete*, or as *over-* and *under-approximate*. We next present some thoughts on these distinctions as well as the terminology they introduce.

2.1   Static and Dynamic Analysis

At first glance it may seem simple to classify an analysis as static or dynamic. The definition in the popular Wikipedia archive claims that:

> *Static code analysis* is the analysis of computer software that is performed without actually executing programs built from that software (analysis performed on executing programs is known as *dynamic analysis*).

This definition is not quite satisfying, however. Program execution only differs from program reasoning at the level of accuracy. This distinction is fairly artificial. First, there are languages where reasoning and execution are often thought of in the same terms (e.g., static analyses of Prolog programs often include steps such as "execute the program in a universe that only includes these values"). Second, even in imperative languages, it is often hard to distinguish between a virtual machine that executes the program and tools that reason about it at some level of abstraction (e.g., model checking tools, or symbolic execution analyses). Finally, it is hard to classify analyses that execute a program with known inputs. Known inputs are by definition "static", in standard terminology, and these analyses give information about the program without executing it under "real" conditions. Yet at the same time, since the program is executed, it is tempting to call such analyses "dynamic".

We believe that there is a continuum of analyses and the static vs. dynamic classification is not always easy to make. Our working definition is as follows:

An analysis is "dynamic" if it emphasizes control-flow accuracy over data-flow richness/generality, and "static" if it emphasizes data-flow richness/generality over control-flow accuracy.

There is always a trade-off between these trends. The undecidability of most useful program properties entails that one cannot make statements about infinitely many inputs without sacrificing some control-flow accuracy.

Although the definition is approximate, we believe that it serves a useful purpose. It reflects the intuitive understanding of the two kinds of analyses, while emphasizing that the distinction is arbitrary. A more useful way to classify analyses is in terms of *what* they claim not *how* they maintain the information that leads to their claims.

2.2   Soundness for Incorrectness

Analyses can be classified with respect to the set of properties they can establish with confidence. In mathematical logic, reasoning systems are often classified as *sound* and *complete*. A sound system is one that proves only true sentences, whereas a complete system proves all true sentences. In other words, an analysis is sound iff $provable(p) \Rightarrow true(p)$ and complete iff $true(p) \Rightarrow provable(p)$. Writing the definitions in terms of what the analysis claims, we can say:

Definition 1 (Sound). $claim_{true}(p) \Rightarrow true(p)$.

Definition 2 (Complete). $true(p) \Rightarrow claim_{true}(p)$.

When we analyze programs we use these terms in a qualified way. For instance, a type system (the quintessential "sound" static analysis) only proves correctness with respect to certain errors.

In our work, we like to view program analyses as a way to prove programs *incorrect*—i.e., to find bugs, as opposed to certifying the absence of bugs. If we escape from the view of program analysis as a "proof of correctness" and we also allow the concept of a "proof of incorrectness", our terminology can be adjusted. Useful program analyses give an answer for all programs (even if the analysis does not terminate, the programmer needs to interpret the non-termination-within-time-bounds in some way). In this setting, an analysis is sound for showing program correctness iff it is complete for showing program incorrectness. Similarly, an analysis is sound for showing program incorrectness iff it is complete for showing program correctness.

These properties are easily seen from the definitions. We have:

Lemma 1. *Complete for program correctness $\equiv$ Sound for program incorrectness.*

Proof. Complete for program correctness
$\equiv correct(p) \Rightarrow claim_{cor}(p)$
$\equiv \neg incorrect(p) \Rightarrow \neg claim_{incor}(p)$
$\equiv claim_{incor}(p) \Rightarrow incorrect(p)$
$\equiv$ Sound for program incorrectness

Lemma 2. *Complete for program incorrectness $\equiv$ Sound for program correctness.*

Proof. Complete for program incorrectness
$\equiv incorrect(p) \Rightarrow claim_{incor}(p)$
$\equiv \neg correct(p) \Rightarrow \neg claim_{cor}(p)$
$\equiv claim_{cor}(p) \Rightarrow correct(p)$
$\equiv$ Sound for program correctness

In the above, we considered the complementary use of the analysis, such that it claims incorrectness whenever the original analysis would not claim correctness. Note that the notion of "claim" is external to the analysis. An analysis either passes or does not pass programs, and "claim" is a matter of interpretation. Nevertheless, the point is that the same base analysis can be used to either soundly show correctness or completely show incorrectness, depending on how the claim is interpreted.

The interesting outcome of the above reasoning is that we can abolish the notion of "completeness" from our vocabulary. We believe that this is a useful thing to do for program analysis. Even experts are often hard pressed to name examples of "complete" analyses and the term rarely appears in the program analysis literature (in contrast to mathematical logic). Instead, we can equivalently refer to analyses that are "sound for correctness" and analyses that are "sound for incorrectness". An analysis does not have to be either, but it certainly cannot be both for interesting correctness properties.

Other researchers have settled on different conventions for classifying analyses, but we think our terminology is preferable. For instance, Jackson and Rinard call a static analysis "sound" when it is sound for correctness, yet call a dynamic analysis "sound" when it is sound for incorrectness [12]. This is problematic, since, as we argued, static and dynamic analyses form a continuum. Furthermore, the terminology implicitly assumes that static analyses always attempt to prove correctness. Yet, there are static analyses whose purpose is to detect defects (e.g., FindBugs by Hovemeyer and Pugh [11]). Another pair of terms used often are "over-" and "under-approximate". These also require qualification (e.g., "over-approximate for incorrectness" means the analysis errs on the safe side, i.e., is sound for correctness) and are often confusing.

2.3   Why Prove a Program Incorrect?

Ensuring that a program is correct is the Holy Grail of program construction. Therefore analyses that are sound for correctness have been popular, even if limited. For instance, a static type system guarantees the absence of certain kinds of bugs, such as attempting to perform an operation not defined for our data. Nevertheless, for all interesting properties, soundness for correctness implies that the analysis has to be pessimistic and reject perfectly valid programs. For some kinds of analyses this cost is acceptable. For others, it is not—for instance, no mainstream programming language includes sound static checking to ensure the lack of division-by-zero errors, exactly because of the expected high rejection rate of correct programs.

Instead, it is perfectly valid to try to be sound for incorrectness. That is, we may want to show that a program fails with full confidence. This is fairly expected for dynamic analysis tools, but it is worth noting that even static analyses have recently adopted this model. For instance, Lindahl and Sagonas's *success typings* [14] are an analogue of type systems but with the opposite trade-offs. Whereas a type system is sound for correctness and, hence, pessimistic, a success typing is sound for incorrectness and, thus, optimistic. If a success typing cannot detect a type clash, the program might work and is permitted. If the system does report a problem, then the problem is guaranteed to be real. This is a good approach for languages with a tradition of dynamic typing, where users will likely complain if a static type system limits expressiveness in the name of preventing unsafety.

Yet the most important motivation for analyses that are sound for incorrectness springs from the way analyses are used in practice. For the author of a piece of code, a sound-for-correctness analysis may make sense: if the analysis is too conservative, then the programmer probably knows how to rewrite the code to expose its correctness to the analysis. Beyond this stage of the development process, however, conservativeness stops being an asset and becomes a liability. A tester cannot distinguish between a false warning and a true bug. Reporting a non-bug to the programmer is highly counter-productive if it happens with any regularity. Given the ever-increasing separation of the roles of programmer and tester in industrial practice, high confidence in detecting errors is paramount.

This need can also be seen in the experience of authors of program analyses and other researchers. Several modern static analysis tools [10, 8, 11] attempt to find program defects. In their assessment of the applicability of ESC/Java, Flanagan et al. write [10]:

> "[T]he tool has not reached the desired level of cost effectiveness. In particular, users complain about an annotation burden that is perceived to be heavy, and about excessive warnings about non-bugs, particularly on unannotated or partially-annotated programs."

The same conclusion is supported by the findings of other researchers. Notably, Rutar et al. [19] examine ESC/Java2, among other analysis tools, and conclude that it can produce many spurious warnings when used without context information (method annotations). For five testees with a total of some 170 thousand non commented source statements, ESC warns of a possible null dereference over nine thousand times. Rutar et al., thus, conclude that "there are too many warnings to be easily useful by themselves."

To summarize, it is most promising to use analyses that are sound for correctness at an early stage of development (e.g., static type system). Nevertheless, for analyses performed off-line, possibly by third parties, it is more important to be trying to find errors with high confidence or even certainty. This is the goal of our analysis tools. We attempt to increase the soundness of existing analyses by combining them in a way that reduces the false error reports. Just like analyses that are sound for correctness, we cannot claim full correctness, yet we can claim that our tools are sound for incorrectness with respect to specific kinds of errors. Such soundness-for-incorrectness topics are analyzed in the next section.

3   Soundness of Automatic Bug Finding Tools

In practice, there are two levels of soundness for automatic bug finding tools. The lower level is being sound with respect to the execution semantics. This means that a bug report corresponds to a possible execution of a program module, although the input that caused this execution may not be one that would arise in normal program runs. We call this *language-level soundness* because it can be decided by checking the language specification alone. Many bug finding tools concern themselves only with this soundness level and several of them do not achieve it. A stronger form of soundness consists of also being sound with respect to the intended usage of the program. We call this *user-level soundness*, as it means that a bug report will be relevant to a real user of the program. This is an important distinction because developers have to prioritize their energy on the cases that matter most to their users. From their perspective, a language-level sound but user-level unsound bug report may be as annoying as one that is unsound at the language level.

We next examine these concepts in the context of the ESC/Java tool. Analysis with ESC/Java is an important step for our tools, and we can contrast them well by looking at what need they fill over the base ESC/Java bug finding ability.

3.1   Background: ESC/Java

The Extended Static Checker for Java (ESC/Java) [10] is a compile-time program checker that detects potential invariant violations. ESC/Java compiles the Java source code under test to a set of predicate logic formulae [10]. ESC/Java checks each method m in isolation, expressing as logic formulae the properties of the class to which the method belongs, as well as Java semantics. Each method call or invocation of a primitive Java operation in m's body is translated to a check of the called entity's precondition followed by assuming the entity's postcondition. ESC/Java recognizes invariants stated in the Java Modeling Language

(JML) [13]. (We consider the ESC/Java2 system [2]—an evolved version of the original ESC/Java, which supports JML specifications and recent versions of the Java language.) In addition to the explicitly stated invariants, ESC/Java knows the implicit pre- and postconditions of primitive Java operations—for example, array access, pointer dereference, class cast, or division. Violating these implicit preconditions means accessing an array out-of-bounds, dereferencing null pointers, mis-casting an object, dividing by zero, etc. ESC/Java uses the Simplify theorem prover [7] to derive error conditions for a method. We use ESC/Java to derive abstract conditions under which the execution of a method under test may terminate abnormally. Abnormal termination means that the method would throw a runtime exception because it violated the precondition of a primitive Java operation. In many cases this will lead to a program crash as few Java programs catch and recover from unexpected runtime exceptions.

Like many other static analysis based bug finding systems, ESC/Java is language-level unsound (and therefore also user-level unsound): it can produce spurious error reports because of inaccurate modeling of the Java semantics. ESC/Java is also unsound for correctness: it may miss some errors—for example, because ESC/Java ignores all iterations of a loop beyond a fixed limit.

3.2 Language-Level Soundness: Program Execution Semantics

Language-level soundness is the lower bar for automatic analysis tools. An analysis that is unsound with respect to execution semantics may flag execution paths that can never occur, under any inputs or circumstances. ESC/Java uses such an analysis. In the absence of pre-conditions and post-conditions describing the assumptions and effects of called methods, ESC/Java analyzes each method in isolation without taking the semantics of other methods into account. For instance, in the following example, ESC/Java will report potential errors for get0() < 0 and get0() > 0, although neither of these conditions can be true.

```
public int get0() {return 0;}

public int meth() {
  int[] a = new int[1];
  return a[get0()];
}
```

In Section 4.1 we describe how our tool Check 'n' Crash eliminates language-level unsoundness from ESC/Java warnings by compiling them to test cases. This enables us to confirm ESC/Java warnings by concrete program execution and suppress warnings we could not confirm. Check 'n' Crash could never generate a test case that confirms the above warning about method meth and would therefore never report such an language-level unsound case to the user.

3.3 User-Level Soundness: Informal Specifications

A user-level sound analysis has to satisfy not only language semantics but also user-level specifications. Thus, user-level soundness is generally impossible to achieve for automated tools since user-level specifications are mostly informal. Common forms of user-level specifications are code comments, emails, or web pages describing the program. Often these informal specifications only exist in the developers' minds. It is clear that user-level soundness implies language-level soundness, since the users care only about bugs that can occur in real program executions. So the user-level sound bug reports are a subset of the language-level sound bug reports.

ESC/Java may produce spurious error reports that do not correspond to actual program usage. For instance, a method `forPositiveInt(int i)` under test may be throwing an exception if passed a negative number as an argument. Even if ESC/Java manages to produce a language-level sound warning about this exception it cannot tell if this case will ever occur in practice. A negative number may never be passed as input to the method in the course of execution of the program, under any user input and circumstances. That is, an implicit precondition that the programmer has been careful to respect makes the language-level sound warning unsound at the user-level.

In Section 4.2 we describe how our tool DSD-Crasher tries to eliminate user-level unsoundness from ESC/Java warnings by inferring the preconditions of intended program behavior from actual program executions. This allows us to exclude cases that are not of interest to the user. In the above example we might be able to infer a precondition of `i > 0` for method `forPositiveInt(int i)`, which would allow ESC/Java to suppress the user-level unsound warning.

4   Turning ESC/Java into a Sound Tool for Automatic Bug Finding

Our two tools attempt to address the two levels of unsoundness exhibited by many static analysis tools like ESC/Java. Check 'n' Crash is a *static-dynamic* (SD) tool, which post-processes ESC/Java's output with a dynamic step. DSD-Crasher is a *dynamic-static-dynamic* (DSD) tool that adds a dynamic step at the beginning, feeding the results of this first dynamic step to the static-dynamic Check 'n' Crash.

4.1   Check 'n' Crash: Making ESC/Java Language-Level Sound

Check 'n' Crash [4] addresses the problem of ESC/Java language-level unsoundness. Figure 1 illustrates the key idea. Check 'n' Crash takes error conditions that ESC/Java infers from the testee, derives variable assignments that satisfy the error condition (using a constraint solver), and compiles them into concrete test cases that are executed with our JCrasher testing tool [3], to determine whether an error truly exists. Compared to ESC/Java alone, Check 'n' Crash's combination of ESC/Java with JCrasher eliminates language-level unsound warnings and improves the ease of comprehension of error reports through concrete Java counterexamples.

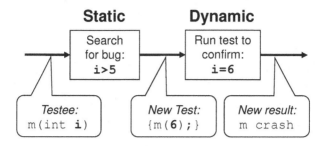

Fig. 1. Check 'n' Crash uses ESC/Java to statically check the testee for potential bugs. It then compiles ESC/Java's bug warnings to concrete test cases to eliminate those warnings that are unsound at the language level.

Check 'n' Crash takes as inputs the names of the Java files under test. It invokes ESC/Java, which derives error conditions. Check 'n' Crash takes each error condition as a constraint system over a method m's parameters, the object state on which m is executed, and other state of the environment. Check 'n' Crash extends ESC/Java by parsing and solving this constraint system. A solution is a set of variable assignments that satisfy the constraint system. Reference [4] discusses in detail how we process constraints over integers, arrays, and reference types in general. Once the variable assignments that cause the error are computed, Check 'n' Crash uses JCrasher to compile some of these assignments to JUnit [1] test cases. The test cases are then executed under JUnit. If the execution does not cause an exception, then the variable assignment was a false positive: no error actually exists. If the execution does result in the error predicted by ESC/Java, an error report is generated by Check 'n' Crash.

4.2 DSD-Crasher: Improving ESC/Java's User-Level Soundness

DSD-Crasher [5] attempts to address the user-level unsoundness of ESC/Java and Check 'n' Crash. This requires recognizing "normal" program inputs. Such informal specifications cannot generally be derived, therefore our approach is necessarily heuristic. DSD-Crasher employs the Daikon tool [9] to infer likely program invariants from an existing test suite. The results of Daikon are exported as JML annotations [13] that are used to guide Check 'n' Crash. Figure 2 illustrates the processing steps of the tool.

Daikon [9] tracks a testee's variables during execution and generalizes their observed behavior to invariants—preconditions, postconditions, and class invariants. Daikon instruments a testee, executes it (for example, on an existing test suite or during production use), and analyzes the produced execution traces. At each method entry and exit, Daikon instantiates some three dozen invariant templates, including unary, binary, and ternary relations over scalars, and relations over arrays (relations include linear equations, orderings, implication, and disjunction) [9, 17]. For each invariant template, Daikon tries several combinations of method parameters, method results, and object state. For example, it might

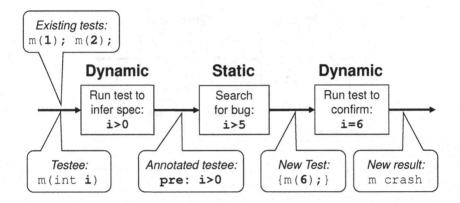

Fig. 2. DSD-Crasher adds a dynamic analysis step at the front to infer the intended program behavior from existing test cases. It feeds inferred invariants to Check 'n' Crash by annotating the testee. This enables DSD-Crasher to suppress bug warnings that are unsound at the user level.

propose that some method m never returns null. It later ignores those invariants that are refuted by an execution trace—for example, it might process a situation where m returned null and it will therefore ignore the above invariant. So Daikon summarizes the behavior observed in the execution traces as invariants and generalizes it by proposing that the invariants might hold in all other executions as well. Daikon can annotate the testee's source code with the inferred invariants as JML preconditions, postconditions, and class invariants. Daikon-inferred invariants are not trivially amenable to automatic processing, requiring some filtering and manipulation (e.g., for internal consistency according to the JML behavioral subtyping rules, see [6]).

In DSD-Crasher we chose to ignore Daikon-inferred invariants as requirements and only use them as assumptions. That is, we deliberately avoid searching for cases in which the method under test violates some Daikon-inferred precondition of another method it calls. (This would be against the spirit of the tool, as it would increase its user-level unsoundness, by producing extra error reports for violations of preconditions that were only heuristically derived.) Instead, we use Daikon-inferred invariants as assumptions. This restricts the number of legal program executions.

5   A Small Case Study

We next discuss in detail a small case study and present examples that illustrate the capabilities of each of our tools. Our test subject is Groovy, an open source scripting language that compiles to Java bytecode.

5.1 Setting

We used the Groovy 1.0 beta 1 version. Table 1 gives an overview of Groovy's main application classes and the subset used in our experiments. Its main application sources contain some eleven thousand non-commented source statements (NCSS) in 182 top-level classes and interfaces. We excluded any testees that led to processing problems in our tools. These were mainly low-level Groovy AST classes. The biggest processing problem was the Daikon component of DSD-Crasher running out of heap space. (We were using Daikon version 4.1.6, which is not the latest version.) The resulting set of testees consisted of 113 top-level types with a total of some five thousand NCSS. These declare a total of 952 methods and constructors, of which our testing tools analyze 757. (We analyze all public non-abstract methods declared by the testees as well as public constructors declared by non-abstract testees.) We used 603 of the unit test cases that came with the tested Groovy version. (The source code of the application and the unit tests are available from http://groovy.codehaus.org/ .) All experiments were conducted on a 2 GHz AMD Athlon 64 X2 dual core 3800+ with 4 GB of RAM, of which 1.5 GB were available for each experiment.

We believe that Groovy is a very representative test application for our kind of analysis: it is a medium-size, third party application. Importantly, its test suite was developed completely independently of our evaluation by the application developers, for regression testing and not for the purpose of yielding good Daikon invariants.

Table 1. Groovy testees

	Total	Analyzed
Top-level classes	171	105
Top-level interfaces	11	8
Non-commented source statements (NCSS)	11k	5k
Public non-abstract methods and constructors	1240	757
Other methods and constructors	441	195

5.2 Baseline: JCrasher

We include JCrasher in the experiment in order to provide a baseline with a dynamic tool. This serves to highlight the advantages of sophisticated static analyses. JCrasher picks its test cases at random, without analyzing the bodies of the methods under test. It examines the type information of a set of Java classes and constructs code fragments that will create instances of different types to test the behavior of public methods under random data. For instance, to test a method, JCrasher will attempt to create sample objects of the receiver type and of each of the argument types. JCrasher begins with a set of types for which it knows how to create instances—e.g., primitive types or types with public no-argument constructors. This set is expanded by finding constructors and methods

that accept as arguments only types that JCrasher knows how to create, and
the process continues until the space is exhaustively explored up to a certain
invocation depth. Once the size of the space is known, test cases are selected at
random, up to a user-defined number.

JCrasher attempts to detect bugs by causing the program under test to
"crash", i.e., to throw an undeclared runtime exception indicating an illegal class
cast, division by zero, or an illegal array expression. The output of JCrasher is a
set of test cases for JUnit (a popular Java unit testing tool) [1]. We only include
those JCrasher reports where a method under test throws such an exception directly (by performing an illegal Java language operation such as an illegal class
cast).

Table 2 shows the total runtime, which includes the steps of compiling the
testee classes (three seconds), generating test cases (about 20 seconds), compiling these test cases (about 40 seconds), and running them with our JUnit
extensions (about 30 seconds). We let JCrasher generate test cases that randomly combine methods and constructors up to a depth of two. We also limited
JCrasher to generate 100 thousand test cases per run. JCrasher picked these
test cases from some $7 * 10^8$ available cases. (This is not an unusually large
number: on the entire Groovy testee, JCrasher has $4 * 10^{12}$ test cases to pick
from.) In three out of five runs JCrasher got lucky and reported an array index
out of bounds exception in the last statement of the following parser look-ahead
method `org.codehaus.groovy.syntax.lexer.AbstractCharStream.la(int)`
when passed -1.

```
public char la(int k) throws IOException {
  if (k > buf.length)
    throw new LookAheadExhaustionException(k);
  int pos = this.cur + k - 1;
  pos %= buf.length;
  if (pos == this.limit) {
    this.buf[pos] = nextChar();
    ++this.limit;
    this.limit %= buf.length;
  }
  return this.buf[pos];
}
```

Clearly this report is language-level sound (like all JCrasher reports), as we
observed an actual runtime exception. On the other hand it is likely that this
report is not user-level sound since look-ahead functions are usually meant to be
called with a non-negative value.

5.3   Check 'n' Crash

For this and the DSD-Crasher experiment we used ESC/Java2 version 2.08a, set
the Simplify timeout to one minute, limited ESC/Java to generate ten warnings
per method under test, and configured ESC/Java to only search for potential

Table 2. Experience with running different automatic bug finding tools on Groovy. ESC/Java warnings may be language-level unsound. Each report generated by JCrasher, Check 'n' Crash, and DSD-Crasher is backed by an actual test case execution and therefore guaranteed language-level sound.

	Runtime [min:s]	ESC/Java warnings	Generated test cases	Reports confirmed by test cases
JCrasher	1:40	n/a	100,000	0.6
Check 'n' Crash	2:17	51	439	7.0
DSD-Crasher	10:31	47	434	4.0

runtime exceptions in public methods and constructors, stemming from illegal class cast, array creation and access, and division by zero. Table 2 shows that ESC/Java produced 51 reports. By manual inspection we classified 14 as language-level unsound and 32 as language-level sound (we hand-wrote eight test cases to convince ourselves of non-trivial sound cases.) We could not classify the remaining five warnings within three minutes each due to their complex control flow. The latter cases are the most frustrating to inspect since several minutes of investigation might only prove that the bug finding tool produced a spurious report. Of the 32 language-level sound warnings Check 'n' Crash could confirm seven. The remaining 24 warnings would require to generate more sophisticated test cases than currently implemented by Check 'n' Crash, supporting method call sequences and generating custom sub-classes that produce bug inducing behavior not found in existing sub-classes.

To our surprise ESC/Java did not produce a warning that would correspond to the runtime exception discovered by JCrasher. Instead it warned about a potential division by zero in the earlier statement `pos %= buf.length`. This warning is language-level unsound, though, since `buf.length` is never zero. `buf` is a private field, all constructors set it to an array of length five, and there are no other assignments to this field. This case is representative of the language-level unsound ESC/Java warnings we observed: a few methods access a private field or local variable and all of these accesses maintain a simple invariant. ESC/Java misses the invariant since it analyzes each method in isolation. When commenting out this line, ESC/Java's analysis reaches the final statement of the method and generates a warning corresponding to JCrasher's finding and Check 'n' Crash confirms this warning as language-level sound.

5.4   DSD-Crasher

For the 603 Groovy test cases Daikon gathers some 600 MB of execution traces, which it distills to 3.6 MB of compressed invariants. Of the total runtime, Daikon took 88 seconds to monitor the existing test suite, 204 seconds to infer invariants from the execution traces, and 130 seconds to annotate the testee sources with the derived invariants. The Check 'n' Crash component of DSD-Crasher used the remaining time.

In our working example, Daikon derived several preconditions and class invariants, including k >= 1 and this.cur >= 0, for the look-ahead method described above. This supports our initial estimate that JCrasher and Check 'n' Crash reported a user-level unsound warning about passing a negative value to this method. The remainder of this example requires a modified version of Daikon since the method under test implements an interface method. Daikon can produce a contradictory invariant in this case—see [6] for a detailed discussion of dealing correctly with JML behavioral subtyping. For this example we manually added a precondition of false to the interface method declaration. When we again comment out the line pos %= buf.length; (but re-using the previously derived invariants, including k >= 1 and this.cur >= 0) ESC/Java reaches the offending statement but uses the derived precondition to rule out the case. Thus, ESC/Java no longer produces the user-level unsound warning and DSD-Crasher does not produce a corresponding report.

6   Related Work

There is clearly an enormous amount of work in the general areas of test case generation and program analysis. We discuss representative recent work below.

There are important surveys that concur with our estimate that an important problem is not just reporting potential errors, but minimizing false positives so that inspection by humans is feasible. Rutar et al. [19] evaluate five tools for finding bugs in Java programs, including ESC/Java 2, FindBugs [11], and JLint. The number of reports differs widely between the tools. For example, ESC reported over 500 times more possible null dereferences than FindBugs, 20 times more than JLint, and six times more array bounds violations than JLint. Overall, Rutar et al. conclude: "The main difficulty in using the tools is simply the quantity of output."

AutoTest by Meyer et al. is a closely related automatic bug finding tool [16]. It targets the Eiffel programming language, which supports invariants at the language level in the form of contracts [15]. AutoTest generates random test cases like JCrasher, but uses more sophisticated test selection heuristics and makes sure that generated test cases satisfy given testee invariants. It can also use the given invariants as its test oracle. Our tools do not assume existing invariants since, unlike Eiffel programmers, Java programmers usually do not annotate their code with formal specifications.

The commercial tool Jtest [18] has an automatic white-box testing mode that generates test cases. Jtest generates chains of values, constructors, and methods in an effort to cause runtime exceptions, just like our approach. The maximal supported depth of chaining seems to be three, though. Since there is little technical documentation, it is not clear to us how Jtest deals with issues of representing and managing the parameter-space, classifying exceptions as errors or invalid tests, etc. Jtest does, however, seem to have a test planning approach, employing static analysis to identify what kinds of test inputs are likely to cause problems.

Xie and Notkin [20] present an iterative process for augmenting an existing test suite with complementary test cases. They use Daikon to infer a specification of the testee when executed on a given test suite. Each iteration consists of a static and a dynamic analysis, using Jtest and Daikon. In the static phase, Jtest generates more test cases, based on the existing specification. In the dynamic phase, Daikon analyzes the execution of these additional test cases to select those which violate the existing specification—this represents previously uncovered behavior. For the following round the extended specification is used. Thus, the Xie and Notkin approach is also a DSD hybrid, but Jtest's static analysis is rather limited (and certainly provided as a black box, allowing no meaningful interaction with the rest of the tool). Therefore this approach is more useful for a less directed augmentation of an existing test suite aiming at high testee coverage—as opposed to our more directed search for fault-revealing test cases.

7   Conclusions

We discussed our thoughts on combinations of static and dynamic reasoning for bug detection, and presented our experience with our tools, JCrasher, Check 'n' Crash, and DSD-Crasher. We argued that static and dynamic analyses form a continuum and that a "sound for correctness"/"sound for incorrectness" terminology is more illuminating than other conventions in the area. We believe that tools that are sound for incorrectness (i.e., complete for correctness) will gain ground in the future, in the entire range of static and dynamic analyses.

Our DSD-Crasher, Check 'n' Crash, and JCrasher implementations are available in source and binary form at http://code.google.com/p/check-n-crash/ and http://code.google.com/p/jcrasher/

Acknowledgments

We thank Tao Xie who offered extensive comments and contributed to early discussions about the generation of test cases from Daikon invariants. We gratefully acknowledge support by the NSF under grant CCR-0238289.

References

[1] Beck, K., Gamma, E.: Test infected: Programmers love writing tests. Java Report 3(7), 37–50 (1998)
[2] Cok, D.R., Kiniry, J.R.: ESC/Java2: Uniting ESC/Java and JML: Progress and issues in building and using ESC/Java2. Technical Report NIII-R0413, Nijmegen Institute for Computing and Information Science (May 2004)
[3] Csallner, C., Smaragdakis, Y.: JCrasher: An automatic robustness tester for Java. Software—Practice & Experience 34(11), 1025–1050 (2004)
[4] Csallner, C., Smaragdakis, Y.: Check 'n' Crash: Combining static checking and testing. In: ICSE 2005, pp. 422–431. ACM, New York (2005)

[5] Csallner, C., Smaragdakis, Y.: DSD-Crasher: A hybrid analysis tool for bug find-ing. In: Proc. ACM SIGSOFT International Symposium on Software Testing and Analysis (ISSTA), pp. 245–254. ACM Press, New York (2006)

[6] Csallner, C., Smaragdakis, Y.: Dynamically discovering likely interface invariants. In: ICSE. Proc. 28th International Conference on Software Engineering, Emerging Results Track, pp. 861–864. ACM Press, New York (2006)

[7] Detlefs, D., Nelson, G., Saxe, J.B.: Simplify: A theorem prover for program check-ing. Technical Report HPL-2003-148, Hewlett-Packard Systems Research Center (July 2003)

[8] Engler, D., Musuvathi, M.: Static analysis versus software model checking for bug finding. In: Steffen, B., Levi, G. (eds.) VMCAI 2004. LNCS, vol. 2937, pp. 191–210. Springer, Heidelberg (2004)

[9] Ernst, M.D., Cockrell, J., Griswold, W.G., Notkin, D.: Dynamically discovering likely program invariants to support program evolution. IEEE Transactions on Software Engineering 27(2), 99–123 (2001)

[10] Flanagan, C., Leino, K.R.M., Lillibridge, M., Nelson, G., Saxe, J.B., Stata, R.: Ex-tended static checking for Java. In: Proc. ACM SIGPLAN Conference on Program-ming Language Design and Implementation (PLDI), pp. 234–245. ACM Press, New York (2002)

[11] Hovemeyer, D., Pugh, W.: Finding bugs is easy. In: Companion to the 19th ACM SIGPLAN Conference on Object-Oriented Programming Systems, Languages, and Applications (OOPSLA), pp. 132–136. ACM Press, New York (2004)

[12] Jackson, D., Rinard, M.: Software analysis: A roadmap. In: Proc. Conference on The Future of Software Engineering, pp. 133–145. ACM Press, New York (2000)

[13] Leavens, G.T., Baker, A.L., Ruby, C.: Preliminary design of JML: A behavioral interface specification language for Java. Technical Report TR98-06y, Department of Computer Science, Iowa State University (June 1998)

[14] Lindahl, T., Sagonas, K.: Practical type inference based on success typings. In: PPDP. Proc. 8th ACM SIGPLAN Symposium on Principles and Practice of Declarative Programming, pp. 167–178. ACM Press, New York (2006)

[15] Meyer, B.: Object-Oriented Software Construction, 2nd edn. Prentice Hall PTR, Englewood Cliffs (1997)

[16] Meyer, B., Ciupa, I., Leitner, A., Liu, L.: Automatic testing of object-oriented software. In: van Leeuwen, J., Italiano, G.F., van der Hoek, W., Meinel, C., Sack, H., Plášil, F. (eds.) SOFSEM 2007. LNCS, vol. 4362, Springer, Heidelberg, 2007 (to appear)

[17] Nimmer, J.W., Ernst, M.D.: Invariant inference for static checking: An empiri-cal evaluation. In: Proc. 10th ACM SIGSOFT International Symposium on the Foundations of Software Engineering (FSE), pp. 11–20. ACM Press, New York (2002)

[18] Parasoft Inc.: Jtest. October 2002 (accessed March 2007), http://www.parasoft.com/

[19] Rutar, N., Almazan, C.B., Foster, J.S.: A comparison of bug finding tools for Java. In: ISSRE. Proc. 15th International Symposium on Software Reliability Engineering, pp. 245–256. IEEE Computer Society Press, Los Alamitos (2004)

[20] Xie, T., Notkin, D.: Tool-assisted unit test selection based on operational viola-tions. In: ASE. Proc. 18th IEEE International Conference on Automated Software Engineering, pp. 40–48. IEEE Computer Society Press, Los Alamitos (2003)

Testable Requirements and Specifications

Jonathan S. Ostroff and Faraz Ahmadi Torshizi

Department of Computer Science and Engineering, York University,
4700 Keele St.,Toronto, ON M3J 1P3, Canada
{jonathan,faraz}@cse.yorku.ca

Abstract. A design *specification* is the artifact intermediate between implemented code and the customer *requirements*. In this paper we argue that customer requirements and design specifications should be testable and testable early in the design cycle leading to early detection of requirement and specification errors. The core idea behind early testable requirements is that the problem is described before we search for a solution that can be tested against the problem description. We also want the problem description to drive the design. We provide a method for describing early testable requirements and specifications and a support tool called ESpec. ESpec allows for the description of testable requirements via Fit tables as well as testable design specifications via contracts written in Eiffel using mathematical models following the single model principle. The tool can mechanically check the requirements and specifications.

1   Introduction

Informal surveys such as those done by the Standish Group [5] show that a minority of software development finish on time and within budget. Many projects fail entirely and have to be abandoned. In their recipe for success the Standish group recommends that shareholders develop the ability to clearly articulate requirements and translate these requirements between the business people (the customers) and the technical people (software developers).

The software developer faces many difficulties in writing and communicating requirements. As one IT specialist wrote [2]:

> I was once in a meeting in which a team had to review a business specification for an application enhancement. The meeting had been scheduled for one hour. It lasted for three painful hours, because the team was stumbling over each paragraph: Verbosity, ambiguity and an avalanche of bullets conspired to hide the meaning of those phrases. ...
>
> UML might be king in academic circles, but English is still the preferred and most-used tool in the field when it comes to communication between business users and developers. I have recently heard a tool vendor trying to score points for his product based on the fact that the product uses plain English, not UML, in order to capture requirements.

B. Meyer and Y. Gurevich (Eds.): TAP 2007, LNCS 4454, pp. 17–40, 2007.

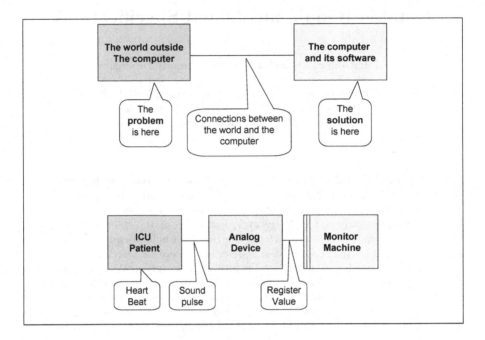

Fig. 1. The Computer (the Machine) and the World Outside the Computer (Problem Domain)

In this paper we use the words "requirements" and "specifications" in the sense of Jackson [7]. A design *specification* is the artifact intermediate between implemented code and the customer *requirements*. We argue that customer requirements and design specifications should be testable and testable early in the design cycle leading to early detection of requirement and specification errors. We provide a method for describing early testable requirements and specifications and a support tool called ESpec. ESpec allows for the description of testable requirements via Fit tables adapted from [8] for Eiffel. Testable design specifications are described via contracts written in Eiffel using mathematical models following the single model principle. The tool can mechanically check the requirements and specifications.

2   Requirements and Specifications

Consider the diagram in Fig. 1 illustrating the problem of measuring vital signs such as the heartbeat of a patient in an ICU taken from [7]. There are four different descriptions of the patient monitoring system.

P – Problem Domain: A patient's heart can beat from 0 to 170 beats per second (predetermined by human physiology).

R – Requirement: Monitor the patient's heart beat and sound an alarm if it is outside of the range from 60 to 100 beats per minute.

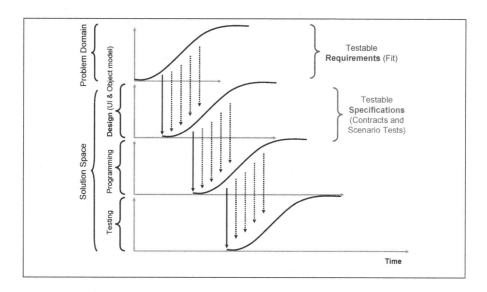

Fig. 2. The role of Early Testable Requirements and Specifications in the design cycle

S – Specification: Alarm-Register := False when the Sound-Pulse-Register is outside the range hexadecimal 3C to hexadecimal 64.

C – Computer Code: The machine code that implements specification **S**.

The central requirement **R** is to monitor the heartbeat – not the sound pulses or the register values in the machine (i.e. the implemented computer code). The requirements are the effects in the problem domain that your customer wants the machine to guarantee. The requirements are all about the phenomena of the problem domain (not the machine). The predicate **P** described the fixed constraints emerging from the problem domain.

The specification **S** refers to phenomena shared by the problem domain and the machine. **S** specifies a design solution that we hope satisfies requirements **R**. Finally, **C** is a description of the computer code needed to implement the design specification **S**. As mentioned earlier, the design specification is the artifact intermediate between implemented code and the customer requirements.

Our core idea behind early testable requirements and specification is as follows. Requirements should be testable as early as possible so that the problem is stated before we search for a solution. We also want the problem to drive the design. We provide a method for describing early testable requirements and specifications and a support tool called ESpec.

ESpec allows for the description of testable requirements via Fit tables adapted from [8] for Eiffel. Testable design specifications are described via contracts written in Eiffel using mathematical models following the single model principle. The tool can mechanically check the requirements and specifications.

Our method and tool does not require a rational software development process as described earlier. The developer may follow agile [1] or big design up front methodologies. Our method does provide a framework for describing testable requirements that can be written as early as possible in the design cycle as shown in Fig. 2.

A rational software development might proceed as follows:

- Elicit and document the Requirements R of the customer in terms of the phenomena in the problem domain. Constraints of the problem domain are described by P.
- From the Requirements, derive a Specification S for the software code that must be developed.
- From the Specification, derive a machine C (the code).

We may describe the development process as follows [10]:

---

1. **Specification correctness:** $P \wedge S \rightarrow R$
2. **Implementation correctness:** $C \rightarrow S$
3. **System correctness:** From (1) and (2) conclude that: $P \wedge C \rightarrow R$

The first equation (specification correctness) asserts that we are developing the right product, i.e. the one desired by the customer as described by R. The second equation (implementation correctness) asserts that the product is being developed correctly, i.e. the implemented code satisfies the design specification.

The third formula (system correctness) is a consequence of formulas (1) and (2). It asserts that the code working in a problem domain P satisfies the customer requirements.

3   Fit Tables as Testable Requirements

How do we make requirements testable? In this section we show how Fit tables may be used to make requirements testable early in the design cycle. We use a small application as a running example in this section and the sequel.

3.1   Informal Requirements for a Chat Application

Suppose our customer is a company that needs a specialized chat application allowing employees to communicate with each other. Chat rooms can be developed for technical support or discussions on various administrative issues. Some of the informal requirements include:

[R1] A chat server has an Administrator and a public room called the Lobby.
[R2] A user may connect to the chat server initially landing in the Lobby.
[R3] A user may add or remove public or private rooms thus becoming the owner of that room.

[R4] An owner may permit or reject other users from accessing rooms.

[R5] A user may enter or exit rooms as allowed by the owner of the room.

[R6] After entering an allowed room, a user may read and post messages in the room.

The requirements are expressed in terms of the phenomena of the problem domain such as chat rooms like the Lobby, users such as the Administrator and owner relationships between users and rooms. Phenomena of the solution domain such as linked lists of users or binary search routines for finding users in the lists should not be part of the requirements.

3.2 A Fit Table to Test the First Requirement

How do we convert the informal requirements into testable requirements? We can make the first requirement testable with the simple Fit table shown in Table 1.

As described in [8], there are three basic tables types: Column, Action and Row. A testable requirements document may contain informal text interleaved with an arbitrary number of Row, Column and Action tables.

For requirement R1 we use an Action table. An Action table checks that a sequence of actions performed on an application works as expected. In the sequel we will also see examples of Row tables. Software developers may also use the Fit framework to specify their own table types.

In the first row of Action table 1 the Customer provides an arbitrary title such as: "R1: Chat Server Setup". In the first column of the table we can see keywords (**start**, **check**, **enter** and **press**) which denote the type of action performed by each row.

The keyword **start** is used to initiate the chat server. Usually there is only one **start** per Action table. Thus the second row of the table starts the business logic for the chat server. The next Action table in the same document will use the current chat server unless there is another **start** in that table (which would re-initialize the server business logic).

The keyword used in the third row is **check**. It checks that a property (designated by the descriptive text in the second column) satisfies some value (specified by the text in the third column). The action in the third row thus states that "Is server running?" must have the value "True".

Properties of the business logic are specified in the second column of the Action table. The customer may use any descriptive string (say *Str*) to denote a property (say *Prop*) in the second column. Once *Str* is specified then it always denotes the same property *Prop* throughout this table and any other Action table. Values in the third column of the Action table are interpreted by the Fit framework as booleans, integers, reals, characters, strings and arrays of the basic types. In Action table 1, "True" is a boolean, "1" is an integer, and "Admin" is a string. As far as the customer is concerned, a value is just a descriptive string.

Consider the check for the property "Is [user] in [room]?" in row 9 of Action table 1. We could have used the descriptive string "Is Admin in Lobby?" for the property. However, that limits this description to the specific property involving

Table 1. Chat Action table for requirement R1

- Start the chat server.
- Check that the chat server is up and running.
- Check that there is one room (the Lobby).
- Check that there is one user (the Administrator).
- Set [user] to "Admin" and [room] to "Lobby".
- Check that [user] "Admin" is connected and in [room] "Lobby".
- Check that the owner of the "Lobby" is "Admin".

R1: Chat Server Setup		
start	Chat Server	
check	Is server running?	True
check	Number of server rooms	1
check	Number of server users	1
enter	[user]	Admin
enter	[room]	Lobby
check	Is [user] connected?	True
check	Is [user] in [room]?	True
check	[room]'s owner	Admin

the specific individuals Admin and Lobby. We would prefer to check for the more generic property that some arbitrary user is in a given room. We use the keyword **enter** to associate a value with a parameter of the property (like an argument of a query). Thus at row 6, the customer associates the value "Admin" with the parameter "[user]". The customer could have chosen "some user" rather than "[user]" in the second column or some other descriptive string. We use the convention of surrounding the parameter with square brackets so that it stands out as a parameter of the property, e.g. in the property "Is [user] in [room]?" at line 9 the parameters are "[user]" and "[room]" entered at lines 6 and 7 respectively.

The keyword **press** is not used in Table 1 but it will be used in the sequel. This keyword denotes an action (like pressing a button) that effects some change in the business logic. The keyword **press** may be used together with **enter** to denote a parameterized action, e.g. we may use **press** together with the parameterized action "[user] adds [room]" as in Action table in Fig. 13. This means that user "Bob" adds the room "Technical Support" to the chat application, and "Bob" is now the owner of the room.

How does the developer satisfy the requirements specified in the Action table? The developer will need to write two kinds of classes: *Fixture* classes and classes of the business logic (see Fig. 3). Fixture code acts as a glue code or bridge between the customer-provided requirements and the business logic. The ESpec

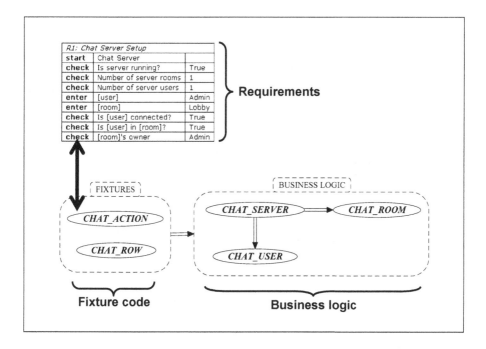

Fig. 3. Relationship between Fit tables, Fixture classes and Business logic

tool provides fixture libraries that allow the developer to easily develop such fixture classes. Fit framework can then use the developer written fixture classes to parse the requirements document, extract the Row Column and Action tables, interpret the tables and invoke the relevant business logic and then reflect the results of running the business logic back to the tables in the requirements document. The rows that succeed are coloured green and those that fail are coloured red.

For example, to run Table 1, the developer writes an Action Fixture class CHAT_ACTION that binds developer defined routines (in the business logic) to the properties in the table. These routines call the appropriate features of the business logic. ESpec takes care of the rest of the processing as explained in more detail in [14].

3.3   Implementation Correctness

Fit tables make the requirements testable. However, at this point, if we run the Fit table in the requirements document it will fail. For example, the checks associated with the value cells in Table 1 will display as red indicating that the requirement is not yet satisfied. As yet there is no implementation code and so we expect failure. Our goal is now to specify a *design* that will satisfy the requirements (i.e. cause each test row in the table to pass).

```
 1    scenario_test: BOOLEAN is
 2        local
 3            server: CHAT_SERVER
 4            mike, anna: CHAT_USER
 5            mike_room: CHAT_ROOM
 6            users: LIST[CHAT_USER]
 7            rooms: LIST[CHAT_ROOM]
 8        do
 9            -- create the chat server and check it
10            create server.make
11            users := server.users
12            rooms := server.rooms
13            check server.user_count = 1 end
14            check server.room_count = 1 end
15
16            -- create 2 users Mike and Anna and connect them to the server
17            create mike.make ("Mike")
18            create anna.make ("Anna")
19            server.connect (mike)
20            server.connect (anna)
21            check server.user_count = 3 and server.room_count = 1 end
22            check mike.room = server.lobby and anna.room = server.lobby end
23            check users.has(mike) and users.has(anna) end
24
25            -- Mike creates and adds a room "Technical Support"
26            mike_room := mike.create_room ("Technical Support")
27            mike.add_room (mike_room)
28            check server.room_count = 2 end
29            check not mike_room.is_private end
30            check rooms.has(mike_room) end
31
32            -- Mike changes the status of his room to private
33            mike.set_private ("Technical Support")
34            check mike_room.is_private end
35            check not server.is_allowed (anna, "Technical Support") end
36
37            -- Mike allows Anna to join the Technical Support room
38            mike.allow_user ("Anna", "Technical Support")
39            check server.is_allowed (anna, "Technical Support") end
40            Result := True
41        end
```

Fig. 4. Scenario Test to start a server, connect users, create a room and set the room permissions

How does the developer specify implementation code that will satisfy the requirements? It is unlikely that the code can be developed all at once. The requirements are described at a relatively high level in terms of the phenomena of the problem domain. Code will have to be developed in small chunks to build up the functionality needed to provide a solution. This functionality is the *design* which is intermediate between the code and the requirements. The Fit table requirements were expressed in terms of the phenomena of the problem domain. The design will be specified in terms of the phenomena of the machine (solution space), i.e. we must specify the relevant classes and features that will solve the problem posed by the requirements.

How do we specify testable designs? We will use a combination of Contracts and Scenario Tests to specify the design. In this section we illustrate Scenario

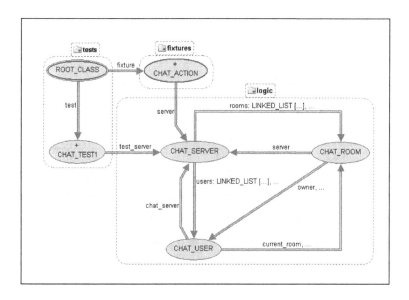

Fig. 5. Design of the chat application as a BON class diagram

Tests and in the next section we will use Contracts. This should not be taken as a description of a step-by-step software development methodology. In the actual development, developers may use any combination of coding, Scenario Tests, contracts and other development techniques in whatever order they choose. Our contribution is to provide a method and tool for specifying designs as early as possible in the design cycle and mechanically testing implementations against the design specification.

Consider the Scenario Test in Fig. 4 expressed in the unit testing framework developed for Eiffel [11]. A Scenario Test is written the same way as a unit test but instead of testing only one unit of functionality, it tests the collaboration between various elements in the business logic. The Scenario Test in Fig. 4 specifies a collaboration between classes CHAT_SERVER, CHAT_ROOM, and CHAT_USER. The test specifies specific features in CHAT_SERVER such as:

- users: LIST[CHAT_USER]
- rooms: LIST[CHAT_ROOM]
- add_room (a_user: CHAT_USER)

If all the classes and features in the Scenario Test are added, the project will compile and the design illustrated in the BON class diagram in Fig. 5 is generated automatically. The class diagram presents the design so far (classes and feature signatures, but not yet code in the bodies of the features).

The ESpec quality workbench will run all the Scenario Tests and show which ones fail with a red bar. The Scenario Test will fail if (a) the collaboration between the various elements fails to satisfy the specified checks or to produce

Table 2. Result of running Table 1 with implementation or contract errors in the business logic. Light grey indicates tests that succeed (green) and dark grey tests that fail (red).

R1: Chat Server Setup		
start	Chat Server	
check	Is server running?	True
check	Number of server rooms	1
check	Number of server users	1
enter	[user]	Admin
enter	[room]	Lobby
check	Is [user] connected?	True *Expected* False *Actual*
check	Is [user] in [room]?	True *Postcondition violated.* *CHAT_SERVER get_user @10 server_has_it:* *<00000000018BC810> Postcondition violated. Fail* -- *CHAT_SERVER get_user @3* *<00000000018BC810> Routine failure. Fail*
check	[room]'s owner	Admin

the anticipated results, or (b) the contracts fail while executing the tests. At this point we have not specified any contracts so failures will be of type (a).

Scenario Tests (as in Fig. 4) thus do two things for us: (1) They specify the design, in a (2) mechanically testable manner. Contracts will likewise specify aspects of the design. With runtime assertion checking turned on the implementations are also checked against the contracts.

There is thus a synergy between the contracts and Scenario Tests. They both specify aspects of the design and both are mechanically checkable. Contracts act as test amplifiers, i.e. when we execute the tests, all contracts will also be executed and tested.

3.4 Specification Correctness

Scenario Tests helped us to specify aspects of the design in an automatically testable format. When these tests run successfully, we obtain a certain amount of confidence that the implementation satisfies the specification. However, there is yet no guarantee that the specified design satisfies the requirements as described in the Fit tables. We may be designing the product right – yet, we still do not know if we have the right product!

How do we test that our specified design satisfies the requirements? We do this by hooking up the Fit tables to our business logic for the chat application and running the Fit table tests. If we run Action table 1 with an incorrect implementation or design, we get error results of the kind shown in Table 2.

Two types of errors are shown in Table 2. The first error (row 8 shown in dark gray) indicates that the routine to check if a user is connected is not doing what

Table 3. Result of running Table 1 after fixing the business logic. All tests succeed (light grey = green).

R1: Chat Server Setup		
start	Chat Server	
check	Is server running?	True
check	Number of server rooms	1
check	Number of server users	1
enter	[user]	Admin
enter	[room]	Lobby
check	Is [user] connected?	True
check	Is [user] in [room]?	True
check	[room]'s owner	Admin

was expected (the value "True" was expected but the actual value returned by the business logic was "False"). We refer to these as *category 1 errors*. Category 1 errors usually indicate that the design was not specified correctly. The implemented code was correct in a sense that it did not trigger any contract violations or Scenario Test errors yet it failed to satisfy the customer requirements. The design specification (via Scenario Tests and contracts) is either incomplete or even incorrect.

The second error (row 9 shown in gray) indicates a postcondition failure in the business logic (in **CHAT_SERVER.get_user**). We refer to these type of errors as *category 2 errors*. Category 2 errors usually indicate an implementation problem in the business logic (i.e., the implementation failed to satisfy its contracts).

We will discuss the differences between these types of errors in the sequel. The result of running Action table 1 (after all fixes) is shown in Table 3. All the cells in the table are shown in light gray (green) indicating that all the Fit tests succeed.

4   Writing Complete Modular Contracts

In the previous section we used Test Scenarios to write testable specifications. In this section we explore the use of contracts for writing testable specifications.

Design by Contract (DbC) is a well-know method for specifying the obligations and benefits of the client of a module (class) and its supplier. Languages such as Eiffel, ESC/Java [4] and Spec# [3] follow the single model principle [12], i.e. specifications (contracts) and implementation details are both an integral part of the program text itself thus also allowing the implementation to be mechanically checked against the specification. The features of a class are described by expressive preconditions, postconditions and class invariants and these contracts can be tested at runtime by checking that the feature implementations satisfy the contracts.

However, the contracting facilities of these languages do not yet allow for complete contracts. We illustrate this lack and describe the use of an implemented mathematical modelling library (ML) for Eiffel that facilitates fully descriptive

```
class CHAT_SERVER ...

feature {NONE} —— private features

    rooms: LIST[CHAT_ROOM]
    users: LIST[CHAT_USER]

feature —— public features

    lobby: CHAT_ROOM
    admin: CHAT_USER

    connect (u: USER) is
        require
            a_user /= Void
            —— user u not already connected
        do
            ...
        ensure
            —— add u to the existing users in the lobby
        end

end
```

Fig. 6. Incomplete contract for routine connect

contracts following the single model principle so that the full contracts are part of the program text.

Consider the contract for the routine connect in class CHAT_SERVER in Fig. 6. This feature allows a user u to connect to the server. A new user is not initially connected. In the precondition of routine connect we would like to specify that a new user u is not yet connected, i.e. is not yet in our list of users. In the postcondition, we would like to specify that the new user u is now added to the existing users of the Lobby.

How do we specify these contracts? One possibility is to use the private implementation data structures users and rooms which are linked lists of chat rooms and chat users (respectively) to write the contracts. This is not ideal because the implementation is low level and might change. We would like the specification of the feature to be independent of low level implementation details. In addition, not all classes are effective. Some classes are deferred (abstract) and thus there is no available implementation.

So the question is: how do we specify complete contracts without depending upon implementation detail?

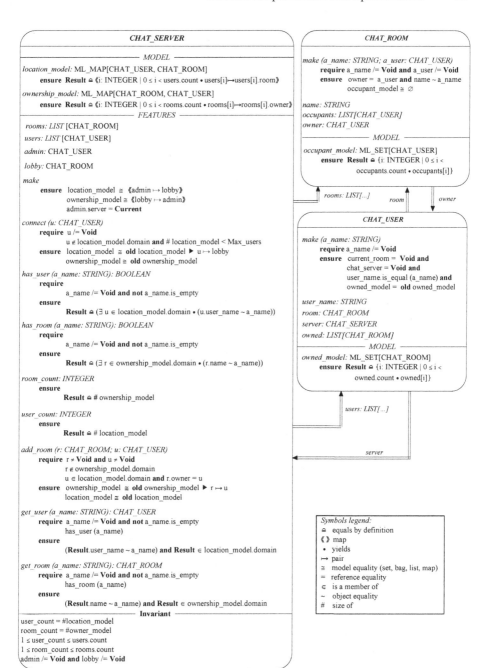

Fig. 7. System Specifications in BON notation

4.1   The Need for Mathematical Models

In order to fully specify the contracts of feature connect the chat application must remember:

1. All the users that are already connected (so that a check can be made that the same user does not connect twice).
2. All the users in the Lobby (so that the list of users of the Lobby can be updated when the new user is connected).

We may use a mathematical model describe the above state of affairs. The *location model* is a function from CHAT_USER to CHAT_ROOM as shown in Fig. 8.

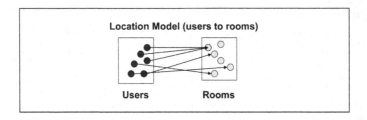

Fig. 8. Location model – mapping from users to rooms

In the location model each user is associated with a room. The location model may be described using the mathematical map class ML_MAP in the ESpec model library (these classes all have the prefix ML) as shown in Fig. 9. The ML classes are immutable. Thus they have no commands that can change their state, only queries that may return new maps constructed from the old maps as in mathematics. These classes are thus mathematically expressive but not efficient. This is not a problem as models are used solely in contracts and contract checking can be turned off in final deliveries.

In Fig. 9, the location model is specified as

location_model: ML_MAP[CHAT_USER,CHAT_ROOM]

The precondition of routine connect is $u \notin location\_model.domain$ which asserts that the user u is not already connected (i.e. the user is not in the domain of the map). The postcondition is

$$location\_model \cong (\text{old } location\_model) \blacktriangleright (u \mapsto lobby) \qquad (1)$$

which asserts that after execution of connect, the *location_model* is extended by (symbol ▶) the pair $u \mapsto lobby$, i.e. the location map in the poststate is the same as it was in the prestate but with the addition that user u is connected and in the Lobby. The symbol $\cong$ is the *model equality* symbol. Two maps are model equal provided they have the same elements in their respective domains and map the same elements in the domain to the associated elements in their respective ranges.

(a) BON mathematical notation

    class CHAT_SERVER **feature**

        location_model: ML_MAP[CHAT_USER,CHAT_ROOM]
        ownership_model: ML_MAP[CHAT_ROOM,CHAT_USER]

        lobby: CHAT_ROOM
        admin: CHAT_USER

        connect (u: USER) **is**
            require
                $u \neq Void \wedge u \notin location\_model.domain$
            ensure
                $location\_model \cong$ **old** $location\_model \blacktriangleright u \mapsto lobby$
                $ownership\_model \cong$ **old** $ownership\_model$
            end
    end

(b) Eiffel notation

    class CHAT_SERVER **feature**

        location_model: ML_MAP[USER,ROOM]
        ownership_model: ML_MAP[ROOM,USER]

        lobby: CHAT_ROOM
        admin: CHAT_USER

        connect (u: USER) **is**
            require
                a_user /= Void
                not location_model.domain.has_key(u)
            ensure
                location_model |=| **old** location_model ^ [u, lobby]
                ownership_model |=| **old** ownership_model
            end
    end

Fig. 9. Complete contracts for routine **connect** using a mathematical model

The BON [13] mathematical notation as in (1) is often convenient to use. The equivalent Eiffel notation has been designed so as to be as close to the mathematical notation as possible. As shown in Fig. 9(b) the Eiffel equivalent of (1) is

$$location\_model \;|=|\; \textbf{old } location\_model \;\hat{}\; [u, lobby]$$

The ML library has mathematical maps, sets, bags and sequences and the normal operators of set theory and predicate logic have been implemented [9]. For example, the postcondition of query **has_user** in Fig. 12 is specified as

$$Result \;\; \widehat{=} \;\; \exists\, u \in location\_model.domain \bullet (u.user\_name \sim a\_name) \quad (2)$$

The symbol $\sim$ denotes object equality. The postcondition thus asserts that the query holds when there exists some connected user whose name (as a string) has the same characters as the query argument **a_user**.

An implementor of class CHAT_SERVER may provide any private implementation code that satisfies the contracts. For example, the implementor may use two linked lists (users and rooms) for the implementation. However, all the contracts are specified in terms of the model. Thus the implementor must link the implementation to the model by providing an abstraction function [6] that maps (or "lifts") the implementation detail to the model as shown in Fig. 12. For example for the location model, the abstraction function is

$$Result \; \widehat{=} \; \langle\!\langle i : INT \mid 0 \leq i < users.count \bullet users[i] \mapsto users[i].room \rangle\!\rangle \qquad (3)$$

The angle brackets $\langle\!\langle \cdots \rangle\!\rangle$ is used for map comprehension (similar to set comprehension). Thus (3) asserts that the location model is a map consisting of pairs $users[i] \mapsto users[i].room$ where $users[i]$ is the item (i.e. the user) at index i in the linked list $users$.

In addition to the location model, we will also need an ownership model which is a map from rooms to users (owners) as shown in Fig. 11. For example, when a user adds a new room it is the ownership model that changes while the location model remains the same (e.g. see routine add_room in Fig. 7). The domain of the ownership model is the set of all rooms in the chat application. The contracts (expressed in terms of the model) for the chat application are shown in more detail in Fig. 7.

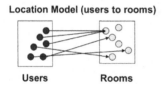

Location Model (users to rooms)

Users   Rooms

Ownership Model (rooms to users)

Rooms   Users

Fig. 10. Location model (mapping from users to rooms)

Fig. 11. Ownership model (mapping from rooms to users)

5   Contract Violations in Fit Tables

Section 3.3 used Scenario Tests to specify the design. Fit tables were able to catch specification errors (as category 1 errors in which the expected value disagreed with the actual values) in the design (category 1 errors may also reflect implementation errors).

Section 4 used contracts to specify the design. The advantage of contracts (as opposed to Scenario Tests for a particular execution) is that contracts specify the complete behaviour of modules (classes). In ESpec, contract violations are reflected back into the Fit tables (these are category 2 errors). This is useful because a contract error in the Fit table indicates that the specification of the design is correct, but the implementation does not satisfy the specified design solution. The contract violation in the Fit table provides precise details as to which feature fails which makes it easier to fix the problem.

```
┌─────────────────────────────────────────────────────────────────┐
                           CHAT_SERVER
 admin: CHAT_USER;
 lobby: CHAT_ROOM;
 connect (u: CHAT_USER)
       require  u /= Void and u ∉ location_model.domain
       ensure   location_model ≅ old location_model ▶ u ↦ lobby
                ownership_model ≅ old ownership_model
 has_user (a_name: STRING): BOOLEAN
       require  a_name /= Void and not a_name.is_empty
       ensure   Result ≙ ∃ u ∈ location_model.domain • (u.user_name ~ a_name)
 ──────────────────────────────── MODEL ────────────────────────────
 location_model: ML_MAP[CHAT_USER, CHAT_ROOM]
       ensure Result ≙ ⟪i: INTEGER | 0 ≤ i < users.count • users[i]↦users[i].room⟫
 ownership_model: ML_MAP[CHAT_ROOM, CHAT_USER]
       ensure Result ≙ ⟪i: INTEGER| 0 ≤ i < rooms.count • rooms[i]↦rooms[i].owner⟫
 ──────────────────────────────── PRIVATE ──────────────────────────
 rooms: LIST [CHAT_ROOM];    users: LIST [CHAT_USER]
 ──────────────────────────────── Invariant ────────────────────────
 user_count = #location_model and room_count = #owner_model
 admin /= Void and lobby /= Void
└─────────────────────────────────────────────────────────────────┘
```

Fig. 12. BON specification of the chat server

We illustrate the use of contract violations in Fit tables with some new Fit tables in our requirement document as shown in Fig. 13 and Fig. 14. These tables convert requirements R2, R3, and R4 into a mechanically testable format.

We use an Action table to specify a sequence of actions such as adding users, rooms and permissions. We then use a Row table to query and check that the underlying database of users, rooms and permissions are as expected.

Row tables allow for powerful descriptions that collections of elements (e.g. in lists, sets, bags and maps) are present as expected. For example, suppose only "Bob" and "Anna" have been allowed to access the room "Technical Support". A single row in a Row table can check that these users alone are in the permitted list by simple enumeration.

Fig. 13 has an Action table and a Row table. The Action table starts a chat server, and adds users, rooms and permissions as shown. Consider the Row table in Fig. 13. The customer specifies the header of the first column in the table as "Room name". This means that the customer will be querying a collection of entities of type room considered as phenomena in the problem space.

It is of course up to the developer to connect the Row table to the business logic via a Row fixture. In our case, the developer uses the fixture to link the

Action table:

- Start a chat server, create three chat users ("Anna", "Bob" and "Tod") and connect them to the server.
- User "Bob" creates a chat room called "Technical Support" and adds it to the chat server.
- "Bob" changes the room status from public to private.
- "Bob" permits user "Anna" to join the room.

R2, R3 and R4: Scenario		
start	Chat Server	
enter	[user]	Anna
press	Connect [user]	
enter	[user]	Bob
press	Connect [user]	
enter	[user]	Tod
press	Connect [user]	
enter	[user]	Bob
enter	[room]	Technical Support
press	[user] adds [room]	
press	[user] makes [room] private	
enter	[user list]	Anna
press	[user] allows [user list] in [room]	
check	Total number of users	4
check	Total number of rooms	2

Row table:

The following Row table checks
the status of the database of users and rooms.

R2, R3 and R4: Scenario Query				
Room name	Owner	Occupants	Is public?	Permitted list
Lobby	Admin	Admin,Anna,Bob,Tod	True	Admin
Technical Support	Bob	Empty	False	Bob,Anna

Fig. 13. Testing requirements R2 – R4

Row table to rooms in the business logic which is a linked list of CHAT_ROOM. The linked list and class CHAT_ROOM are of course phenomena in the machine.

Each row in the Row table describes the properties of a room in the collection. In the Row table of Fig. 13 the first row deals with room "Lobby" and the second row deals with room "Technical Support". These are the only two rows because the customer has not created any other rooms. Suppose there are other rooms but they are not expected in the table. Then execution of the Row table would yield an error stating that there are surplus rooms in the business logic that

– User "Anna" enters room "Technical Support"

R2, R3 and R4: Scenario		
enter	[user]	Anna
enter	[room]	Technical Support
press	move [user] to [room]	

– Checking the status of chat server using a Row Fixture

R2, R3 and R4: Scenario Query				
Room name	Owner	Occupants	Is public?	Permitted list
Lobby	Admin	Admin,Bob,Tod	True	Admin
Technical Support	Bob	Anna	False	Bob,Anna

Fig. 14. Moving a user from one room to another

were not expected in the requirements. Thus Row tables represent *exhaustive* descriptions of the collection.

The other column headings of the Row table in Fig. 13 describe properties that each room must satisfy. The second column, for example, specifies who is the owner of the room, the third column describes who are the occupants of the room, the fourth column asserts whether the room is public (anybody may enter), and the last column checks the permitted list. If the room is public then the permitted list contains only the owner of the room.

Fig. 14 is a continuation of the requirement document described in Fig. 13, i.e. it refers to the same chat server initialized and acted upon in Fig. 13. Subsequent to the actions of Fig. 13, our customer uses the Action table in Fig. 14 to specify that user Anna moves from the Lobby to Technical Support. As shown in the Row table, our customer expects that user Anna is transferred from the Lobby to Technical Support.

Do the Fit tests pass given the design developed in previous sections of this paper? If we execute the Fit requirement tests described in Fig. 13 and Fig. 14 we obtain the results shown in Fig. 15 and Fig. 16.

Both tables in Fig. 15 succeed whereas the Row table in Fig 16 fails with a category 1 error indicating that Anna is in two locations at the same time (in the Lobby and Technical Support). According to the Row table, after moving from one room to another, the customer's expectation is that Anna is solely in Technical Support and not in the Lobby anymore.

An investigations of the code shows an implementation error in the body of routine CHAT_SERVER.enter_room. The developer simply forgot to remove the user from the original room while adding this user to the new room thus causing the user to be in two locations at the same time. This category 1 error in the Fit table is an indication of an incomplete specification as the error should have been caught by a contract violation (a category 2 error).

The fix for this problem is to convert a category 1 error into a category 2 contract error. Consider the specification of routine enter_room in Fig. 17. The postcondition is:

R2, R3 and R4: Scenario		
start	Chat Server	
enter	[user]	Anna
press	Connect [user]	
enter	[user]	Bob
press	Connect [user]	
enter	[user]	Tod
press	Connect [user]	
enter	[user]	Bob
enter	[room]	Technical Support
press	[user] adds [room]	
press	[user] makes [room] private	
enter	[user list]	Anna
press	[user] allows [user list] in [room]	
check	Total number of users	4
check	Total number of rooms	2

R2, R3 and R4: Scenario Query				
Room name	Owner	Occupants	Is public?	Permitted list
Lobby	Admin	Admin,Anna,Bob,Tod	True	Admin
Technical Support	Bob	Empty	False	Bob,Anna

Fig. 15. Success: Result of executing tables in Fig. 13

$$location\_model \quad \cong \quad (\textbf{old } location\_model) \oplus (u \mapsto get\_room(r))$$

where $\oplus$ is the symbol for map override. The postcondition asserts that the location model in the poststate is the same as in the prestate except that the room associated with user u is now changed to $get\_room(r)$ where query get_room returns the chat room object associated with string r (this is a search routine). The ownership model is left unchanged by the routine enter_room.

The postcondition is correct but incomplete (as the error was category 1 and not category 2). As shown in Fig. 7, class CHAT_ROOM has an occupant model (ML_SET[CHAT_USER]) that keeps track of the occupants of each room. There is no assertion that ensures that the models of CHAT_SERVER and CHAT_ROOM are consistent with each other. The consistency assertions are best written as invariants in class CHAT_SERVER as shown in Fig. 17.

The invariant disjoint_users asserts that any two rooms are pairwise disjoint, i.e. a user may be in at most one room at a time. The second invariant coverage asserts that the domain of the location model (i.e. all chat users) consists of the union of the occupant model sets, i.e. all users specified in the location model must be occupants of some room.

Fig. 18 shows how the invariants are written using the ML Eiffel library. The invariant disjoint_users is captured by enumerating through the list of all rooms collecting, pairwise, intersections of the room occupants and then checking

R2, R3 and R4: Scenario			
enter	[user]	Anna	
enter	[room]	Technical Support	
press	move [user] to [room]		

R2, R3 and R4: Scenario Query					
Room name	Owner	Occupants		Is public?	Permitted list
Lobby	Admin	Admin,Bob,Tod *Expected* [Admin, Anna, Bob, Tod] *Actual*		True	Admin
Technical Support	Bob	Anna		False	Bob,Anna

Fig. 16. Failure: Result of executing tables in Fig 14

```
class CHAT_SERVER
    ...
    enter_room (u: CHAT_USER; r: STRING) is
            -- Move user 'u' into room with string name 'r'
        require
            (u ≠ Void) ∧ (r ≠ Void) ∧ ¬(r.is_empty)
            u ∈ location_model.domain
        ensure
            user_entered: location_model ≅ (old location_model ⊕ (u ↦ get_room(r)))
            ownerships_not_changed: ownership_model ≅ old ownership_model
        end

    get_room (r: STRING): CHAT_ROOM is
            -- returns a room with name 'r'
        require
            (r ≠ Void) ∧ ¬(r.is_empty)
            has_room (r)
        ensure
            (∃ room ∈ ownership_model.domain | room.name ∼ Result.name)
        end

    ...
    location_model: ML_MAP [CHAT\_USER, CHAT\_ROOM]
    ownership_model: ML_MAP [CHAT\_ROOM, CHAT\_USER]
invariant
    disjoint_users:
    (∀ r₁, r₂ ∈ own_model.domain | r₁ ≠ r₂ • r₁.occupant_model ∩ r₂.occupant_model ≅ ∅)
    coverage: (∪ r ∈ own_model.domain • r.occupant_model) ≅ location_model.domain
end
```

Fig. 17. BON specification of the invariant for the CHAT_SERVER

that the resulting set is empty. Queries `forall_rooms` and `empty_intersection` are agent routines that are used for this purpose (see lines 6–19 in Fig. 18). The * infix operator is used for the intersection of two sets. The `coverage` property is implemented using the `multi_union` recursive agent. This agent collects the union of all users in all rooms using the `occupant_model` of each room and then

```
1    class CHAT_SERVER
2        ...
3        location_model: ML_MAP [USER, ROOM]
4        ownership_model: ML_MAP [ROOM, USER]
5
6        forall_rooms (r1: CHAT_ROOM): BOOLEAN is
7            do
8                Result := ownership_model.domain.for_all
9                                        (agent empty_intersection (r1, ?))
10           end
11
12       empty_intersection (r1, r2: CHAT_ROOM): BOOLEAN is
13           do
14               if r1 /= r2 then
15                   Result := (r1.occupant_model * r2.occupant_model) |=| create {
                         ML_SET[CHAT_USER]}.make
16               else
17                   Result := true
18               end
19           end
20
21       multi_union (s: ML_SEQ[CHAT_ROOM]): ML_SET[CHAT_USER] is
22           do
23               if s.count = 1 then
24                   Result := s.head.occupant_model.to_set
25               else
26                   Result := (multi_union (s.tail) |++ (s.head.occupant_model)).to_set
27               end
28           end
29
30   invariant
31     pairwise_disjoint: ownership_model.domain.for_all (agent forall_rooms (?))
32     coverage: multi_union (ownership_model.domain.to_seq) |=| location_model.domain
```

Fig. 18. Implementing the invariant using ML

Table 4. Specification violations are reflected to the Fit table

R2, R3 and R4: Scenario		
enter	[user]	Anna
enter	[room]	Technical Support
press	move [user] to [room]	*Class invariant violated.* *CHAT_SERVER enter_room @7 pairwise_disjoint:* *Class invariant violated. Fail* --- *CHAT_SERVER enter_room @11* *Routine failure. Fail*

returns a set composed of all those users. The |++ infix operator is used for the union of two sets.

The Fit table now reports an invariant error in class CHAT_SERVER (i.e. a category 2 error) thus indicating an implementation problem in routine enter_room in class CHAT_SERVER. This contract error is reported in the Fit table 4.

As shown in Fig. 19 a category 1 error (expected vs. actual discrepancy) may indicate that the specification is either incomplete or even incorrect. A complete

		Fit Table Violations
Specification Correctness	$P \wedge S \rightarrow R$	Actual vs. Expected (cat. 1)
Implementation Correctness	$C \rightarrow S$	Contract Violation (cat. 2)
System Correctness	$P \wedge C \rightarrow R$	

Fig. 19. Interpreting Fit table violations

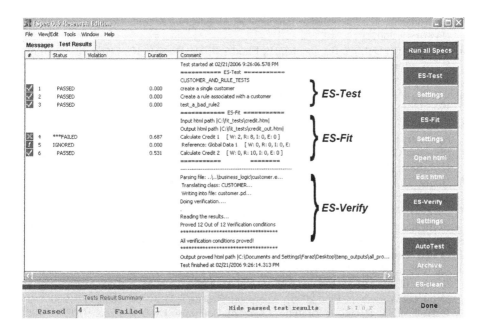

Fig. 20. The Espec software quality workbench

specification (via contracts) would have been flagged with a contract error in the Fit table. In the absence of a contractual specification error that pinpoints the faulty routine, there may either be an implementation error or specification error. By fixing the contracts we can pinpoint the precise routine that is not implemented correctly.

6   ESpec Tool

Fig. 20 shows the ESpec tool[1] in action. The tool allows the user to write testable customer requirements and design specifications that can be checked mechanically. ESpec provides feedback to the developer for Fit table requirement tests, Scenario Tests and unit tests as shown in the figure under a unified green bar

---

[1] www.cse.yorku.ca/~sel/espec

(i.e. if all the various tests run correctly then a green bar is displayed). The tool also allows formal verification of implementations with respect to contracts using a theorem prover as described in [9].

References

1. Ambler, S.: Agile Model Driven Development is Good Enough. IEEE Software 20(5), 71–73 (2003)
2. Andronache, T.: The english language as an effective it tool. Computerworld, 18 (February 2007)
3. Barnett, M., DeLine, R., Jacobs, B., Fhndrich, M., Rustan, K., Leino, M., Schulte, W., Venter, H.: The Spec# Programming System: Challenges and Directions. Position paper at VSTTE (2005)
4. Chalin, P., Kiniry, J.R., Leavens, G.T., Poll, E.: Beyond Assertions: Advanced Specification and Verification with JML and ESC/Java2. In: de Boer, F.S., Bonsangue, M.M., Graf, S., de Roever, W.-P. (eds.) FMCO 2005. LNCS, vol. 4111, Springer, Heidelberg (2006)
5. Standish Group. Project management: The criteria for success. Software Magazine (February 2001)
6. Hoare, C.A.R.: Proof of correctness of data representations. Acta Inf. 1, 271–281 (1972)
7. Jackson, M.: Problem frames: analyzing and structuring software development problems. Addison-Wesley Longman Publishing Co., Inc., Boston, MA, USA (2001)
8. Mugridge, R., Cunningham, W.: Fit for Developing Software: Framework for Integrated Tests. Prentice-Hall, Englewood Cliffs (2005)
9. Ostroff, J., Wang, C.-W., Kerfoot, E., Torshizi, F.A.: Automated model-based verification of object oriented code. In: Verified Theories: Theories, Tools, Experiments (VSTTE Workshop, Floc 2006). Microsoft Research MSR-TR-2006-117 (2006)
10. Ostroff, J.S., Paige, R.F.: The Logic of Software Design. Proc. IEE - Software 147(3), 72–80 (2000)
11. Ostroff, J.S., Paige, R.F., Makalsky, D., Brooke, P.J.: E-tester: a contract-aware and agent-based unit testing framework for eiffel. Journal of Object Technology 4(7) (September-October 2005)
12. Paige, R., Ostroff, J.S.: The Single Model Principle. Journal of Object Oriented Technology 1(5) (2002)
13. Paige, R.F., Ostroff, J.S.: Developing BON as an Industrial-Strength Formal Method (Developing BON as an Industrial-Strength Formal Method). In: Wing, J.M., Woodcock, J.C.P., Davies, J. (eds.) FM 1999. LNCS, vol. 1708, Springer, Heidelberg (1999)
14. Torshizi, F.A., Ostroff, J.S.: ESpec – a Tool for Agile Development via Early Testable Specifications. Technical Report CS-2006-04, York University, Toronto (2006)

Proving Programs Incorrect Using a Sequent Calculus for Java Dynamic Logic

Philipp Rümmer[1] and Muhammad Ali Shah[2]

[1] Department of Computer Science and Engineering,
Chalmers University of Technology and Göteborg University
`philipp@cs.chalmers.se`
[2] Avanza Solutions ME, Dubai - 113116, United Arab Emirates
`muhammad.ali@avanzasolutions.com`

Abstract. Program verification is concerned with proving that a program is correct and adheres to a given specification. Testing a program, in contrast, means to search for a witness that the program is incorrect. In the present paper, we use a program logic for Java to prove the *incorrectness* of programs. We show that this approach, carried out in a sequent calculus for dynamic logic, creates a connection between calculi and proof procedures for program verification and test data generation procedures. Starting with a program logic enables to find more general and more complicated counterexamples for the correctness of programs.

Keywords: Disproving, Program logics, Program verification, Testing.

1 Introduction

Testing and program verification are techniques to ensure that programs behave correctly. The two approaches start with complementary assumptions: when we try to verify correctness, we implicitly expect that a program *is* correct and want to confirm this by conducting a proof. Testing, in contrast, expects incorrectness and searches for a witness (or *counterexample* for correctness):

"Find program inputs for which something bad happens."

In the present paper, we want to reformulate this endeavour and instead write it as an existentially quantified statement:

"There are program inputs for which something bad happens." (1)

Written like this, it becomes apparent that we can see testing as a proof procedure that attempts to eliminate the quantifier in statements of form (1). When considering functional properties, many program logics that are used for verification are general enough to formalise (1), which entails that calculi for such program logics can in fact be identified as testing procedures.

The present paper discusses how the statement (1), talking about a Java program and a formal specification of safety-properties, can be formalised in

B. Meyer and Y. Gurevich (Eds.): TAP 2007, LNCS 4454, pp. 41–60, 2007.

dynamic logic for Java [1,2]. Through the usage of algebraic datatypes, this formalisation can be carried out without leaving first-order dynamic logic. Subsequently, we use a sequent calculus for automatic reasoning about the resulting formulae. The component of the calculus that is most essential in this setting is quantifier elimination. Depending on the way in which existential quantifiers are eliminated—by substituting ground terms, or by using metavariable techniques—we either obtain proof procedures that much resemble automated white-box test generation methods, or we arrive at procedures that can find more general and more complicated solutions (program inputs) of (1), but that are less efficient for "obvious" bugs. We believe that this viewpoint to incorrectness proofs can both lead to a better understanding of testing and to more powerful methods for showing that programs are incorrect.

Organisation of the Paper. Sect. 2 introduces dynamic logic for Java and describes how (1) can be formalised. In Sect. 3, we show how different versions of a sequent calculus for dynamic logic can be used to reason about (1). Sect. 4 discusses how solutions of (1) can be represented. Sect. 5 provides further details about incorrectness proofs using the incremental closure approach. Sect. 6 discusses related work, and Sect. 7 gives future work and concludes the paper.

Running Example: Erroneous List Implementation. The Java program shown in Fig. 1 is used as example in the whole paper. It is interesting for our purposes because it operates on a heap datastructure and contains unbounded loops, although it is not difficult to spot the bug in the method `delete`.

2   Formalisation of the Problem in Dynamic Logic

In the scope of this paper, the only "bad things" that we want to detect are violated post-conditions of programs. Arbitrary broken safety-properties (like assertions) can be reduced to this problem, whereas the violation of liveness-properties (like looping programs) falls in a different class and the techniques presented here are not directly applicable. This section describes how the statement that we want to prove can be formulated in dynamic logic:

> There is a pre-state—possibly subject to pre-conditions—such that the program at hand violates given post-conditions. (2)

Dynamic Logic. First-order dynamic logic (DL) [1] is a multi-modal extension of first-order predicate logic in which modal operators are labelled with programs. There are primarily two kinds of modal operators that are dual to each other: a diamond formula $\langle \alpha \rangle \phi$ expresses that ϕ holds in at least one final state of program α. Box formulae can be regarded as abbreviations $[\alpha] \phi \equiv \neg \langle \alpha \rangle \neg \phi$ as usual. The DL formulae that probably appear most often have the form $\phi \rightarrow \langle \alpha \rangle \psi$ and state, for a deterministic program α, the total correctness of α concerning a precondition ϕ and a postcondition ψ. In this paper, we will only use dynamic logic for Java [2] (JavaDL) and assume that α is a list of Java statements.

```
public class IntList {                    class ListNode {
  private ListNode head;                    public int        val;
  public void add (int n) { ... }           public ListNode next;
                                          }

  /*@
    @ public normal_behavior
    @ ensures !contains(n);
    @*/
  public void delete(int n) {
    ListNode cur = head, prev = head;
    while (cur != null) {
      if (cur.val == n) prev.next = cur.next;
      else              prev = cur;
      cur = cur.next;
    }
  }

  public /*@ pure @*/ boolean contains(int n) {
    ListNode temp = head;
    while (temp != null) {
      if (temp.val == n) return true;
      temp = temp.next;
    }
    return false;
  }
}
```

Fig. 1. The running example, a simple implementation of singly-linked lists, annotated with JML [3] constraints. We concentrate on the method `delete` for removing all elements with a certain value, which contains bugs.

Updates. JavaDL features a notation for updating functions in a substitution-like style [4], which is primarily useful because it allows for a simple and natural memory representation during symbolic execution. For our purposes, *updates* can be seen as a simplistic programming language and are defined by the grammar:

$$Upd ::= \text{skip} \mid f(s_1, \ldots, s_n) := t \mid Upd|Upd \mid \text{if } \phi \{Upd\} \mid \text{for } x \{Upd\}$$

in which $s_1, \ldots, s_n, t$ range over terms, f over function symbols, ϕ over formulae and x over variables. The update constructors denote effect-less updates, assignments, parallel composition, guarded updates and quantified updates. Updates u can be attached to terms and formulae (like in $\{u\} t$) for changing the state in which the expression is supposed to be evaluated:

Expression with update:	Equivalent update-free expr.:
$\{a := g(3)\} f(a)$	f(g(3))
$\{x := y \mid y := x + 1\} (x < y)$	$y < x + 1$
$\{a := 3 \mid \text{for } x \{f(x) := 2 \cdot x + 1\}\} f(f(a))$	15

As illustrated here, it is always possible to apply updates to terms and formulae like a substitution, unless a formula contains further modal operators. In the latter case, the application has to be delayed until the modal operator is eliminated.

2.1 Heap Representation in Dynamic Logic for Java

Reasoning in JavaDL always takes place in the context of a system of Java classes, which is supposed to be free of compile-time errors. From this context, a vocabulary of sorts and function symbols is derived that represents variables and the heap of the program in question [2].

Most importantly, in JavaDL objects of classes are identified with natural numbers. For each class C, a sort with the same name and a (injective) function $C.get : nat \rightarrow C$ are introduced. $C.get(i)$ is the ith object of class C (i is the index or "address"). For distinct classes C and D, $C.get(i)$ and $D.get(j)$ are never the same object. Each sort C representing a class also contains a distinguished individual denoted by $null$, which is used to represent undefined references. Attributes of type T of a class C are modelled by functions $C \rightarrow T$. Instead of the infix notation $attr(o)$, we mostly write $o.attr$ for attribute accesses.

C can be seen as a reservoir containing both those objects that are already created and those that can possibly be created later by a program: JavaDL uses a constant-domain semantics in which modal operators never change the domains of existing individuals. In order to distinguish existing and non-existing objects, for each class C also a constant $C.nextToCreate : nat$ is declared that denotes the lowest index of a non-created object. All objects $C.get(i)$ with $i < C.nextToCreate$ are created, all others are not.

For the program in Fig. 1, the vocabulary is as follows:

Sorts:	Functions:	
$IntList, ListNode,$	$IntList.get$	$:\ nat \rightarrow IntList$
$int, nat, \ldots$	$ListNode.get$	$:\ nat \rightarrow ListNode$
	$IntList.nextToCreate$	$:\ nat$
	$ListNode.nextToCreate$	$:\ nat$
	$head$	$:\ IntList \rightarrow ListNode$
	$next$	$:\ ListNode \rightarrow ListNode$
	val	$:\ ListNode \rightarrow int$

2.2 Formalising the Violation of Post-conditions

We go back to (2). It is almost straightforward to formalise the part of (2) that comes after the existential quantifier "there is a pre-state":

$$\neg(\textit{pre-conditions} \rightarrow \langle \textit{statements} \rangle \textit{ post-conditions}) \tag{3}$$

Formula (3) is true if and only if the pre-conditions hold, the program fragment does not terminate, or terminates and the post-conditions do not hold in the final state.

Property (2) does not mention termination, which could be interpreted in different ways. If in (3) the box operator $[\alpha]\,\phi$ was used instead of a diamond, we would also specify that the program has to terminate for the inputs that we search for. JavaDL does, however, not distinguish between non-termination due to looping and abrupt termination due to exceptions (partial correctness model). Because we, most likely, will consider abrupt termination as a violation of the post-conditions, the diamond operator appears more appropriate.

2.3   Quantification over Program States

In order to continue formalising (2), it is necessary to close the statement (3) existentially and to add quantifiers that express "there is a pre-state":

$$\exists\,\text{pre-state}.\;\{\text{pre-state}\}\,\neg\,(\text{pre-conditions} \rightarrow \langle\,\text{statements}\,\rangle\,\text{post-conditions}) \quad (4)$$

Because state quantification is not directly possible in JavaDL, we use an update $\{\text{pre-state}\}$ to define the state in which (3) is to be evaluated. For a Java program, the pre-state covers (i) variables that turn up in a program, and (ii) the heap that the program operates on. Following Sect. 2.1, at a first glance this turns out to be a second-order problem, because the heap is modelled by functions like *head*, *next*, etc.[1] A second glance reveals, fortunately, that a proper Java program and proper pre- and post-conditions[2] will only look at the values $C.get(i).attr$ of attributes for $i < C.nextToCreate$: the state of non-existing objects is irrelevant. Quantification of $C.nextToCreate$ and the finite prefix

$$C.get(0).attr,\; C.get(1).attr,\; \ldots,\; C.get(C.nextToCreate - 1).attr$$

can naturally be realised through quantification over algebraic datatypes like lists. Note, that the number of quantified locations is finite, but unbounded.

Attributes of Primitive Types. The simplest case is an attribute *attr* of a primitive Java type. If *attr* has type *int*, the quantification can be performed as follows:

$$\exists\,attr_V : intList.\;\{\texttt{for } x : nat\;\{C.get(x).attr := attr_V \downarrow x\}\}\,\ldots$$

Apart from the actual quantifier, an update is used for copying the contents of the list variable $attr_V$ to the attribute. The expression also contains an operator for accessing lists $[a_0, \ldots, a_n]$, which we define by

$$[a_0, \ldots, a_n] \downarrow i \;:=\; \begin{cases} a_i & \text{for } i \leq n \\ 0 & \text{otherwise} \end{cases} \quad (i : nat)$$

The fact that the operator returns a default value (0, but any other value would work equally well) for accesses outside of the list bounds simplifies the overall treatment and basically renders the length of lists irrelevant. Instead of lists, one could also talk about functions with finite support.

---

[1] JavaDL does not provide higher-order quantification.

[2] In the whole paper, we assume that pre- and post-conditions only talk about the program state, and only about created objects.

Attributes of Reference Types. The quantification is a bit more involved for attributes *attr* of type D, where D is a reference type like a class: (i) attributes can be undefined, i.e., have value *null*, (ii) attributes of created objects must not point to non-created objects, and (iii) attributes of type D can also point to objects of type D', provided that D' is a subtype of D. We capture these requirements by overloading the function $D.get$. Assuming that $D_0 (= D), \ldots, D_k$ is an arbitrary, but fixed enumeration of D's subtypes, we define:

$$D.get(s, i) := \begin{cases} D_s.get(i) & \text{for } i < D_s.nextToCreate,\ s \le k \\ null & \text{otherwise} \end{cases} \qquad (s, i : nat)$$

Apart from the object index i, we also pass $D.get(s, i)$ the index s of the requested subtype of D. The result of $D.get(s, i)$ is either a created object (if i and s are within their bounds $D_s.nextToCreate$ and k) or *null*. With this definition, the quantification part for a reference attribute boils down to

$$\exists a_S, a_V : natList.\ \{\text{for } x : nat\ \{C.get(x).attr := D.get(a_S \downarrow x, a_V \downarrow x)\}\} \ldots$$

In case of a class D that does not have proper subclasses, the list a_S can of course be left out (and the first argument of $D.get$ can be set to 0).

Example. We show the formalisation of (2) for the method `delete` in the program of Fig. 1. Apart from the values of the attributes *head*, *next* and *val*, which are treated as discussed above, one also has to quantify over the number of created objects (*IntList.nextToCreate* and *ListNode.nextToCreate*), over the receiver o of the method invocation and over the argument n. o is assumed to be either an arbitrary created object or *null* (*IntList.get*$(0, o_V)$). The pre- and post-conditions correspond to the JML specification: initially, o is not *null*, and `delete` in fact removes the elements with value n.

$$\exists k_{IL}, k_{LN}, o_V : nat.\ \exists n_V : int.\ \exists head_V, next_V : natList.\ \exists val_V : intList.$$
$$\{IntList.nextToCreate := k_{IL} \mid ListNode.nextToCreate := k_{LN}\}$$
$$\{\text{for } x : nat\ \{IntList.get(x).head := ListNode.get(0, head_V \downarrow x)\} \mid$$
$$\text{for } x : nat\ \{ListNode.get(x).next := ListNode.get(0, next_V \downarrow x)\} \mid \qquad (5)$$
$$\text{for } x : nat\ \{ListNode.get(x).val := val_V \downarrow x\} \mid$$
$$o := IntList.get(0, o_V) \mid n := n_V\}$$
$$\neg(\ o \ne null \rightarrow \langle o.\texttt{delete}(n)\rangle\,\langle b = o.\texttt{contains}(n)\rangle\, b = FALSE\ )$$

3   Constructing Proofs for Program Incorrectness

A Gentzen-style sequent calculus for JavaDL is introduced in [2], which has been implemented in the KeY system and is used by us as test-bed. Fig. 2 shows a small selection of the rules. Relevant for us are the following groups of rules: (i) rules for a sequent calculus for first-order predicate logic with metavariables (the first 5 rules of Fig. 2), (ii) rules that implement symbolic execution [5] for Java (the

$$\frac{\Gamma \vdash \phi, \Delta \quad \Gamma \vdash \psi, \Delta}{\Gamma \vdash \phi \wedge \psi, \Delta} \wedge R \qquad \frac{\Gamma, \phi, \psi \vdash \Delta}{\Gamma, \phi \wedge \psi \vdash \Delta} \wedge L \qquad \frac{\Gamma, \phi \vdash \Delta}{\Gamma \vdash \neg\phi, \Delta} \neg R$$

$$\frac{\Gamma \vdash \phi[x/f(X_1, \ldots, X_n)], \Delta}{\Gamma \vdash \forall x.\phi, \Delta} \forall R \qquad (X_1, \ldots, X_n \text{ all metavariables in } \phi)$$

$$\frac{\Gamma \vdash \phi[x/X], \exists x.\phi, \Delta}{\Gamma \vdash \exists x.\phi, \Delta} \exists R \qquad (X \text{ a fresh metavariable})$$

$$\frac{\Gamma, \{u\} \{r := l\} \langle \ldots \rangle \phi \vdash \Delta}{\Gamma, \{u\} \langle r = l; \ldots \rangle \phi \vdash \Delta} \text{ ASSIGN-L} \qquad (r, l \text{ side-effect-free})$$

$$\frac{\Gamma, \{u\} \langle \alpha_1; \ldots \rangle \phi, \{u\} b \vdash \Delta \quad \Gamma, \{u\} \langle \alpha_2; \ldots \rangle \phi \vdash \{u\} b, \Delta}{\Gamma, \{u\} \langle \texttt{if } (b) \ \alpha_1 \texttt{ else } \alpha_2 \ \ldots \rangle \phi \vdash \Delta} \text{ IF-L} \qquad (b \text{ side-effect-free})$$

$$\frac{\Gamma, \{u\} \langle \texttt{if } (b) \ \{\alpha; \ \texttt{while } (b) \ \alpha\} \ldots \rangle \phi \vdash \Delta}{\Gamma, \{u\} \langle \texttt{while } (b) \ \alpha \ \ldots \rangle \phi \vdash \Delta} \text{ WHILE-L}$$

Fig. 2. Examples of (simplified) sequent calculus rules for JavaDL. In the last three rules, the update u can also be empty (**skip**) and disappear. Γ and Δ denote arbitrary sets of formulae (side-formulae).

last three rules of Fig. 2), and (iii) rewriting rules for applying and simplifying updates (not shown here, see [4]). The rule ASSIGN-L turns a Java assignment into an update, which subsequently can be merged with the former preceding update u and simplified. In IF-L, a case analysis for an if-statement is performed by splitting on the branch predicate b evaluated in the current program state u. Both rules require that expressions with side-effects are simplified first. Finally, the rule WHILE-L unwinds a loop once.

The fact that the calculus directly integrates symbolic execution—and covers all important features of Java like dynamic object creation and exceptions—is most central for us. When symbolically executing a program, the proof tree resembles the *symbolic execution tree* of the program [5] and reflects the (feasible) paths through the program. Branch predicates that describe, in terms of the pre-state, when a certain path is taken are accumulated as formulae in a sequent. JavaDL introduces such predicates for conditional statements and for statements that might raise exceptions. A simple example is the following proof:

$$\frac{\begin{array}{c}\vdots \\ p+1 \leq 0, p \geq 0 \vdash \\ \hline \{p := p+1\} \langle\rangle \, p \leq 0, p \geq 0 \vdash \\ \hline \langle p = p+1; \rangle \, p \leq 0, p \geq 0 \vdash \end{array} \text{ ASSIGN-L} \qquad \begin{array}{c}\vdots \\ -p \leq 0 \vdash p \geq 0 \\ \hline \{p := -p\} \langle\rangle \, p \leq 0 \vdash p \geq 0 \\ \hline \langle p = -p; \rangle \, p \leq 0 \vdash p \geq 0 \end{array}}{\langle \texttt{if } (p \geq 0) \ p = p+1; \texttt{ else } p = -p; \rangle \, p \leq 0 \vdash} \text{ IF-L}$$

Symbolic execution and update application can usually be automated easily—in contrast to reasoning in first-order logic—because in each proof situation only few rules are applicable, and because the application order does not matter.

This section discusses how the sequent calculus can be used to prove formulae (4). The first and essential task is always to eliminate the existential quantifiers, i.e., to provide the programs inputs, which can be concrete or symbolic. Assuming that pre- and post-conditions only talk about the program state, it is sufficient to apply ∃R once (and not multiple times) for each quantifier in ∃ *pre-state*, because the validity of (4) only depends on the program fragment and the pre- and post-conditions, not on the values of other symbols.

We focus on and propose two methods for constructing proofs: the usage of metavariables and depth-first search (Sect. 3.2) and the usage of metavariables and backtracking-free search with constraints (Sect. 3.3, Sect. 5). In our experiments, we have concentrated on the latter method, because the implementation KeY follows this paradigm. As a comparison, Sect. 3.1 shortly discusses how a ground calculus would handle (4), which resembles common test generation techniques.

3.1   Construction of Proofs Using a Ground Proof Procedure

The simplest approach is *ground reasoning*, i.e., to not use metavariables. Therefore, a ground version of ∃R can be used: (t is an arbitrary term)

$$\frac{\Gamma \vdash \phi[x/t], \exists x.\phi, \Delta}{\Gamma \vdash \exists x.\phi, \Delta} \; \exists\mathrm{R}_g$$

Equivalently, also the normal rule ∃R can be applied, immediately followed by a *substitution step* that replaces the introduced metavariable X with a concrete term t. For (4), the usage of rule $\exists\mathrm{R}_g$ encompasses that a concrete pre-state has to be chosen up-front that satisfies the pre-condition and makes the program violate its post-condition. If we consider (5), for instance, we see that a proof can be conducted with the following instantiations:

$$
\begin{array}{ccccccc}
k_{IL} & k_{LN} & o_V & n_V & head_V & next_V & val_V \\
\hline
1 & 1 & 0 & 5 & [0] & [7] & [5]
\end{array}
\tag{6}
$$

The instantiations express that the classes *IntList* and *ListNode* have one created object each (k_{IL}, k_{LN}), that the object *IntList.get*(0) receives the method invocation (o_V) with argument 5 (n_V), that *IntList.get*(0).*head* points to the object *ListNode.get*(0) ($head_V$), that *ListNode.get*(0).*next* is *null* ($next_V$, because of $7 \geq k_{LN}$), i.e., that the receiving list has only one element, and that *ListNode.get*(0).*val* is 5 (val_V).

A ground proof of a formula (4) is the most specific description of an erroneous situation that is possible. For debugging purposes, this is both an advantage and a disadvantage: (i) it is possible to concretely follow a program execution that leads to a failure, but (ii) the description does not distinguish between those inputs (or input features) that are relevant for causing a failure and those that are irrelevant. The disadvantage can partly be undone by looking at more than one ground proof, and by searching for proofs with "minimal" input data (e.g., [6]). Technically, the main advantage of a ground proof is that program

$$
\cfrac{
  \cfrac{
    \cfrac{
      \cfrac{
        \cfrac{
          \cfrac{*}{[P \mapsto 2]}
        }{P+1 > 3, P \geq 0 \vdash}
      }{\{p := P+1\}\,\langle\rangle\,p > 3, p \geq 0 \vdash}
    }{\{p := P\}\,\langle p = p+1;\rangle\,p > 3, P \geq 0 \vdash}
    \qquad
    \cfrac{
      \cfrac{*}{[P \mapsto 2]}
    }{\{p := P\}\,\langle p = -p;\rangle\,p > 3 \;\vdash\; P \geq 0}
  }{\{p := P\}\,\langle \texttt{if } (p \geq 0)\ p = p+1;\ \texttt{else } p = -p;\rangle\,p > 3 \vdash}\ \text{{\scriptsize IF-L}}
  }{\vdash\ \neg\{p := P\}\,\langle \texttt{if } (p \geq 0)\ p = p+1;\ \texttt{else } p = -p;\rangle\,p > 3, \ \ldots}\ \text{{\scriptsize ¬R}}
}{\vdash\ \exists p_V : int.\ \{p := p_V\}\,\neg\langle \texttt{if } (p \geq 0)\ p = p+1;\ \texttt{else } p = -p;\rangle\,p > 3}\ \text{{\scriptsize ∃R}}
$$

Fig. 3. Proof that a program violates its post-condition $p > 3$. The initial (quantified) formula is derived as described in Sect. 2. The application of updates is not explicitly shown in the proof.

execution (and checking pre- and post-conditions) is most efficient for a concrete pre-state. The difficulty, of course, is to find the *right* pre-state, which is subject of techniques for automated test data generation. Common approaches are the generation of *random* pre-states (e.g., [6]), or the usage of backtracking, symbolic execution and constraint techniques in order to optimise coverage criteria and to reach the erroneous parts of a program (see, e.g., [7]).

3.2 Construction of Proofs Using Metavariables and Backtracking

The most common technique for efficient automated proof search in tableau or sequent calculi are rigid metavariables (also called free variables) and backtracking (depth-first search), for an overview see [8]. The rules shown in Fig. 2, together with a global substitution rule that allows to substitute terms for metavariables in a proof tree, implement a corresponding sequent calculus. Because, in particular, the substitution rule is destructive and a wrong decision can hinder the subsequent proof construction, proof procedures usually carry out a depth-first search with iterative deepening and backtrack when earlier rule applications appear misleading.

The search space of a proof procedure can be seen as an and/or search tree: (i) And-nodes occur when the proof branches, for instance when applying $\wedge$R, because each of the new proof goals has to be closed at some point. (ii) Or-nodes occur when a decision has to be drawn about which rule to apply next, or about a substitution that should be applied to a proof; in general, only one of the possible steps can be taken.

Metavariables and backtracking can be used to prove formulae like (4). The central difference to the ground approach is that metavariables can be introduced as place-holders for the pre-state, which can later be refined and made concrete by applying substitutions. A simple example is shown in Fig. 3, where the initial value of the variable p is represented by a metavariable P. After symbolic execution of the program, it becomes apparent that the post-condition $p > 3$ can be violated in the left branch by substituting 2 for P. The right branch can then be closed immediately, because this path of the program is not executed for $P = 2$: the branch predicate $P \geq 0$ allows to close the branch. Generally, the composition of the substitutions that are applied to the proof can be seen as a description of the pre-state that is searched for. A major difference to the ground case is that a substitution also can describe *classes* of pre-states, because it is not necessary that concrete terms are substituted for all metavariables.

Branch Predicates. Strictly speaking, the proof branching that is caused by the rule IF-L (or by similar rules for symbolic execution) falls into the "and-node" category: all paths through the program have to be treated in the proof. The situation differs, however, from the branches introduced by $\wedge$R, because IF-L performs a cut (a case distinction) on the branch predicate $\{u\}\, b$. As the program is executed with symbolic inputs (metavariables), it is possible to turn $\{u\}\, b$ into *true* or *false* (possibly into both, as one pleases), by applying substitutions and choosing the pre-state appropriately. Coercing $\{u\}\, b$ in this way will immediately close one of the two branches.

There are, consequently, two principal ways to close (each of) the proof branches after executing a conditional statement: (i) the program execution can be continued until termination, and the pre-state can be chosen so that the post-condition is violated, or (ii) one of the two branches can be closed by making the branch predicate *true* or *false*, which means that the program execution is simply forced *not* to take the represented path. Both cases can be seen in Fig. 3, in which the same substitution $P \mapsto 2$ leads to a violation of the post-condition in the left branch and turns the branch predicate in the right branch into *true*.

Proof Strategy. The proof construction consists of three parts: (i) pre-conditions have to be proven, (ii) the program has to be executed symbolically in order to find violations of the post-conditions, and (iii) it has to be ensured that the program execution takes the right path by closing the remaining proof branches with the help of branch predicates. These steps can be performed in different orders, or also interleaved. Furthermore, it can in all phases be necessary to backtrack, for instance when a violation of the post-conditions was found but the pre-state does not satisfy the pre-condition, or if the path leading to the failure is not feasible.

Example. Formula (5) can be proven by choosing the following values, which could be found using metavariables and backtracking:

$$\begin{array}{ccccccc} k_{IL} & k_{LN} & o_V & n_V & head_V & next_V & val_V \\ \hline 1 & 1 & 0 & N_V & [0,\ldots] & [7,\ldots] & [N_V,\ldots] \end{array} \tag{7}$$

Comparing this solution to (6), the main difference is that no concrete value has to be chosen for n_V. It suffices to state that the value of n_V coincides with the first element of the list val_V: when calling `delete`, the actual parameter coincides with the first element of the receiving linked list. Likewise, the parts of the pre-state that are described by lists do not have to be determined completely: the tail of lists can be left unspecified by applying substitutions like $VAL_V \mapsto \mathrm{cons}(N_V, VAL_{tail})$ (which is written as $[N_V,\ldots]$ in the table). Sect. 4 discusses how the representation of solutions can further be generalised.

3.3   Construction of Proofs Using Incremental Closure

There are alternatives to proof search based on backtracking: one idea is to work with metavariables, but to delay the actual application of substitutions to the proof tree until a substitution has been found that closes all branches. The idea is described in [9] and worked out in detail in [10]. While backtracking-free proof search is, in principle, also possible when immediately applying substitutions, removing this destructive operation vastly simplifies proving without backtracking. Because KeY implements this technique, it is used in our experiments.

The approach of [10] works by explicitly enumerating and collecting, for each of proof goals, the substitutions that would allow to close the branch. Substitutions are represented as *constraints*, which are conjunctions of unification conditions $t_1 \equiv t_2$. A generalisation is discussed in Sect. 4. For the example in Fig. 3, the "solutions" of the left branch could be enumerated as $[\,P \equiv 2\,]$, $[\,P \equiv 1\,]$, $[\,P \equiv 0\,]$, $[\,P \equiv -1\,]$, ..., and the solutions of the right branch as $[\,P \equiv 0\,]$, $[\,P \equiv 1\,]$, $[\,P \equiv 2\,]$, ... In this case, we would observe that, for instance, the substitution represented by $[\,P \equiv 0\,]$ closes the whole proof. Generally, the conjunction of the constraints for the different branches describes the substitution that allows to close a proof (provided that it is consistent).

When proving formulae (4) using metavariables, a substitution (i.e., pre-state) has to be found that simultaneously satisfies the pre-conditions, violates the post-conditions in one (or multiple) proof branches and invalidates the branch predicates of all remaining proof branches. The constraint approach searches for such a substitution by enumerating the solutions of all three in a fair manner. In our experiments, we also used breadth-first exploration of the execution tree of programs, which simply corresponds to a fair selection of proof branches and formulae that rules are applied to. For formula (5), the method could find the same solution (7) as the backtracking approach of Sect. 3.2.

Advantages. Compared to backtracking, the main benefits of the constraint approach are that duplicated rule applications (due to removed parts of the proof tree that might have to be re-constructed) are avoided, and that it is possible to search for different solutions in parallel. Because large parts of the proofs in question—the parts that involve symbolic execution—can be constructed algorithmically and do not require search, the first point is particularly significant here. The second point holds because the proof search does never commit to one particular (partial) solution by applying a substitution. Constraints also naturally lead to more powerful representations of classes of pre-states (Sect. 4).

Disadvantages. Destructively applying substitutions has the effect of *propagating* decisions that are made in one proof branch to the whole proof. While this is obviously a bad strategy for wrong decisions, it is by far more efficient to *verify* a substitution that leads to a solution (by applying it to the whole proof and by closing the remaining proof branches) than to hope that the remaining branches can independently come up with a compatible constraint. In Fig. 3, after applying the substitution $[\,P \mapsto 2\,]$ that is found in the left branch, the only work left in the right branch is to identify the inequation $2 \geq 0$ as valid. Finding a common solution of $P + 1 \not> 3$ and $P \geq 0$ by enumerating partial solutions, in contrast, is more naive and less efficient. One aspect of this problem is that unification constraints are not a suitable representation of solutions when arithmetic is involved (Sect. 4).

3.4   A Hybrid Approach: Backtracking and Incremental Closure

Backtracking and non-destructive search using constraints do not exclude each other. The constraint approach can be seen as a more fine-grained method for generating substitution candidates: while the pure backtracking approach always looks at a single goal when deriving substitutions, constraints allow to compare the solutions that have been found for multiple goals. The number of goals that can simultaneously be closed by one substitution, for instance, can be considered as a measure for how reasonable the substitution is. Once a good substitution candidate has been identified, it can also be applied to the proof destructively and the proof search can continue focussing on this solution candidate. Because the substitution could, nevertheless, be misleading, backtracking might be necessary at a later point. Such hybrid proof strategies have not yet been developed or tested, to the best of our knowledge.

4   Representation of Solutions: Constraint Languages

In Sect. 3.2 and 3.3, classes of pre-states are represented as substitutions or unification constraints. These representations are well-suited for pure first-order problems [10], but they are not very appropriate for integers (or natural numbers) that are common in Java: (i) Syntactic unification does not treat interpreted functions like $+$, $-$ or literals in special way. This rules out too many constraints, for instance $[X + 1 \equiv 2]$, as inconsistent. (ii) Unification conditions $t_1 \equiv t_2$ cannot describe simple classes of solutions that occur frequently, for instance classes that can be described by linear conditions like $X \geq 0$.[3]

The constraint approach of Sect. 3.3 is not restricted to unification constraints: we can see constraints in a more semantic way and essentially use any sublanguage of predicate logic (also in the presence of theories like arithmetic) that is closed under the connective $\wedge$ as constraint language. For practical purposes, validity should be decidable in the language, although this is not strictly necessary. The language that we started using in our experiments is a combination of unification conditions (seen as equations) and linear arithmetic:

$$ C ::= C \wedge C \mid t_{int} = t_{int} \mid t_{int} \neq t_{int} \mid t_{int} < t_{int} \mid t_{int} \leq t_{int} \mid t_{oth} = t_{oth} $$

in which t_{int} ranges over terms of type int and t_{oth} over terms of other types. The constraints are given the normal model-theoretic semantics of first-order formulae (see, for instance, [9]):

---

[3] Depending on the representation of integers or natural numbers, certain inequations like $X \geq 1 \Leftrightarrow X \equiv \mathrm{succ}(X')$ might be expressible, but this concept is rather restricted.

Definition 1. *A constraint C is called* consistent *if for each arithmetic struc-ture (interpreting the symbols $+$, $-$, $\neq$, $<$, $\leq$ and literals as is common over the integers, and all other function symbols arbitrarily), there is an assignment of values to metavariables such that C is evaluated to tt.*

Example 1. Of the following constraints, C_1, C_2 and C_3 are consistent, while the others are not. C_4 is inconsistent because the ranges of f and g could be disjoint, C_5 because f could be the identity, and C_6 because 5 could be outside of the range of the function $\cdot\downarrow\cdot$. Our constraint language does not know about lists, so that $\cdot\downarrow\cdot$ is just an arbitrary function symbol in this regard.

$$
\begin{array}{llll}
C_1 & := & X = 5 \wedge 2 = Y + 1 \qquad & C_2 & := & h(A, 2) = h(h(c, Y), Y + 1) \\
C_3 & := & c < X \wedge d \leq X & C_4 & := & f(X) = g(Y) \\
C_5 & := & X < f(X) & C_6 & := & (ATTR \downarrow O) = 5
\end{array}
$$

We are in the process of working out details of this language—so far, we do not know whether consistency of constraints is decidable. Using a prototypical implementation of the constraints in KeY (as part of the constraint approach of Sect. 3.3), it is possible to find the following solution of (5) automatically:

k_{IL}	k_{LN}	o_V	n_V	$head_V$	$next_V$	val_V
K_{IL}	K_{LN}	0	N_V	$[0,\ldots]$	$[E,\ldots]$	$[N_V,\ldots]$

$$
\begin{array}{l}
K_{IL} > 0 \wedge \\
K_{LN} > 0 \wedge \\
E \geq K_{LN}
\end{array}
$$

Compared to (7), this description of pre-states is more general and no longer con-tains the precise number of involved objects of *IntList* and *ListNode*. It is enough if at least one object of each class is created ($K_{IL} > 0$, $K_{LN} > 0$). Further, the so-lution states that *IntList.get*(0) receives the invocation of **delete** with arbitrary argument N_V, that *IntList.get*(0).*head* points to the object *ListNode.get*(0), that the attribute *ListNode.get*(0).*next* is *null* ($E \geq K_{LN}$), i.e., the receiving list has only one element, and that the value of this element coincides with N_V.

5 Reasoning About Lists and Arithmetic

The next pages give more (implementation) details and treat some further as-pects of the backtracking-free method from Sect. 3.3. As incremental closure works by enumerating the closing constraints of all proof branches, the central issue is to design suitable goal-local rules that produce such constraints, and to develop an application strategy that defines which rule should be applied at which point in a proof. The solutions shown here are tailored to the constraint language of the previous section.

5.1 Rules for the Theory of Lists

For proof obligations of the form (4), the closing constraints of a goal mostly describe the values of metavariables X_1, X_2, ... over lists—the lists that in Sect. 2.3 are used to represent program states—and usually have the form:

$$X_1 = cons(X_1^1, cons(X_1^2, \ldots)) \wedge X_2 = cons(X_2^1, cons(X_2^2, \ldots)) \wedge \cdots$$
$$\wedge\, C(X_1^1, X_1^2, \ldots, X_2^1, X_2^2, \ldots)$$

Such constraints consist of a first part that determines to which depth the lists X_1, X_2, ... have been "expanded," and of a part $C(X_1^1, X_1^2, \ldots, X_2^1, X_2^2, \ldots)$ (which is again a constraint, e.g. in the language from Sect. 4) that describes the values of list elements. As each of the list elements X_1^1, X_1^2, ... belongs to one object of a class (following Sect. 2.3), this intuitively means that a constraint always represents one fixed arrangement of objects in the heap. One constraint in the language from Sect. 4 cannot represent multiple isomorphic heaps (like heaps that only differ in the order of objects), because the constraints are not evaluated modulo the theory of lists. As it is explained in Example 1, a constraint like $(ATTR \downarrow O) = 5$, telling that the value of an instance attribute is 5 for the object with index O, is inconsistent and has to be written in a more concrete form like $ATTR = cons(ATTR^1, T) \wedge O = 0 \wedge ATTR^1 = 5$.

The expansion of lists is handled by a single rule that introduces fresh metavariables H, T for the head and the tail of a list. We use the *constrained formula* approach from [10] to remember this decomposition of a list L into two parts. A constrained formula is a pair $\phi \ll C$ consisting of a formula ϕ and a constraint C. The semantics of a formula $\phi \ll C$ that occurs in the antecedent of a sequent is (roughly) the same as of the implication $C \to \phi$, and in the succedent the semantics is $C \wedge \phi$: intuitively, the presence of ϕ can only be assumed if the constraint C holds. C has to be kept and propagated to all formulae that are derived from $\phi \ll C$ during the course of a proof. If $\phi \ll C$ is used to close a proof branch, the closing constraint that is created has to be conjoined with C.

The rule for expanding lists is essentially a case distinction on whether the head ($i = 0$) or a later element ($i > 0$) of a list is accessed. An attached constraint $[L = cons(H, T)]$ expresses that the name H is introduced for the head of the list and T for its tail. In practice, the rule is only applied if an expression $L \downarrow i$ occurs in the sequent $\Gamma \vdash \Delta$, where L is a metavariable. As described in Sect. 2.3, the length of lists is irrelevant, so that the case $L = nil$ does not have to be taken into account:

$$\frac{\Gamma, (i = 0 \wedge (L \downarrow 0) = H) \ll [L = cons(H, T)] \vdash \Delta \qquad \Gamma, (i > 0 \wedge (L \downarrow i) = (T \downarrow (i - 1))) \ll [L = cons(H, T)] \vdash \Delta}{\Gamma \vdash \Delta} \text{ EXPAND-LIST}$$

$$(H, T \text{ fresh metavariables})$$

Fig. 4 shows an example how EXPAND-LIST is used to enumerate the solutions of the formula $L \downarrow X > 3$.

By repeated application of EXPAND-LIST, all list access expressions $L \downarrow i$ in a sequent can be replaced with scalar metavariables, which subsequently can be handled with other rules for first-order logic and arithmetic. The fact that different goals are created for all possible heap arrangements (because EXPAND-LIST splits on the value of the list index i) obviously leads to a combinatorial

$$\cfrac{\cfrac{\cfrac{\cfrac{\overset{*}{[\,H > 3 \wedge C\,]}}{X = 0 \ll C, L{\downarrow}0 = H \ll C, H \leq 3 \ll C \;\vdash} \;\leq_{\mathrm{L}}}{X = 0 \ll C, L{\downarrow}0 = H \ll C \;\vdash\; H > 3 \ll C}}{X = 0 \ll C, L{\downarrow}0 = H \ll C \;\vdash\; L{\downarrow}X > 3}}{(X = 0 \wedge L{\downarrow}0 = H) \ll C \;\vdash\; L{\downarrow}X > 3}$$

$$\mathcal{D}$$

$$\mathcal{D} \qquad \cfrac{\cfrac{\cfrac{\cfrac{\overset{*}{[\,X < 1 \wedge C\,]}}{X \geq 1 \ll C, L{\downarrow}X = T{\downarrow}(X - 1) \ll C \;\vdash\; L{\downarrow}X > 3} \;\geq_{\mathrm{L}}}{X > 0 \ll C, L{\downarrow}X = T{\downarrow}(X - 1) \ll C \;\vdash\; L{\downarrow}X > 3}}{(X > 0 \wedge L{\downarrow}X = T{\downarrow}(X - 1)) \ll C \;\vdash\; L{\downarrow}X > 3}}{\vdash\; L{\downarrow}X > 3} \;\text{EXPAND-LIST}$$

Fig. 4. Example for a proof involving lists and metavariables $L, T : intList$, $H : int$, $X : nat$. We write C as abbreviation for the constraint $[\,L = cons(H, T)\,]$. The first solution (shown here) that is produced by the proof is $[\,L = cons(H, T) \wedge X < 1 \wedge H > 3\,]$ and stems from the formulas $X \geq 1 \ll C$ and $H \leq 3 \ll C$ in the two branches. When applying further rules to the proof—instead of closing it—and expanding the list more than once, further solutions like $[\,L = cons(H, cons(H', T')) \wedge X = 1 \wedge H' > 3\,]$ can be generated. Concerning the handling of inequations in the proof, see Sect. 5.3.

explosion, however, when the number of considered objects is increased. This is not yet relevant for programs like the one in Fig. 1. Generally, two possibilities to handle this issue (which we have not investigated yet) are (i) to work with a constraint language that directly supports the theory of lists, or to (ii) use the approach suggested in Sect. 3.4 to focus on one particular heap arrangement, ignoring isomorphic heaps. In this manner, it is, for instance, possible to simulate the lazy-initialisation approach from [11].

5.2   Fairness Conditions

As the different branches (and formulae) of a proof are expanded completely independently when using incremental closure, it is important to choose a fairness strategy that ensures an even distribution of rule applications. When proving program incorrectness, there are two primary parameters that describe how far a problem has been explored: (i) how often loops have been unwound on a branch (the number of applications of the rule WHILE-L from Fig. 2), and the (ii) the depth to which lists have been expanded (the size of the heap under consideration, or the number of applications of the rule EXPAND-LIST from the previous section).

In the KeY prover, automatic reasoning is controlled by *strategies*, which are basically cost computation functions that assign each possible rule application in a proof an integer number as cost. The rule application that has been given the least cost (for thewhole proof) is carried out first. In this setting, we achieve fairness in the following way:

- Applications of WHILE-L are given the cost $c_w = \alpha_w \cdot k_w + o_w$, where k_w is the number of applications of WHILE-L that have already been performed on a proof branch, and $\alpha_w > 0$, o_w are constants. This means that the cost for unwinding a loop a further time grows linearly with the number of earlier loop unwindings.
- Applications of EXPAND-LIST are given the cost $c_e = \alpha_e \cdot k_e + o_e$, where k_e is the sum of the depths to which each of the list metavariables has been expanded on a proof branch. This sum can be computed by considering the constraints C that are attached to formulae $\phi \ll C$ in a sequent that contain list access expressions $L \downarrow i$: one can simply count the occurrences of *cons* in the terms that have to be substituted for the original list metavariables when solving the constraint C.[4]

Good values for the constants α_w, α_e are in principle problem-dependent, but in our experience it is meaningful to choose α_e (a lot) bigger than α_w. When proving the formula (5), yielding the constraint shown in Sect. 4, we had chosen $\alpha_w = 50$, $o_w = 200$, $\alpha_e = 2500$, $o_e = -2000$.

A slightly different approach is to choose a fixed upper bound either for the number of loop unwindings or for the heap size, and to let only the other parameter grow unboundedly within one proof attempt. If the proof attempt fails, the bound can be increased and a new proof is started. In the experiments so far, we have not found any advantages of starting multiple proof attempts over the method described first, however.

5.3   Arithmetic Handling in KeY

The heap representation that is introduced in Sect. 2.3 heavily uses arithmetic (both natural and integer numbers). After the elimination of programs using symbolic execution, of updates and of list expressions, the construction of solutions or closing constraints essentially boils down to handling arithmetic formulae. Although KeY is in principle able to use the theorem prover Simplify [12] as a back-end for discharging goals that no longer contain modal operators and programs, this does not provide any support when reasoning with metavariables (Simplify does not use metavariables). In this section, we shortly describe the native support for arithmetic that we, thus, have added to KeY.

Linear Arithmetic. Equations and inequations over linear polynomials is the most common and most important fragment of integer arithmetic. We use Fourier-Motzkin variable elimination to handle such formulae—inspired by the Omega test [13], which is an extension of Fourier-Motzkin. Although Fourier-Motzkin

---

[4] The actual computation of c_e is more complicated, because smaller costs are chosen when applying EXPAND-LIST for terms $L \downarrow i$ in which i is a concrete literal, or when the rule has already been applied for the same list L earlier.

does not yield a complete procedure over the integers, in contrast to the Omega test, we have so far not encountered the need to create a full implementation of the Omega test.

As a pre-processing step, the equations and inequations of a sequent are always moved to the antecedent and are transformed into inequations $c \cdot x \leq s$ or $c \cdot x \geq s$, where c is a positive number and s is a term. Further, in order to ensure termination, we assume the existence of a well-ordering on the set of variables of a problem and require that x is strictly bigger than all variables in s. Fourier-Motzkin variable elimination can then be realised by the following rule:

$$\frac{\Gamma, c \cdot x \geq s, d \cdot x \leq t, d \cdot s \leq c \cdot t \vdash \Delta}{\Gamma, c \cdot x \geq s, d \cdot x \leq t \vdash \Delta} \text{ TRANSITIVITY} \qquad (c > 0, d > 0)$$

Apart from the rule for eliminating variables from inequations, we also have to provide rules for generating closing constraints (using the constraint language from Sect. 4):

$$\frac{[s = t]}{\Gamma \vdash s = t, \Delta} =\text{R} \qquad \frac{[s \neq t]}{\Gamma, s = t \vdash \Delta} =\text{L} \qquad \frac{[s > t]}{\Gamma, s \leq t \vdash \Delta} \leq\text{L} \qquad \frac{[s < t]}{\Gamma, s \geq t \vdash \Delta} \geq\text{L}$$

Non-Linear Arithmetic. In order to handle multiplication, division- and modulo-operations that frequently occur in programs, we have also added some support for non-linear integer arithmetic to KeY. Our approach is similar to that of the ACL2 theorem prover [14] and is based on the following rule (together with the rules for handling linear arithmetic):

$$\frac{\Gamma, s \leq s', t \leq t', 0 \leq (s' - s) \cdot (t' - t) \vdash \Delta}{\Gamma, s \leq s', t \leq t' \vdash \Delta} \text{ MULT-INEQUATIONS}$$

Often, it is also necessary to perform a systematic case analysis. The rule MULT-INEQUATIONS alone is, for instance, not sufficient to prove simple formulae like $x \cdot x \geq 0$. Case distinctions can be introduced with the following rules:

$$\frac{\Gamma, x < 0 \vdash \Delta \quad \Gamma, x = 0 \vdash \Delta \quad \Gamma, x > 0 \vdash \Delta}{\Gamma \vdash \Delta} \text{ SIGN-CASES} \qquad \frac{\Gamma, s < t \vdash \Delta \quad \Gamma, s = t \vdash \Delta}{\Gamma, s \leq t \vdash \Delta} \text{ STRENGTHEN}$$

We can now prove $x \cdot x \geq 0$ by first splitting on the sign of x. The rules SIGN-CASES and STRENGTHEN are in principle sufficient to find solutions for arbitrary solvable polynomial equations and inequations. Combined with the rules =R, =L, $\leq$L, $\geq$L from above, this guarantees that the calculus can always produce solutions and closing constraints for satisfiable sequents that (only) contain such formulae.

6 Related Work

Proof strategies based on metavariables and backtracking are related to common approaches to test data generation with symbolic execution, see, e.g., [5,7]. Conceiving the approach as *proving* provides a semantics, but also opens up for new optimisations like backtracking-free proof search. Likewise, linear arithmetic is frequently used to handle branch predicates in symbolic execution, e.g. [15]. This is related to Sect. 4, although constraints are in the present paper not only used for branch predicates, but also for the actual pre- and post-conditions.

As discussed in Sect. 3.1, there is a close relation between ground proof procedures and test data generation using actual program execution. Constructing proofs using metavariables can be seen as exhaustive testing, because the behaviour of a program is examined (simultaneously) for all possible inputs. When using the fairness approach of limiting the size of the initial heap that is described in Sect. 5.2, the method is related to bounded exhaustive testing, because only program inputs up to a certain size are considered.

A technique that can be used both for proving programs correct and incorrect is abstraction-refinement model checking (e.g., [16,17,18]). Here, the typical setup is to abstract from precise data flow and to prove an abstract version of a program correct. If this attempt fails, usually symbolic execution is used to extract a precise witness for program incorrectness or to increase the precision of the employed abstraction. Apart from abstraction, a difference to the method presented here is the strong correlation between paths in a program (reachability) and counterexamples in model checking. In contrast, our approach can potentially produce classes of pre-states that cover multiple execution paths.

Related to this approach is the general idea of extracting information from failing verification attempts, which can be found in many places. ESC/Java2 [19] and Boogie [20] are verification systems for object-oriented languages that use the prover Simplify [12] as back-end. Simplify is able to derive counterexamples from failed proof attempts, which are subsequently used to create warnings about possible erroneous behaviour of a program for certain concrete situations. Another example is [21], where counterexamples are created from unclosed sequent calculus proofs. Making use of failing proof attempts has the advantage of reusing work towards verification that has already been performed, which makes it particularly attractive for interactive verification systems. At the same time, it is difficult to obtain completeness results and to guarantee that proofs explicitly "fail," or that counterexamples can be extracted. In this sense, our approach is more systematic.

7 Conclusions and Future Work

The development of the proposed method and of its prototypical implementation has been driven by working with (small) examples [22], but we cannot claim to have a sufficient number of benchmarks and comparisons to other approaches yet. It is motivating, however, that our method can handle erroneous programs like in Fig. 1 (and similar programs operating on lists) automatically, which we found to be beyond the capabilities of commercial test data generation tools like JTest [23,22]. This supports the expectation that the usage of a theorem prover for finding bugs (i) is most reasonable for "hard" bugs that are only revealed when running a program with a non-trivial pre-state, and (ii) has the further main advantage of deriving more general (classes of) counterexamples than testing methods. The method is probably most useful when combined with other techniques, for instance with test generation approaches that can find "obvious" bugs more efficiently.

For the time being, we consider it as most important to better understand the constraint language of Sect. 4 for representing solutions, and, in particular, to investigate the decidability of consistency. Because of the extensive use of lists in Sect. 2.3, it would also be attractive to have constraints that directly support the theory of lists. As explained in Sect. 5.1, such constraints would introduce a notion of *heap isomorphism*, which is a topic that we also plan to address. Further, we want to investigate the combination of backtracking and incremental closure (as sketched in Sect. 3.4). A planned topic that conceptually goes beyond the method of the present paper are proofs about the termination behaviour of programs.

Acknowledgements

We want to thank Wolfgang Ahrendt for many discussions that eventually led to this paper, and Tobias Nipkow for comments on an older version of the paper. Thanks are also due to the anonymous referees for helpful comments and hints.

References

1. Harel, D., Kozen, D., Tiuryn, J.: Dynamic Logic. MIT Press, Cambridge (2000)
2. Beckert, B., Hähnle, R., Schmitt, P.H. (eds.): Verification of Object-Oriented Software: The KeY Approach. LNCS (LNAI), vol. 4334. Springer, Heidelberg (2007)
3. Leavens, G.T., Poll, E., Clifton, C., Cheon, Y., Ruby, C.: JML Reference Manual (August 2002)
4. Rümmer, P.: Sequential, parallel, and quantified updates of first-order structures. In: Hermann, M., Voronkov, A. (eds.) LPAR 2006. LNCS (LNAI), vol. 4246, pp. 422–436. Springer, Heidelberg (2006)
5. King, J.C.: Symbolic execution and program testing. Communications of the ACM 19(7), 385–394 (1976)
6. Claessen, K., Hughes, J.: QuickCheck: a lightweight tool for random testing of Haskell programs. ACM SIGPLAN Notices 35(9), 268–279 (2000)
7. Edvardsson, J.: A survey on automatic test data generation. In: ECSEL. Proceedings of the Second Conference on Computer Science and Engineering in Linkping, pp. 21–28 (October 1999)
8. Hähnle, R.: Tableaux and related methods. In: Robinson, A., Voronkov, A. (eds.) Handbook of Automated Reasoning, vol. 1, pp. 101–178. Elsevier Science B.V, Amsterdam (2001)
9. Fitting, M.C.: First-Order Logic and Automated Theorem Proving, 2nd edn. Springer, New York (1996)
10. Giese, M.: Incremental closure of free variable tableaux. In: Goré, R.P., Leitsch, A., Nipkow, T. (eds.) IJCAR 2001. LNCS (LNAI), vol. 2083, pp. 545–560. Springer, Heidelberg (2001)

11. Khurshid, S., Pasareanu, C.S., Visser, W.: Generalized symbolic execution for model checking and testing. In: Garavel, H., Hatcliff, J. (eds.) ETAPS 2003 and TACAS 2003. LNCS, vol. 2619, pp. 553–568. Springer, Heidelberg (2003)
12. Detlefs, D., Nelson, G., Saxe, J.B.: Simplify: a theorem prover for program checking. J. ACM 52(3), 365–473 (2005)
13. Pugh, W.: The omega test: a fast and practical integer programming algorithm for dependence analysis. In: Supercomputing '91. Proceedings of the 1991 ACM/IEEE conference on Supercomputing, pp. 4–13. ACM Press, New York, USA (1991)
14. Kaufmann, M., Moore, J.S.: An industrial strength theorem prover for a logic based on common lisp. IEEE Trans. Softw. Eng. 23(4), 203–213 (1997)
15. Gupta, N., Mathur, A.P., Soffa, M.L.: Automated test data generation using an iterative relaxation method. In: SIGSOFT '98/FSE-6. Proceedings of the 6th ACM SIGSOFT international symposium on Foundations of software engineering, pp. 231–244. ACM Press, New York (1998)
16. Cimatti, A., Clarke, E.M., Giunchiglia, F., Roveri, M.: NUSMV: A new symbolic model checker. International Journal on Software Tools for Technology Transfer 2(4), 410–425 (2000)
17. Visser, W., Havelund, K., Brat, G.P., Park, S., Lerda, F.: Model checking programs. Automated Software Engineering 10(2), 203–232 (2003)
18. Ball, T., Majumdar, R., Millstein, T.D., Rajamani, S.K.: Automatic predicate abstraction of C programs. In: Proceedings PLDI, pp. 203–213 (2001)
19. Flanagan, C., Leino, K.R.M., Lillibridge, M., Nelson, G., Saxe, J.B., Stata, R.: Extended Static Checking for Java. In: Proceedings PLDI, pp. 234–245 (2002)
20. Barnett, M., Leino, K.R.M., Schulte, W.: The Spec# programming system: an overview. In: Barthe, G., Burdy, L., Huisman, M., Lanet, J.-L., Muntean, T. (eds.) CASSIS 2004. LNCS, vol. 3362, pp. 49–69. Springer, Heidelberg (2005)
21. Reif, W., Schellhorn, G., Thums, A.: Flaw detection in formal specifications. In: Goré, R.P., Leitsch, A., Nipkow, T. (eds.) IJCAR 2001. LNCS (LNAI), vol. 2083, pp. 642–657. Springer, Heidelberg (2001)
22. Shah, M.A.: Generating counterexamples for Java dynamic logic. Master's thesis (November 2005)
23. Parasoft: JTest (2006),
    www.parasoft.com/jsp/products/home.jsp?product=Jtest

Testing and Verifying Invariant Based Programs in the SOCOS Environment

Ralph-Johan Back[1], Johannes Eriksson[1], and Magnus Myreen[2]

[1] Åbo Akademi University, Department of Information Technologies
Turku, FI-20520, Finland
{backrj,joheriks}@abo.fi
[2] University of Cambridge, Computer Laboratory
Cambridge CB3 0FD, UK
magnus.myreen@cl.cam.ac.uk

Abstract. SOCOS is a prototype tool for constructing programs and reasoning about their correctness. It supports the invariant based programming methodology by providing a diagrammatic environment for specification, implementation, verification and execution of procedural programs. Invariants and contracts (pre- and postconditions) are evaluated at runtime, following the Design by Contract paradigm. Furthermore, SOCOS generates correctness conditions for static verification based on the weakest precondition semantics of statements. To verify the program the user can attempt to automatically discharge these conditions using the Simplify theorem prover; conditions which were not automatically discharged can be proved interactively in the PVS theorem prover.

Keywords: Invariant based programming, static program verification, verification conditions, state charts.

1 Introduction

This paper presents tool support for an approach to program construction, which we refer to as *invariant based programming* [1,2]. This approach differs from most conventional programming paradigms in that it lifts specifications and invariants to the role of first-class citizens. The programmer starts by formulating the specifications and the internal loop invariants before writing the program code itself. Expressing the invariants first has two main advantages: firstly, they are immediately available for evaluation during execution to identify invalid assumptions about the program state. Secondly, if strong enough, invariants can be used to prove the correctness of the program. To mechanize the second step, we have previously developed a static checker [3], which generates verification conditions for invariant based programs and sends them to an external theorem prover. In this paper we continue on the topic by presenting the SOCOS tool, an effort to extend this checker into a fully diagrammatic programming environment.

The syntax of SOCOS programs is highly visual and based on a precise diagrammatic syntax. We use *invariant diagrams* [1], a graphical notation for

B. Meyer and Y. Gurevich (Eds.): TAP 2007, LNCS 4454, pp. 61–78, 2007.

describing imperative programs, to model procedures. The notation is intuitive and shares similarities with both Venn diagrams and state charts—invariants are described as nested sets and statements as transitions between sets. As a means for constructing programs, the notation differs from most programming languages in that invariants, rather than control flow blocks, serve as the primary organizing structure.

SOCOS has been developed in the Gaudi Software Factory [4], our experimental software factory for producing research software. The tool is being developed in parallel with the theory for incremental software construction with refinement diagrams [5], and the project has undergone a number of shifts in focus to accommodate the ongoing research. By using an agile development process [6] we have been able to keep the software up to date with the changing requirements.

1.1 Related Work

Invariant based programming originates in Dijkstra's ideas of constructing the program and its proof hand in hand [7]. Invariant based programming (Reynolds [8], Back [9,2] and van Emden [10]) takes this approach one step further, so that program invariants are determined before the program code or even the control structures to be used have been determined.

There exists a number of methods and tools for formal program verification, some with a long standing tradition. Verification techniques typically include a combined specification and programming language, supported by software tools for verification condition generation and proof assistance. For the construction of realistic software systems, a method for reasoning on higher levels of abstraction becomes crucial; some approaches, such as the B Method [11], support correct refinement of abstract specifications into executable implementations. This method has had success in safety-critical and industrial applications and shows the applicability of formal methods to software systems of realistic scales.

Equipping software components with specifications (contracts) and assertions is the central idea of *Design by Contract* [12]. This method is either supported by add-on tools or integrated into the language. Most tools supporting Design by Contract do not, however, provide static correctness checking.

A host of tools have been developed for Java and the JML specification language, for both runtime and static correctness checking [13]. In particular, ESC/Java2 [14] enables programmers to catch common errors by sending verification conditions to an automatic theorem prover. However, it is fully automatic and thus not powerful enough for full formal verification. The LOOP tool [15], on the other hand, translates JML-annotated Java programs into a set of PVS theories, which can be proved interactively using the PVS proof assistant. Another tool called JACK, the Java Applet Correctness Kit [16], allows the use of both automatic and interactive provers from an Eclipse front end.

1.2 Contribution

Many tools for verifying programs work by implementing a weakest precondition calculus for an existing language. Due to complex language semantics,theproof obligations generated for invariant-enriched existing languages often become quite elaborate. This can make it difficult to know which part of the code a condition was generated from, and to see the relationship between code and proof obligation. Rather than adding specifications and invariants to an existing language, we start with a simpler notation for programs and their proofs, *invariant diagrams* with nested invariants. Our belief is that an intuitive notation where the proof conditions are easily seen from the program description decreases the mental gap between programming and verification. Since the notation requires the programmer to carefully describe the intermediate situations (invariants), invariant based programs provide as a side effect automatic documentation of the design decisions made when constructing the program, and are thus easier to inspect than ordinary programs.

We describe here a tool to support invariant based programming, the *SOCOS environment,* which supports the construction, testing, verification and visualization of invariant based programs by providing an integrated editor, debugger and theorem prover interface. An invariant based program is developed in SOCOS in an incremental manner, so that we continually check that each increment preserves the correctness of the program built thus far. Both testing and verification techniques are used to check the correctness of program extensions. In the early phases of development, exercising the behavior of the program with test cases is an efficient way to detect invariant violations. To achieve higher assurance, the programmer can perform automated static correctness analysis to prove that some part of each invariant holds for all input. Total correctness is achieved by proving that remaining parts of the invariants hold, using an interactive proof assistant. Our preliminary experience indicates that the tool is quite useful for constructing small programs and reasoning about them. It removes the tedium of checking trivial verification conditions, it automates the run-time checking of contracts and invariants, and it provides an intuitive visual feedback when something goes wrong.

The remainder of this paper is structured as follows. In Section 2 we describe the diagrammatic notations used to implement SOCOS programs and give an overview of the SOCOS invariant diagram editor. In Section 3 we describe how programs are compiled, executed and debugged. In Section 4 we discuss the formal semantics of SOCOS programs and the generation of proof conditions. Section 5 provides a use case of SOCOS as we demonstrate the implementation of a simple sorting program. Section 6 concludes with some general observations and a summary of on-going research.

2   Invariant Diagrams

Invariant based programs are constructed using a new diagrammatic programming notation, *nested invariant diagrams* [1], where specifications and invariants provide the main organizing structure. To illustrate the notation we will consider as an example a naive summation program which calculates the sum of the integers 0..n using simple iteration, accumulating the result in the program variable sum. An invariant diagram describing this program is given in Figure 1.

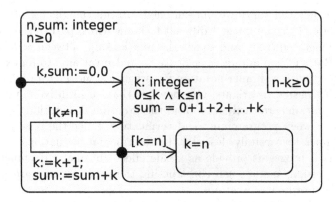

Fig. 1. Summation program

Rounded boxes in the diagram are called *situations*. A situation represents the set of program states that satisfy a given predicate. One or more boolean expressions, all of which should hold, may be written inside the box. Furthermore, nested situations inherit the predicates of enclosing situations. Inside the largest box in Figure 1, variables n and sum are of type integer and n is greater than or equal to 0. Due to nesting this is also true in the middle-sized box, and additionally the variable k is an integer between 0 and n, and the variable sum has the value $0 + 1 + 2 + \dots + k$. In the most deeply nested situation, all these predicates hold and in addition $k = n$.

A transition is a sequence of arrows that start in one situation and end in the same or another situation. Each arrow can be labeled with:

1. A *guard* $[g]$, where g is a Boolean expression - g is assumed when the transition is triggered.
2. A *program statement* S - S is executed when the transition is triggered. S can be a sequence of statements, but loop constructs are not allowed.

To simplify the presentation and logic of transitions, we can add intermediate choice points (forks) to branch the transition. However, joins and cycles between choice points are not allowed. The transitions described by the tree are all the paths in the tree, from the start situation to some end situation. A choice point in the tree can be seen as a conditional branching statement.

It should be noted that the nesting semantics of invariant diagrams that apply to situations do not apply to transitions. The program state is not required to satisfy any situation while executing a transition, even if the arrow itself is drawn inside a situation box.

In general, any situation that does not have an incoming transition is considered an *initial situation*. Conversely, we will consider a situation without outgoing transitions a *terminal situation*.

To prove the correctness of a program described by an invariant diagram, we need to prove consistency and completeness of the transitions, and that the program cannot start an infinite loop. A transition from situation I_1 to situation I_2 using program statement S is *consistent* if and only if $I_1 \Rightarrow wp.S.I_2$ where wp is Dijkstra's weakest-precondition predicate transformer [17]. The program is *complete* if there is at least one enabled transition in each state, with the exception of terminal situations. We show that a program terminates by providing a *variant*, a function which is bounded from below and which is decreased by every cycle in the diagram. In the summation example the variant is indicated in the upper right corner of the situation box.

The notion of correctness for invariant diagrams is further discussed in Section 4 where we consider formal verification of SOCOS programs. For a more general treatment of invariant diagrams and invariant based programming we refer to [1].

2.1   Invariant Diagrams in SOCOS

Figure 1 shows an example of a purely conceptual invariant diagram. SOCOS diagrams, which we will use in this paper, are annotated with some additional elements. Some restrictions have also been introduced to simplify the implementation. Figure 2 shows the equivalent summation program implemented as a SOCOS procedure.

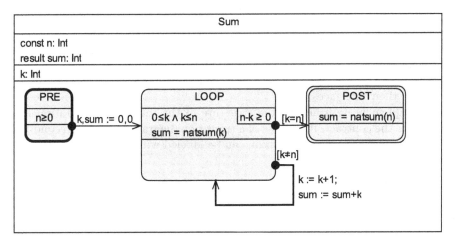

Fig. 2. Summation program, SOCOS syntax

Compared to the conceptual notation, the main differences are:

- The outer situation is a *procedure box*, which represents a procedure declaration with a procedure name, parameters and local variables.
- Each situation is labeled with a descriptive name, such as LOOP for a recurring situation. The name is used as a general situation identifier in error reports and generated proof conditions.
- To prove termination sufficient for one transition in a cycle to *strictly decrease* the variant. Such transitions are selected by the user and rendered in the diagram as thicker arrows. This is further discussed in Section 4.

– We provide an initial and a terminal situation representing the entry and exit point of the procedure, respectively. These situations constitute the contract of the procedure. The precondition situation is called PRE and is additionally marked with a thick outline, while the postcondition is called POST and marked with a double outline. Note that in the example POST is not nested within LOOP, but instead part of the invariant is repeated. Since the contract constitutes an external interface to other procedures, it may only talk about the formal parameters and not, e.g., the local variable k.

– Local variables have procedural scope and it is presently not possible to introduce new variables in nested situations.

– SOCOS supports declaration of global predicates and functions. In this case we assume that natsum has been defined to give the sum from 0 up to its argument, e.g. based on a recursive definition or using the direct formula $\frac{k(k+1)}{2}$.

The procedure is the basic unit of decomposition in SOCOS. A procedure consists of two parts: an externally visible *interface*, and a hidden *implementation*. The interface can further be divided into a *signature* and a *contract*. A signature is a list of formal input and output parameters that describes the name, type and qualifier of each parameter. Five primitive types (natural numbers, integers, Booleans, characters, strings) along with one composite type (array) are presently supported; the four available parameter qualifiers are listed in Table 1. The contract defines the obligations and benefits of the procedure as a pre- and postcondition pair. Recursive procedures are supported. As in the case of cyclic transitions, all procedures in a recursion cycle must provide a common variant as part of their interfaces.

The implementation defines the structure of the internal computation that establishes the contract. It consists of a transition diagram from the precondition to the postcondition. Each transition can be labeled with a statement according to the syntax:

$$S ::= \text{magic} \mid \text{abort} \mid$$
$$x_1,...,x_m := v_1,...,v_m \mid$$
$$S_0; S_1 \mid$$
$$[b] \mid \{b\} \mid$$
$$P(a_1,...,a_n)$$

Here magic is the miraculous statement, which satisfies every postcondition. abort represents the aborting program, which never terminates. The assignment statement assigns a list of values $v_1, ..., v_m$ to a list of variables $x_1, ..., x_m$. The; operator represents sequential composition of two statements S_0 and S_1. An assume statement $[b]$ means that we can assume the predicate b at that point in the transition, while an assert statement $\{b\}$ tells us that we have to show that b holds at that point in the transition. A procedure call $P(a_1,...,a_n)$ stands for a call to procedure P with the actual parameters $a_1,...,a_n$. The type of an actual parameter a_i depends on how the parameter type is qualified: for unqualified and const parameters, an expression is accepted. For result and valres parameters, the

Table 1. Parameter qualifiers

Qualifier	Role	Keyword	Description
Value	In	-	Can be read and updated by the implementation, but updates are not reflected back to the caller
Constant	In	const	Can only be read by the implementation
Value-result	In, out	valres	Can be read as well as updated by the implementation. Updates are not reflected back to caller until the procedure returns
Result	Out	result	Like value-result, but may not occur in preconditions

actual must be a simple variable. The formal weakest precondition semantics of these statements are the standard ones [18].

2.2 Diagram Editor

Programs are constructed in the SOCOS invariant diagram editor. A program is represented by a collection of procedure diagrams. A screen shot of the diagram editor is shown in Figure 3. The highlighted tab below the main toolbar indicates that an invariant diagram is currently being edited. On the left is an outline editor for browsing model elements, and the bottom pane holds property editors and various communication windows.

The SOCOS diagram editor is implemented on top of another project developed in the Gaudi software factory, the Coral *modeling framework* [19]. Coral is a metamodel-independent toolkit which can easily be extended to custom graphical notations.

3   Run-Time Checking of Invariant Diagrams

3.1 Compilation

An invariant diagram is executed by compiling it into a Python program which is executed by the standard Python interpreter. We use a simple approach for code generation; the generated program is effectively a goto-program. Each situation is represented by a method. The body of a situation's method executes the transition statements and returns a reference to the next method to be executed as well as an updated environment (a mapping from variable names to values). The main loop of the program is simply:

```
while s:
    s,env = s(env)
```

where s is the currently executing situation and env is the environment.

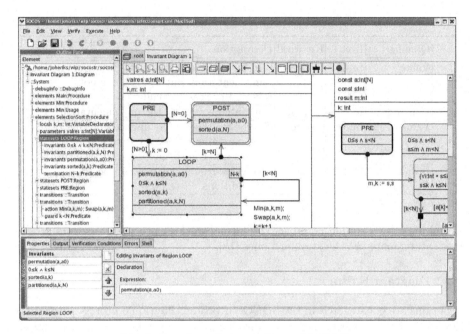

Fig. 3. Invariant diagram editor of SOCOS

If run-time checking is enabled, invariants and assertions are evaluated during execution of a situation's method. For situations that are part of a cycle, the variant is compared to its lower bound, as well as to its value in the previous cycle to ensure that it is decreasing. If any of these checks evaluate to false, an exception is raised. While SOCOS automatically evaluates only a pre-defined subset of all expressible invariants (namely arithmetic expressions and Boolean expressions containing only bounded quantifiers), it is possible to extend the dynamic evaluation capabilities for special cases by adding a side-effect free Python script to perform the evaluation.

3.2 Translating Conditions to Python

SOCOS uses a set of translation rules to produce an executable Python program. In order to make the compilation easily extensible we provide the user with the capability to define new translations. The translation of a mathematical expression is done through simple rewrite rules. The user may define new translation rules. Here are a few of the predefined translation rules:

rule Py00[group=python] $python(\top) \equiv$ **True**.
rule Py03[group=python] $python(a \land b) \equiv python(a)$ **and** $python(b)$.
rule Py13[group=python] $python(m + n) \equiv python(m) + python(n)$.

All translation rules are similar in shape. They push a translation function ($python$ above) through the expression to be translated. The translation of an expression e is performed by repeatedly applying the rewrite rules to the expression $python(e)$ until the function symbol $python$ does not occur in the resulting expression. Compilation succeeds if all expressions of the program are translated successfully.

3.3 Debugging

SOCOS provides a graphical debugger for tracking the execution of invariant diagrams. A program can be run continuously or stepped through transition by transition. During execution the current program state, consisting of the procedure call stack, the values of allocated variables and the current situation, can be inspected. It is possible to set *breakpoints* to halt the execution in specific situations.

Program execution is visualized by highlighting diagram elements in the editor. Active procedures, i.e. procedures on the call stack, as well as the current situation and the currently executing transition are highlighted. The values of local variables in each stack frame are displayed in a call stack view. Invariants are evaluated at run-time and are highlighted in red, green or gray depending on the result: for invariants that evaluate to true the highlight color is green, for invariants that evaluate to false it is red, and if SOCOS is unable to evaluate the invariant it is gray. The program execution is halted whenever an invariant evaluates to false.

4   Proving Correctness of Invariant Diagrams

The SOCOS environment supports interactive and non-interactive verification of program diagrams. It generates the verification conditions and sends them to proof tools. At the time of writing two proof tools are supported: Simplify [20] and PVS [21]. Simplify is a validity checker that suffices to automatically discharge simple verification conditions such as conditions on array bounds. PVS is an interactive proof environment in which the remaining conditions can be proved interactively.

4.1   Verification Condition Generation

SOCOS generates verification conditions using MathEdit [3]. Three types of verification conditions are generated: consistency, completeness and termination conditions. All of these use the weakest precondition semantics as their basis [17]. The consistency conditions ensure that the invariants are preserved; completeness conditions that the program is live; and termination conditions that the program does not diverge.

Consistency

A program is consistent whenever each transition is consistent. A transition from I_1 to I_2 realized by program statement S is consistent iff

$$I_1 \Rightarrow wp.S.I_2$$

Completeness

A program is complete whenever each non-terminal situation is complete. A situation I is complete iff

$$I \Rightarrow wp.S^*.\text{false}$$

where S^* is the statement that we get from the transition tree from I when each branching with branches $[b_1]; S_1, \ldots, [b_k]; S_k$ is treated as an if $b \rightarrow_1 S_1 [] \ldots [] b \rightarrow_k S_k$ fi statement and each leaf statement is replaced with magic [1,2].

Termination

A program does not diverge if the program graph can be divided into subgraphs, such that the transitions in between the subgraphs constitute an acyclic graph and each subgraph is terminating. A subgraph of the program diagram is terminating if (i) it is acyclic or (ii) has a bounded variant that decreases on each cycle within that subgraph.[3]

The cycles considered in case (ii) can consist of any number of transitions that do not increase the subgraph's variant (v below)

$$I_1 \wedge (v_0 = v) \Rightarrow wp.S.(0 \le v \le v_0) \tag{1}$$

as long as each cycle contains one transition (indicated by the user) that strictly decreases the subgraph's variant:

$$I_1 \wedge (v_0 = v) \Rightarrow wp.S.(0 \le v < v_0). \tag{2}$$

The termination conditions are generated for the transitions that make up cycles in the program graph.[4]

The interested reader is referred to [1] for a more detailed presentation of the notion of correctness of invariant diagrams.

---

[1] A single guard statement $[b]; S_1$ without an alternative branch has also to be written as an if ... fi statement, if $b \rightarrow S_1$ fi.

[2] We disregard the statements at the leaves by replacing them with miracles. A simple example may be useful here:

The completeness condition for I in this case is:
$I \Rightarrow wp.(\text{if } g_1 \rightarrow (S; \text{if } h_1 \rightarrow \text{magic } [] h_2 \rightarrow \text{magic fi}) [] g_2 \rightarrow \text{magic fi}). \text{false}$,
which is equivalent to: $I \Rightarrow (g_1 \Rightarrow wp.S.(h_1 \vee h_2)) \wedge (g_1 \vee g_2)$

[3] SOCOS will automatically divide the program graph into the smallest possible subgraphs that constitute an acyclic graph and then require that the situations within the subgraph are annotated with identical variants.

[4] Termination and consistency conditions are actually merged together so as to avoid duplication of proof efforts. Their structure allows them to be merged: $I_1 \wedge (v_0 = v) \Rightarrow wp.S.(I_2 \wedge (0 \le v < v_0))$ and similarly for the case $v \le v_0$.

4.2 Interaction with External Tools

SOCOS communicates through MathEdit with external proofs tools. Interfaces to PVS and Simplify are currently implemented in MathEdit. The interface to Simplify is from the users point of view non-interactive. Behind the scenes MathEdit runs an interactive session with Simplify. MathEdit sets up the logical context and then checks the validity of each verification in turn, splitting the verification conditions to pinpoint problematic cases. For a more detailed description of the interaction with Simplify see [3].

Interaction with PVS is made simple. By clicking a button in SOCOS, MathEdit produces a theory file containing the verification conditions and starts PVS which opens the generated theory file. A non-interactive mode for using PVS is also supplied. In the non-interactive mode PVS is run in batch mode behind the scenes. PVS applies a modified version of the `grind` tactic to all verification conditions and reports success or failure for each verification condition. The output is shown to the user of SOCOS.

4.3 Translation of Verification Conditions

The verification conditions are translated using rewrite rules similar to those used for compilation into Python code. The user may define new translation rules for translation into PVS and Simplify.

The verification conditions sent to Simplify and PVS differ in more than just syntax. PVS has a stronger input language, which among other things supports partial functions well. Simplify's input language is untyped, which means that some expressions require side conditions to ensure that they are well defined, for example k div m requires the side condition $m \neq 0$. We cannot guarantee that the generated side conditions are strong enough for user defined operands. Hence we recommend that Simplify is used for spotting bugs early in the design and PVS is used for formal verification of the final components.

Please note that care must be taken while writing new translation rules for the verification conditions. Mistakes in the translation rules can jeopardize the validity of the correctness proof.

5 Example: Sorting

In this section we demonstrate how a procedure specification, consisting of a procedure interface and given pre- and postconditions, is implemented in SOCOS. We choose a simple sorting algorithm as our case study. The focus is mainly on the tool and how invariant based programming is supported in practice—for a more detailed treatment of the methodology itself, we refer to [1].

5.1 Specification

We start by introducing a procedure specification consisting of a signature and a contract. A standard sorting specification is shown in Figure 4. The procedure accepts one parameter, an integer array a with N elements. Indexes are 0-based; the first element is at position 0 and the last element is at position $N - 1$. The valres keyword indicates that a is a value-result parameter. The array a is updated by the sorting routine, but should remain a permutation of the original array, so the postcondition relates the old and new values of a by the permutation predicate. We use the convention of appending 0 to a parameter name to refer to the original value of the parameter. The sorted predicate says that each element is less than or equal to its successor in the array.

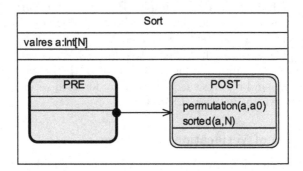

Fig. 4. A specification of a sorting procedure

A SOCOS integer array is modeled as a function from the interval $[0, N)$ to Int, where N is the size of the array. N is assumed to be a positive natural number. Access to an array element at index i is defined as function application: $a[i] = a.i$. We then define the predicates sorted and permutation as follows:

$$\text{sorted}(a, n) \mathrel{\hat{=}} (\forall i : \text{Int} \bullet 0 < i \wedge i < n \Rightarrow a[i - 1] \leq a[i])$$
$$\text{permutation}(a, b) \mathrel{\hat{=}} (\exists f \bullet \text{bijective}.f \wedge a = b \circ f)$$

Some invariants are guaranteed by the system and thus implicit. The precondition as given above is empty, however, during verification condition generation the additional assumption a = a0 is added automatically. Furthermore, arrays are assumed to be non-empty and have an implicit type invariant that allows us to assume $N > 0$ in every situation in Sort.

5.2   Implementation

Given the above specification, the next task is to provide an executable program which transforms any state in PRE to a state in POST. For brevity we implement a simple sorting algorithm, selection sort, which performs in-place sorting in $O(n^2)$ time. Selection sort works by partitioning an array into two portions, one sorted followed by one unsorted. Each iteration of the main loop exchanges the smallest element from the unsorted portion with the element immediately after the already sorted portion, thus extending the sorted portion by one. The loop terminates when no elements are left in the unsorted portion.

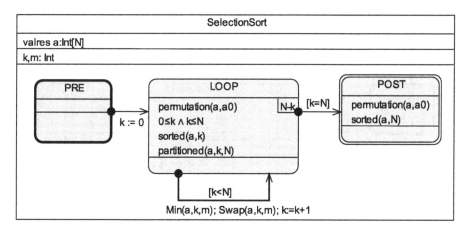

Fig. 5. Selection sort

The implementation SelectionSort can be seen in Figure 5; the two helper procedures, Min and Swap, are given in Figure 6. Min finds the smallest element in the subarray a[s..N) and returns its index, while Swap exchanges the two elements at indexes m and n in the array a.

5.3 Testing the Implementation

We can gain an understanding of how selection sort works by implementing a simple test case and examining the transitions between program states by single-stepping through the call to SelectionSort in the SOCOS debugger. Figure 7 shows such a debugging session.

The current situation is highlighted with a blue outline. The LOOP situation has been marked as a breakpoint (indicated by a red dot in the upper left corner). This causes the execution flow to temporarily halt at this point, and the current program state is shown in the pane to the right. Both the original value of the array prior to the call, a0, and the partially sorted array, a, are shown. Furthermore, invariants are evaluated and color-coded. In the absence of a breakpoint, execution also halts whenever an invariant evaluates to false.

SOCOS can translate simple invariants automatically to Python based on built-in rules. However, permutation is not automatically translatable, but we can add a Python function to check whether the array xs is a permutation of the array ys:

```
def permutation( xs, ys ):
    xs,ys = list(xs),list(ys)
    xs.sort()
    ys.sort()
    return xs==ys
```

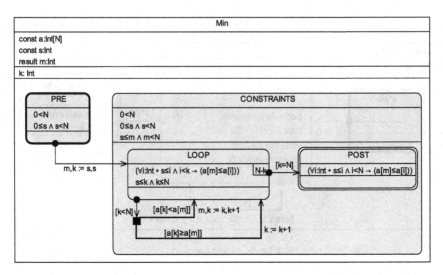

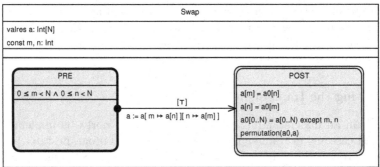

Fig. 6. Utility procedures Min and Swap

In addition to the code snippet we also need to provide a rewrite rule to make SOCOS generate a call to this function whenever it encounters permutation during evaluation of an invariant.

5.4   Verifying the Implementation

While dynamic checking of invariants is valuable in that it catches many common programming errors, its usefulness is highly dependent on good test cases. Since we have put much effort into writing down the invariants, we can go one step further and attempt formal verification. In this mode, SOCOS generates verification conditions for consistency, completeness and termination as described in the previous section. The automatic correctness checking command, Verify ▷ Check Correctness (Simplify), employs Simplify to attempt automatic discharging of verification conditions. If we run this command on the example, SOCOS will tell us that Simplify was able to discharge 99.7 percent of the conditions

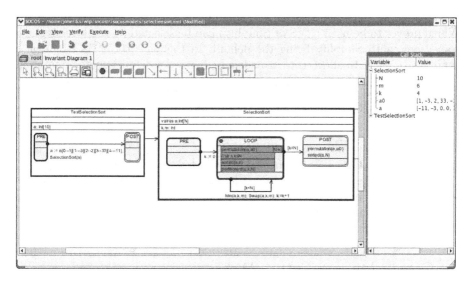

Fig. 7. Stepping through a test case of selection sort

Verification initiated for SelectionSort, Swap and Min.
99.7% of the verifications were proved automatically.
Condition: POST (Swap)
Assumptions:
    $0 < N$
    $0 \leq m$
    $m < N$
    $0 \leq n$
    $n < N$
    $a0 = a$
Imply:
    $permutation(a0, a[m \mapsto a[n]][n \mapsto a[m]])$

Fig. 8. Remaining condition for Swap

(Figure 8). While all conditions for SelectionSort and Max are discharged, problems occur due to the use of permutation in Swap.

SOCOS has pinpointed a specific verification condition that we need to check. However, since permutation is a higher-order property, we can not give a definition of permutation that Simplify can use. In this situation we have two options—firstly, we can get rid of the error temporarily by adding an assumption: in the case of Swap we would add the assumption statement [permutation(a, a0)] directly after the assignment statement in the transition from PRE to POST if we believe that $a[m \mapsto a[n]][n \mapsto a[m]]$ is indeed a permutation of a. This could correspond to simple "belief". During initial development of a procedure it is a useful way of postponing proofs until the final structure of invariants has been established. SOCOS will always warn that an assumption is being used.

Secondly, we can start proving the remaining conditions interactively in PVS. Which prover to be used (PVS or Simplify) can be selected on the level of single transitions, with Simplify being the default. In this case the PVS language is expressive enough to allow us to provide a higher-order definition of permutation:

```
index: type = {i:nat|i<N}
permutation( a:index, b:index ): bool =
    exists(f:(bijective[index,index])): a = b o f
```

This definition is actually part of the SOCOS background theory which is automatically loaded when PVS verification is initiated.[5] In addition the background theory includes useful, already proved lemmas about arrays and permutations to facilitate new proofs. Given the PVS definition of permutation it is easy to prove the remaining Swap condition interactively; however, to conserve space we have not included the actual PVS proofs here.

6   Conclusion and Future Work

We have here presented SOCOS, a tool for constructing and verifying invariant based programs. In the early phases of development simple errors are found by testing. At later stages the programmer can prove, using formal reasoning, that the program is *error-free*. All but the most trivial programs generate a large number of lemmas to be proved. SOCOS translates these lemmas into the PVS and Simplify input languages. Most of the generated lemmas are rather trivial and automatically discharged by Simplify or the PVS grind tactic. For more difficult lemmas, the proofs can be completed interactively in PVS.

The SOCOS system is currently in early stages and the framework is still being worked on. Most importantly, the issues of applicability and scalability require more attention We have so far limited our focus to programming "in the small", which is indeed the main target for invariant based programming. However, to make SOCOS suitable for systems of realistic scales, support for classes and other software decomposition mechanisms becomes critical. As a first step we are currently adding support for object-orientation in SOCOS. Introducing objects makes the verification problem significantly harder; the challenge here is to equip a formalism for classes and objects with an intuitive diagrammatic notation, and provide means for reasoning in terms of these diagrams. Refinement diagrams [5], a diagrammatic representation of lattice theory, will provide the basis for the SOCOS class notation.

Another issue of key importance is performance; SOCOS is currently rather slow—generating and checking (with Simplify) the proof conditions of the example in Section 5 takes several seconds on a modern PC.[6] Replaying PVS

---

[5] It should be pointed out that in this example a (much simpler) background theory is also sent to Simplify; part of this theory is that permutation is reflexive—this property explains how Simplify was able to prove the transition between PRE and LOOP in SelectionSort.

[6] 2.8 GHz Intel Pentium 4 with 1 GB of random access memory.

proofs is even slower. This limits the use of SOCOS to simple programs. While our implementation is in some cases sub-optimal, it is inevitable that automated verification of correctness conditions is computationally taxing. We are currently working on *background checking* to alleviate this problem—instead of requiring a separate verification cycle, the proof checker runs continuously in the background and discharges conditions as they are generated while the user is entering the program, much like how many programming environments semantically analyze programs as the user is typing.

We are carrying out a number of case studies in invariant based programming. These case studies are conducted on two different levels: firstly, we are building a larger example of higher complexity with many interacting components; secondly, we are teaching invariant based programming to a group of undergraduate students, using SOCOS as the programming tool. The objective of the first experiment is to evaluate the feasibility of the method for constructing larger programs. In the second experiment, we explore the educational merits of invariant based programming—it is our belief that the direct connection to logic, together with the use of diagrams and visualization, will make it a useful method for teaching the use of formal methods in programming.

SOCOS currently supports basic program proof management, but does not provide adequate facilities for managing program proofs in a way that accommodates continuous change. PVS proofs must be managed by hand by the user, and if a procedure is changed, however slightly, all proofs must be replayed. It would be desirable if the tool kept track of dependencies between program elements, and in the event of a change, only replayed proofs of possibly invalidated transitions. A nice feature of interactive provers like PVS is that advanced proof strategies work on the high-level structure of a formula. So, in the case of slight changes, chances are good that an existing proof is reusable.

Finally, there is a need for a way to make incremental software extensions and reason about their correctness. Stepwise Feature Introduction [22], a sound layered extension mechanism based on superposition refinement, is intended to be the main method by which a SOCOS program is extended with new functionality.

References

1. Back, R.J.: Invariant based programming. In: Donatelli, S., Thiagarajan, P.S. (eds.) ICATPN 2006. LNCS, vol. 4024, pp. 1–18. Springer, Heidelberg (2006)
2. Back, R.J.: Invariant based programs and their correctness. In: Biermann, W., Guiho, G., Kodratoff, Y. (eds.) Automatic Program Construction Techniques, pp. 223–242. MacMillan Publishing Company, NYC (1983)
3. Back, R.J., Myreen, M.: Tool support for invariant based programming. In: The 12th Asia-Pacific Software Engineering Conference, Taipei, Taiwan (December 2005)
4. Back, R.J., Milovanov, L., Porres, I.: Software development and experimentation in an academic environment: The Gaudi experience. In: Bomarius, F., Komi-Sirviö, S. (eds.) PROFES 2005. LNCS, vol. 3547, Springer, Heidelberg (2005)
5. Back, R.J.: Incremental software construction with refinement diagrams. In: Broy Gunbauer, H., Hoare (eds.) Engineering Theories of Software Intensive Systems.

NATO Science Series II: Mathematics, Physics and Chemistry, pp. 3–46. Springer, Marktoberdorf, Germany (2005)

6. Back, R.J., Milovanov, L., Porres, I., Preoteasa, V.: XP as a framework for practical software engineering experiments. In: Wells, D., Williams, L. (eds.) Extreme Programming and Agile Methods - XP/Agile Universe 2002. LNCS, vol. 2418, Springer, Heidelberg (2002)

7. Dijkstra, E.W.: A constructive approach to the problem of program correctness. BIT 8, 174–186 (1968)

8. Reynolds, J.C.: Programming with transition diagrams. In: Gries, D. (ed.) Programming Methodology, Springer, Berlin (1978)

9. Back, R.J.: Program construction by situation analysis. Research Report 6, Computing Centre, University of Helsinki, Helsinki, Finland (1978)

10. van Emden, M.H.: Programming with verification conditions. In: IEEE Transactions on Software Engineering, vol. SE–5, IEEE Computer Society Press, Los Alamitos (1979)

11. Abrial, J.R., Lee, M.K.O., Neilson, D.S., Scharbach, P.N., Sorensen, I.H.: The B-method (software development). In: Prehn, S., Toetenel, W.J. (eds.) VDM 1991. LNCS, vol. 552, pp. 398–405. Springer, Heidelberg, Germany (1991)

12. Meyer, B.: Object-Oriented Software Construction, 2nd edn. Prentice-Hall, Englewood Cliffs (1997)

13. Burdy, L., Cheon, Y., Cok, D., Ernst, M., Kiniry, J., Leavens, G.T., Leino, K.R.M., Poll, E.: An overview of JML tools and applications. International Journal on Software Tools for Technology Transfer (STTT) 7(3), 212–232 (2005)

14. Flanagan, C., Leino, K.R.M., Lillibridge, M., Nelson, G., Saxe, J.B., Stata, R.: Extended static checking for Java. In: PLDI '02. Proceedings of the ACM SIGPLAN 2002 Conference on Programming language design and implementation, pp. 234–245. ACM Press, New York, USA (2002)

15. van den Berg, J., Jacobs, B.: The LOOP compiler for Java and JML. In: Margaria, T., Yi, W. (eds.) ETAPS 2001 and TACAS 2001. LNCS, vol. 2031, p. 299+. Springer, Heidelberg (2001)

16. Burdy, L., Requet, A., Lanet, J.L.: Java applet correctness: A developer-oriented approach. In: Araki, K., Gnesi, S., Mandrioli, D. (eds.) FME 2003. LNCS, vol. 2805, pp. 422–439. Springer, Heidelberg (2003)

17. Dijkstra, E.W.: A Discipline of Programming. Prentice-Hall, Englewood Cliffs (1976)

18. Back, R.J., von Wright, J.: Refinement Calculus: A Systematic Introduction (Graduate Texts in Computer Science). Springer, Heidelberg (1998)

19. Alanen, M., Porres, I.: The Coral Modelling Framework. In: Koskimies, K., Kuzniarz, L., Lilius, J., Porres, I. (eds.) NWUML'2004. Proceedings of the 2nd Nordic Workshop on the Unified Modeling Language, Turku Centre for Computer Science, July 2004, vol. 35, General Publications (2004)

20. Detlefs, D., Nelson, G., Saxe, J.B.: Simplify: a theorem prover for program checking. J. ACM 52(3), 365–473 (2005)

21. Owre, S., Rajan, S., Rushby, J.M., Shankar, N., Srivas, M.K.: PVS: Combining specification, proof checking, and model checking. In: Alur, R., Henzinger, T.A. (eds.) CAV 1996. LNCS, vol. 1102, pp. 411–414. Springer, Heidelberg (1996)

22. Back, R.J.: Software construction by stepwise feature introduction. In: Bert, D., Bowen, J.P., Henson, M.C., Robinson, K. (eds.) B 2002 and ZB 2002. LNCS, vol. 2272, pp. 162–183. Springer, Heidelberg (2002)

Testing and Proving Distributed Algorithms in Constructive Type Theory

Qiao Haiyan*

Department of Computer Science
Sun Yat-Sen University
Guangzhou 510275, China
qiaohy@mail.sysu.edu.cn

Abstract. We report our experiences to verify distributed algorithms in constructive type theory by testing and proving. Properties can be tested to eliminate bugs before proving, thus saving expensive proof effort. Both deadlock property and liveness property are proven after testing. The verified algorithm can be executed in Cayenne, a functional programming language with dependent types.

1 Introduction

We all know examples of sound looking manual proofs which turned out to be wrong when the proof becomes long and delicate. Thus proving the correctness of algorithms formally has become a practice because machine proofs cannot contain subtle arguments and cannot neglect details which may contain errors. Proving correctness of distributed algorithms can be more difficult because the inherent complexity of the problems [15]. Proof assistants based on various theories can be used to reason about algorithms. However, proving properties of algorithms can be time consuming. Furthermore, errors in the implementation of an algorithm or its specification may be found in later stage of proving, and proving has to be started over from scratch after correction. Absence of counterexamples also makes debugging difficult.

Testing before proving can find counter examples which make debugging easier. Eliminating possible errors in implementation and specification save proving effort. Testing and proving are complementary. Proving can decompose a goal into subgoals which then can be tested and proved. When f is defined in terms of component functions $f_1, f_2, \cdots$, proving is used to decompose the property P of the function f into sub-properties P_i of components f_i and to show why P_i's are sufficient for P. Testing each f_i with respect to P_i increases confidence in test code coverage and locates potential bugs more precisely.

In this article we show how the dining philosophers problem can be modelled quite naturally in Agda/Alfa, a proof assistant based on constructive type theory [19]. Both the deadlock property and liveness property can be proven after

---

* This research is supported by the National Natural Science Foundation of China under Grant No.60673050.

B. Meyer and Y. Gurevich (Eds.): TAP 2007, LNCS 4454, pp. 79–94, 2007.

testing. Furthermore, the verified algorithm is a program in Cayenne [1], and it can be compiled and executed, and therefore provides a demonstration of the protocol.

The article is organized in the following way: Section 2 is a brief introduction to the proof assistant Agda/Alfa, Section 3 describes how testing and proving can be done in Agda/Alfa, Section 4 introduces the dining philosophers problem, Section 5 gives the first version of the protocol using trace semantics and shows how some properties can be tested before proving, Section 6 gives another version of the protocol using graph semantics, and shows how the problem is modelled in Agda/Alfa, and how the correctness properties are proven, and finally in Section 7 we conclude the article.

2   The Proof Assistant Agda/Alfa

This section briefly describes the proof assistant Agda/Alfa. The reader familiar with Agda/Alfa can skip it.

Constructive type theory [19] is a theory about logic and computation. It is based on the idea "specifications as types" and "proofs (or programs) as objects". It can be seen as a programming language and specification language as well. As a specification language we can describe problems and properties, and as a programming language we can write programs or proofs. Agda [6] is an implementation of such a theory, and Alfa [16] is a window interface for Agda. We quote from the Alfa home page [16]:

> Alfa is a successor of the proof editor ALF, i.e., an editor for di-
> rect manipulation of proof objects in a logical framework based on Per
> Martin-Löf's Type Theory. It allows you to, interactively and incremen-
> tally, define theories (axioms and inference rules), formulate theorems
> and construct proofs of the theorems. All steps in the proof construction
> are immediately checked by the system and no erroneous proofs can be
> constructed.

That "no erroneous proofs can be constructed" only means that a completed proof is indeed correct. It does not help you to avoid blind alleys.

The syntax of Agda/Alfa has been strongly influenced by the syntax of Haskell and also of Cayenne [1], a functional programming language with dependent types. In addition to the function types a -> b available in ordinary functional languages, there are dependent function types written (x :: a) -> b, where the type b may depend on x :: a.

Agda/Alfa also has dependent record types (signatures) written

```
sig {x1 :: a1; x2 :: a2; ...; xn :: an}
```

where a2 may depend on x1 :: a1 and an may depend on x1 :: a1, x2 :: a2, etc. Elements of signatures are called structures written

```
struct{x1 = e1; x2 = e2; ...; xn = en}
```

Signatures are much like iterated Σ-types $\Sigma x1 :: a1.\Sigma x2 :: a2. \ldots an.$ and structures are much like iterated tuples (e1, (e2, ..., en)) inhabiting them.

Furthermore, Agda/Alfa has a type Set of sets in Martin-Löf's sense. Such sets are built up from basic inductive data structures, using dependent function types and signature types. A basic example is the set of natural numbers. Its definition in Agda/Alfa is

```
data Nat = Zero | Succ (n :: Nat)
```

More generally, constructors for sets may have dependent types, see for example the definition of finite sets in Section 7.

Remark. The reader is warned that the dependent type theory code given here is not accepted verbatim by the Agda/Alfa system, although it is very close to it. To get more readable notation and avoiding having to discuss some of the special choices of Agda/Alfa we borrow some notations from Haskell, such as writing [a] for the set of lists of elements in a. In particular, we use Haskell-style overloading although this feature is not present in Agda/Alfa.

Predicates on a set D are propositional functions with the type D -> Set by the identification of propositions as sets. Decidable predicates have the type D -> Bool. To convert from decidable to general predicates we use the function

```
T :: Bool -> Set
T True  = Truth
T False = Falsity
```

where Truth = Unit is the type with one element and represents the trivially true proposition, and Falsity is the empty set representing the false proposition.

For a more complete account of the logical framework underlying Agda/Alfa including record types see the paper about structured type theory [8] and for the inductive definitions available in type theory, see Dybjer [10] and Dybjer and Setzer [13,14].

3   Testing and Proving in Constructive Type Theory

Testing and proving in constructive type theory is explored in [12]. The general points about how testing and proving help each other are:

[a] The essence of creative user interaction is the introduction of lemmas. This is often a speculative process. If a user fails to prove a conjecture or its hypotheses, she must backtrack and try another formulation. Testing before proving is a quick and effective way to discard wrong or inapplicable conjectures.

[b] Analysis of failed tests gives useful information for proving. We call a counterexample to a conjecture *spurious* if it lies outside the intended domain of application of the conjecture. Having those at hand, the user can formulate

a sharper lemma that excludes them. Genuine counterexamples on the other hand helps locating bugs in programs or in the formalisation of intended properties.

[c] A given goal may not be (efficiently) testable. When interaction with the proof assistant produces testable subgoals, it is guaranteed that testing all of them is at least as good as testing the original goal; we know that no unintended logical gaps are introduced.

[d] Interactive proving increases confidence in the coverage and rationality of testing. Suppose a program consists of various components and branches, and it passes a top-level test for a property. When we try to prove the goal, the proof assistant typically helps us derive appropriate subgoals for the different components or branches. Testing these subgoals individually reduces the risk of missed test cases in the top-level testing.

The basic idea of Testing is borrowed from QuickCheck [5], an automatic random testing tool for Haskell. To test whether a boolean property

```
p[x1, ..., xn] :: Bool
```

is True for random instances of the variables x1 :: D1, ..., xn :: Dn. (The notation p[x1,...,xn] means that the expression p may contain occurrences of the free variables x1,...,xn. The reader is warned not to confuse this notation with Haskell's list notation!)

For example, if we wish to test that

```
reverse (reverse xs) == xs
```

for arbitrary integer lists xs, we write a property definition

```
prop_RevRev xs = reverse (reverse xs) == xs
    where types = xs :: [Int]
```

Then we call QuickCheck

```
Main> quickCheck prop_RevRev
OK, passed 100 tests.
```

QuickCheck here uses a library test data generator for integer lists. It is also possible for the user to define her own test data generator.

More generally, QuickCheck can test conditional properties written

```
p[x1,...,xn] ==> q[x1,...,xn]
```

where p[x1,...,xn], q[x1,...,xn] :: Bool. QuickCheck performs a sequence of tests as follows (at least conceptually):

1. A random instance r1 :: D1, ..., rn :: Dn is generated.
2. p[r1, ..., rn] is computed. If it is False, the test is discarded and a new random instance is generated. If on the other hand it is True, then

3. `q[r1, ..., rn]` is computed. If it is `False`, QuickCheck stops and reports the counterexample. If it is `True` the test was successful and a new test is performed.

QuickCheck repeats this procedure 100 times, by default. Only tests which are not discarded at step 2 are counted.

Another example of a QuickCheckable property is the following correctness property of a search algorithm `binSearch` for binary search trees. The property states that the algorithm correctly implements membership in binary search trees:

```
isBST lb ub t ==> binSearch t key == member t key
```

Here `t` is a binary tree of type `BT`, the type of binary trees with integers in the nodes; in Haskell:

```
data BT = Empty | Branch Int BT BT
```

`isBST lb ub t` holds if `t` is a binary search tree with elements strictly between `lb` and `ub`, (see Appendix A for the definitions in Haskell).

Before we can use QuickCheck we need a suitable test data generator. A generator for `BT` could be used, but is inappropriate. The reason is that most randomly generated binary trees will not be binary search trees, so most of them will be discarded. Furthermore, the probability of generating a binary search tree decreases with the size of the tree, so most of the generated trees would be small. Thus the reliability of the testing would be low. A better test case generator generates binary search trees only.

For more information about QuickCheck, see Claessen and Hughes [5] and the homepage `http://www.cs.chalmers.se/~rjmh/QuickCheck/`. Much of the discussion about QuickCheck, both about pragmatics and concerning possible extensions seems relevant to our context.

We have extended Agda/Alfa with a testing tool similar to QuickCheck, a tool for random testing of Haskell programs. However, our tool can express a wider range of properties and is integrated with the interactive reasoning capabilities of Agda/Alfa.

Our testing tool can test properties of the following form:

```
(x1 :: D1) -> ... -> (xn :: Dn[x1, ..., x(n-1)]) ->
  T (p1[x1, ..., xn]) -> ... -> T (pm[x1, ..., xn]) ->
  T (q[x1, ..., xn])
```

Under the identification of 'propositions as types', this reads

$$\forall x_1 \in \mathtt{D1}. \cdots \forall x_n \in \mathtt{Dn}[x_1, \cdots, x_{n-1}].$$
$$\mathtt{p1}[x_1, \cdots, x_n] \Longrightarrow \cdots \Longrightarrow \mathtt{pm}[x_1, \cdots, x_n] \Longrightarrow$$
$$\mathtt{q}[x_1, \cdots, x_n]$$

This is essentially the form of properties that QuickCheck can test, except that in dependent type theory the data domains `Di` can be dependent types.

The user chooses an option "test" in one of the menus provided by Alfa. The plug-in calls a test data generator and randomly generates a number of cases for which it checks the property.

Consider again the correctness property of binary search. It is the following Agda/Alfa type (using `Nat` rather than `Int` for simplicity):

```
(lb, ub, key :: Nat) -> (t :: BT) ->  T (isBST lb ub t) ->
T (binSearch t key == member t key)
```

If testing fails, a counterexample is returned. For example, if we remove the condition `T (isBST lb ub t)`, then the property above is not true any more, and the plug-in will report a counterexample.

4   The Dining Philosophers Problem

The dining philosophers problem is a classical multi-process synchronisation problem. Five (or some other number) philosophers spend their whole lives thinking and eating. The philosophers sit at a round table. In the centre of the table is a bowl of rice, and the table is laid with five chopsticks between philosophers. When a philosopher thinks, he does not interact with his colleagues. From time to time, a philosopher gets hungry and tries to pick up the two chopsticks that are closest to him. A philosopher may pick up only one chopstick at a time. When he obtains his two chopsticks at the same time, he eats without releasing his chopsticks. When he is finished eating, he puts both his chopsticks down and starts thinking again.

A solution to the Dining Philosophers' Problem is an algorithm which each philosopher follows and ensures that the hungry philosophers will eventually eat. A solution must be

- deadlock free: if at any time there is a hungry philosopher then eventually some philosophers will eat, and
- lockout free: every hungry philosopher eventually gets to eat.

5   Dining Philosophers, the Version Using Trace Semantics

In this section we formalise the protocol using trace semantics [7], then show how some properties can be tested and then proved.

5.1   The Protocol

Suppose that we have a set of philosophers P. There is a relation `s :: P -> P -> Bool` meaning if two philosophers are neighbors.

There are three possible events for every philosopher, which are modelled by the following set:

```
data Ev =  G (a::P) | E (a::P) | L (a::P)
```

whose meaning is G a: a goes to the table, E a: a starts eating, and L a: a leaves the table.

The protocol is defined via some observation functions on the traces of the system, which are lists of events:

```
Evt = List Ev
```

We have the following observation functions:

```
eat :: Evt -> P -> Bool
eat []          p = False
eat (G a : xs) p = eat xs p
eat (E a : xs) p = eat xs p || a == p
eat (L a : xs) p = eat xs p && a /= p
```

where eat evt p represents that p is eating.

```
table  :: Evt -> P -> Bool
table []          p = False
table (G a : xs) p = table xs p || a == p
table (E a : xs) p = table xs p
table (L a : xs) p = table xs p && a /= p
```

where table evt p represents that p is at the table.

R s evt a b represents that both a and b are hungry but b has priority over a:

```
R :: (s :: P -> P -> Bool) -> Evt -> P -> P -> Bool
R s []          a b = False
R s (G a' : xs) a b = R s xs a b || (a' == a && table xs b  && s a' b)
R s (E a' : xs) a b = R s xs a b
R s (L a' : xs) a b = R s xs a b && a' /= b
```

A possible trace is also called a state of the system. The possible traces we are interested in are called *valid*, and are defined recursively:

```
val :: (s :: P -> P -> Bool) -> Evt -> Bool
val s []        = True
val s (e : es) = val s es && pos s es e
```

where pos s xs x means that the event e is possible in the state es:

```
pos :: (s :: P -> P -> Bool) -> Evt -> Ev -> Bool
pos s es (G a) = not (table es a)
pos s es (E a) = table es a && fa (\h -> not (R s es a h))
pos s es (L a) = eat es a
```

where fa is supposed to be a **forall** function on P:

```
fa :: (P -> Bool) -> Bool
```

5.2   Testing and Proving Safety Properties of the Protocol

We will prove the following safety properties of the system:

1. No neighbors are eating simultaneously;
2. No deadlock, i.e. the relation R s es is acyclic for any valid trace es

Let us first look at the first property, which takes the following form

```
(s :: P -> P -> Bool) -> (evt :: Evt) -> T(val evt) -> (x,y :: P)
   -> T(s x y) -> T(not(eat evt x && eat evt y))
```

To make this property testable, P must be a concrete finite set because of the function fa. We will take F5 (the set with five elements) as P:

```
data F5 = r0 | r1 | r2 | r3 | r4
```

To use the testing tool, we will need to write some generators for those parameter types, i.e. F5, Evt and F5 -> F5 -> Bool. The generator for F5 has the following type:

```
genF5 :: Rand -> F5
```

where Rand is the type of random seeds which is implemented as the set of trees with random natural numbers for simplicity.

```
data Rand = Leaf Nat | Node Nat Rand Rand
```

A possible generator is

```
genF5 :: Rand -> F5
genF5 (Leaf n)     = fre5 n
genF5 (Node n l r) = fre5 n
```

where fre5 n takes the ith element ri if mod n 5 == i.

Similarly, we can write a generator for Evt:

```
genEvt :: Rand -> Evt
genEvt (Leaf n)     = Nil
genEvt (Node n l r) = (genEv l) : genEvt r
```

where genEv is a generator for Ev.

A possible generator for genPPB is

```
genPPB :: Rand -> F5 -> F5 -> Bool
genPPB r a b = genBool r
```

We now can invoke the testing tool. It will generate test cases and check if the property holds.

Testing showed that there was a counterexample, that is when x == y. This is of course not a counter example. So we add the condition x /= y, and reformulate the property as follows:

```
(s :: F5 -> F5 -> Bool)-> (evt :: Evt)-> T(val s evt)
  -> (x,y :: F5) -> T (s x y && not (x == y))
  -> T(not( eat evt x && eat evt y))
```

Now the property passed the test.

The acyclic property has the following form

```
(s :: P -> P -> Bool) -> (evt :: Evt) -> T(val s evt)
  -> T (acyclic s evt)
```

where

```
acyclic (s :: P -> P -> Bool)(evt :: Evt) :: Bool =
 fa (\(x :: P) -> not(R s evt x x))
```

This property passed the test.

Having tested the properties, we can now try to prove the properties by induction on `evt`. The proofs are short in these cases.

The liveness property is formulated as follows

```
(a :: P) -> (evt :: Evt) -> T(val s evt) -> T(table evt a)
   -> Sigma Evt (\(h :: Evt) -> T(extend evt h && eat h a))
```

where `extend evt h` means that `evt` is an initial of `h`.

The property cannot be tested directly. However, we can test the following property:

```
(a :: P) -> (evt :: Evt) -> T(val s evt) -> T(table evt a)
  -> (h :: Evt) -> T(extend evt h) -> T(not(eat h a))
```

Any counterexample to this property gives a solution to the liveness property.

We may also want to check that if some philosopher is eating, then he must be at the table.

```
(s :: P -> P -> Bool)-> (evt :: Evt) -> T(val s evt)
  -> (x :: P) -> T (eat evt x) -> T(table evt x)
```

This property passed the test and the proof is done by induction on `evt`.

6   Modelling the Protocol Using Graph Semantics

6.1   Precedence Graphs

We will describe our problem by using a graph model of conflict [4]. A distributed system is represented by an undirected graph G with a one-to-one correspondence between vertices in G and processes in the system. An edge (u, v) is in G if and only if there may be a conflict between vertices u and v. We assume that there is some mechanism that, in every state of the system, ascribes a precedence ordering to every pair of potentially conflicting processes so that one of the processes in the pair has precedence over the other. If there is a conflict between a pair of processes, the process with the lower precedence must yield to the process with greater precedence in finite time.

We represent precedences between pairs of potentially conflicting processes by directed edges: an edge in G is directed from the process with less precedence toward the process with greater precedence. We call G a precedence graph.

A directed graph is a pair (A, R), where A is the set of nodes and R is a relation on A. When the set of nodes is clear, we will simply say a graph is a relation on the set of nodes.

We will assume the following on the graph (A, R):

1. there is a decidable equality on A, i.e. for any two nodes we can decide if they are the same node;
2. there is a reversing operation on relations on A;
3. the relation R is well-founded, i.e. there is no infinite descending chains.

Under these assumptions, we define a distributed algorithm on directed graphs: for any node u, if it is a sink, then reverses all the edges which are incident to u, otherwise do nothing.

We will use R' to denote the resulting relation after the above operation on R, and $R^{(m)}$ to the result after iterating the operation m times.

We will prove the following:

1. If R is well-founded, then it is acyclic, i.e. there is no path from a node to itself.
2. If R is acyclic, then R' is also acyclic, thus any $R^{(m)}$ is also acyclic for any m (safety property).
3. If R is well-founded, then for any node u, there exists a natural number m such that u is a sink in $R^{(m)}$ (liveness property).

Thus, deadlock and liveness properties are proved.

6.2   Modelling the Problem in Agda/Alfa

We will think of a relation on A as a function from elements of A to subsets of A, the set of elements of A to which it is related. We use `List A` to model subsets of A. So a relation on A has the following type:

```
R :: A -> List A
```

where `R u` is interpreted as a multi-set, consisting of the successors of u.

The membership relation $a \in S$ is easily defined:

```
isIn :: A -> List A -> Bool
isIn a s =
    case s of
      (Nil) -> False
      (Cons x xs) -> eq a x || isIn a xs

IsIn (a :: A)(s :: List A) :: Set = T (isIn a s)
```

where `eq :: A -> A -> Bool` is the decidable equality on A. We will also use `Nxt R a b` to denote $(a, b) \in$ R.

A node u is a sink in R if R u is the empty list:

```
sink (R :: Rel A)(a :: A) :: Bool = null A (R a)
```

If u is a sink in R, then by reversing all the edges incident to u the resulting graph R_1 is such a relation: $R_1 u$ will be $R^{-1}u$, otherwise $R_1 v$ is $Rv - \{u\}$, which is the set deleting u from Rv.

The distributed algorithm to perform 'reversing all sinks' is the following function:

```
revSinks :: Rel A -> Rel A
revSinks R =
    if (List A) (sink R h) (rev R h) (deleSinks  (R h) R)
```

where `rev R` will be R^{-1}, the operation to reverse all edges, and `deleSinks` perform the operation to delete all sinks from any R h:

```
deleSinks  :: List A -> Rel A -> List A
deleSinks h R =
    case h of
      (Nil) -> Nil;
      (Cons x xs) -> let ys :: List A = deleSinks xs R
                     in  if (List A) (sink R x) ys (Cons x ys)
```

6.3   Proving the Safety Property

We can prove the following facts:

1. if b is a sink in R, then $(a, b) \notin R'$ for any $a \in$ A;
2. if $(b, a) \in$ R and a is not a sink in R, then $(b, a) \in R'$;
3. if $(b, a) \notin$ R and a is not a sink in R, then $(b, a) \notin R'$

These properties are formulated as follows:

```
(R :: Rel A) -> (b :: A) -> (q :: Sink R b) ->
            (a :: A) -> Not (IsIn b (revSinks R a))

(R :: Rel A) -> (a, b :: A) -> (p :: IsIn a (R b))
  -> (q :: Not (Sink R a)) -> IsIn a (revSinks R b)

(R :: Rel A) -> (a, b :: A) -> (p :: Not(Sink R a))
   -> (q :: Not(IsIn b (R a)))
   -> Not(IsIn b ((revSinks R) a))
```

These properties have the testable form and can be tested for some concrete A before proving.

To prove that acyclic is an invariant of the operation $(')$ we introduce the notion of paths:

```
data Path (R :: A -> List A)(a, b :: A) =
        Pedge (h :: Nxt R a b)
      | Parc (c :: A) (h :: Nxt R a c)(h' :: Path R c b)
```

and the notion of acyclic:

```
Acyclic (R :: Rel A) :: Set = (a :: A) -> Not (Path R a a)
```

Then the invariant is proved by the fact that if there is a ring in R', then it is already in R because no edge was reversed on the ring as no node was a sink on the ring.

```
(R :: Rel A) -> (p :: Acyclic R) -> Acyclic (revSinks R)
```

and hence

```
(R :: Rel A) -> (p :: Acyclic R)
  -> (m :: Nat) -> Acyclic (rept_revSinks R m)
```

6.4   Proving the Liveness Property

To prove that every node will become a sink, we will use the assumption that R is well-founded and use well-founded induction. Intuitively, if for all $(a, b) \in R$, b becomes a sink in $R^{(m_b)}$, then a will becomes a sink in $R^{(m)}$ if a is not a sink in any $R^{(i)}$ for any $i < m$, where $m = \max\{m_b\}$.

The function max is defined on subsets in the following way:

```
max :: (l :: List A) -> (f :: (a :: A) -> (p :: IsIn a l) -> Nat) -> Nat
max l f  = max' ( map2 l f)
```

where max' takes a set of naturals and returns the maximum and map2 maps a function on a subset of A, on which the function is defined to natural numbers, to a set of natural numbers:

```
map2:: (l :: List A) -> (f :: (a :: A) -> IsIn a l -> Nat)-> List Nat
```

We need to prove that the function max really returns the maximum in the set:

```
(l :: List A) -> (f :: (a ::  A) -> (p :: IsIn a l) -> Nat)
  -> (a :: A) ->(q ::  IsIn a l) -> LessOrEq (f a q) (max l f)
```

Notice that a function with a proof argument is involved in the definition of max, we will need to prove that proof argument is irrelevant during the computation of the maximum by the following properties:

```
(l :: List A) -> (f :: (a ::  A) -> (p :: IsIn a l)-> Nat)
  -> (a :: A) -> (p, q :: IsIn a l) -> T(eqNat (f a p)(f a q))

(xs :: List A) -> (f :: (a :: A) -> (p :: IsIn a xs) -> Nat)
```

```
-> (g :: (a :: A) -> (p :: IsIn a xs) -> Nat)
-> (r :: (a :: A) -> (p :: IsIn a xs)
-> (q :: IsIn a xs) -> T(eqNat (f a p)(g a q)))
-> T(eqNat (max xs f)(max xs g))
```

We use the fact that if u is not a sink in any $R^{(i)}$ $(0 \leq i \leq m)$, then $R^{(i+1)} \subseteq R^{(i)}$ $(0 \leq i \leq m)$.

```
(R :: Rel A) -> (p :: WF R) -> (a :: A)
  -> Sigma Nat (\(h :: Nat) -> T(empty (rept_revSinks R h a)))
```

This property cannot be tested directly because there is an existential quantifier . However, we could test the following negation, and a counter example for the negation gives a solution to the property above:

```
(R :: Rel A) -> (p :: WF R) -> (a :: A)
  -> (h :: Nat) -> T(not(empty (rept_revSinks R h a)))
```

provided we can write generators for dependent types WF R, which defines the well-foundedness for relations. In this case, however, generating a proof that R is well-founded is not that easy.

We have assumed there is a reversing operation on relations R^{-1}, which will require that the set A must be finite for the reversing operation constructed. Then well-foundedness will be equivalent to acyclicity of relations on finite sets.

We have chosen our representation of relations to make sinks and sources more explicit, and after every run of the algorithm a sink becomes a source and the algorithm is distributed. The price we pay for the representation is that we have an expensive reversing operation R^{-1}.

We can run the verified Agda/Alfa program in Cayenne, a programming language with dependent types.

For example, for $n = 5$, the relation is defined as:

```
R5 ::   (Fin n5) -> List (Fin n5);
R5  = \ (h :: Fin n5 ) -> case h of {
     (One) -> r52: Nil;
     (Next h1) ->  case h1 of {
            (One) ->   r53: Nil;
            (Next h2) -> case h2 of {
                  (One) -> Nil;
                  (Next h3) -> case h3 of {
                        (One) ->   r53 : Nil;
                        (Next h4) -> One : r54: Nil; }}}};
```

or

```
R5:  1->2; 2->3; 3->[]; 4->3; 5->1,4
```

meaning that the five elements are 1, 2, 3, 4, 5, and 1 is related to 2, and 3 is related to nothing (a sink), and so on.

Running **revSinks** on R5 repeatedly, we get

```
1->2;       2-> [];    3->2, 4;   4-> [];     5->1, 4
1-> [];     2->1, 3;   3-> [];    4->3, 5;    5->1
1->2, 5;    2-> [];    3->2, 4;   4-> 5;      5-> []
1-> [];     2->1, 3;   3->4;      4-> [];     5->1, 4
1->2, 5;    2->3;      3-> [];    4->3, 5;    5-> []
1->2;       2-> [];    3->2, 4;   4-> [];     5->1, 4
```

After the first round, for example, nodes 2 and 4 become sinks.

We have used lists to represent graphs. Alternatively, we could use matrixes to represent graphs. Then reversing a sink will be done by switching the corresponding line and column.

```
swap_rc ::(r :: Matrix ) -> (i:: A) -> Matrix
swap_rc r i  =
    \(h::A) -> \(h'::A)
    -> if Bool ((eqA h i)|| (eqA h' i)) (r h' h) (r h h')
```

where

```
Matrix :: Set = A -> A -> Bool
```

and the function if has the type of the two branches as its first argument:

```
if :: (a::Set) -> Bool -> a -> a -> a
```

The algorithm will be

```
revSinks :: Matrix -> Matrix
revSinks h = \(h'::Fi n) -> \(h0::Fi n) ->
    if Bool (notsink h h' && notsink h h0) (h h' h0) (h h0 h')
```

In this representation, we have a cheap reversing operation R^{-1}, but it is not so clear a sink becomes a source after the operation.

7   Related Work and Future Work

We have shown how a distributed protocol can be modelled using both trace semantics and graph semantics quite naturally in constructive type theory, and both safety properties and liveness property can be tested and proven. Testing before proving can eliminate errors and thus prevent doing unsuccessful proofs. Safety properties can be tested directly and liveness property can be tested by testing a negation property. Verified code can be executed and gives a demonstration of the protocol.

Considerable work has been done on verification of distributed systems by using general proof checkers e.g. Coq, HOL, Isabelle, Lego etc. and other framework, here we mention a few [3,15,21]. Our work should be compared to those using testing and proving. Combining testing and proving for Haskell program verification is part of the objective of the Cover project at Chalmers University of Technology [9], which aims at combining verification methods including testing, model checking automatic theorem and interactive theorem proving. The idea of combining proving and testing is also part of the Programatica project currently under development at Oregon Graduate Centre [20]. Some early work on combining proving and testing was done by Hayashi, who used testing to debug lemmas while doing proofs in his PX-system [17]. Hayashi is currently pursuing the idea of testing proofs and theorems in his foundationally oriented project on "proof animation" [18]. Dybjer, Qiao and Takeyama [12] explored using testing and proving for algorithm verification in type theory. Testing and proving is also used in Isabelle/HOL [2].

It will be interesting to look at more case studies to see how often and how much we can test in the process of distributed program verification. Future work would also include generators for dependent types that appear in this context [11]. We have only used generators for simple types in this article. In general, we will need generators for dependent types. For example, F5 could be defined as a simple type, as we did in this article. We could also define a family of types (or a dependent type), for which F5 is an instance.

```
Fin (m::Nat) :: Set
  = case m of {
      (Zero) -> Empty;
      (Succ m') -> data One | Next (Fin m');}
```

In this case, we could define a generator for Fin n for any n which is not Zero. However, generators for dependent types turn out to be more difficult in general. It will also be interesting to see if generators for some simple types and dependent types can be generated themselves.

References

1. Augustsson, L.: Cayenne: a language with dependent types. In: Berman, M., Berman, S. (eds.) Proceedings of the third ACM SIGPLAN International Conference on Functional Programming (ICFP-98). ACM SIGPLAN Notices, vol. 34, 1, pp. 239–250. ACM Press, New York (1998)
2. Berghofer, S., Nipkow, T.: Random testing in Isabelle/HOL. In: Cuellar, J., Liu, Z. (eds.) Software Engineering and Formal Methods (SEFM 2004), IEEE Computer Society Press, Los Alamitos (2004)
3. Chou, C.-T.: Mechanical verification of distributed algorithms in higher-order logic. In: Melham, T.F., Camilleri, J. (eds.) Higher Order Logic Theorem Proving and Its Applications. LNCS, vol. 859, pp. 158–176. Springer, Heidelberg (1994)
4. Chandy, K.M., Misra, J.: The drinking philosopher's problem. ACM Transactions on Programming Languages and Systems 6(4), 632–646 (1984)
5. Claessen, K., Hughes, J.: QuickCheck: a lightweight tool for random testing of Haskell programs. In: Proceedings of the ACM SIGPLAN International Conference on Functional Programming (ICFP-00), NY, september 18–21, 2000. ACM Sigplan Notices, vol. 35.9, pp. 268–279. ACM Press, New York (2000)
6. Coquand, C.: The Agda homepage, http://www.cs.chalmers.se/~catarina/agda

7. Coquand, T.: Inductive definitions and type theory: an introduction, http://www-sop.inria.fr/certilab/types-sum-school02/Lnotes/
8. Coquand, T., Pollack, R., Takeyama, M.: A logical framework with dependently typed records. In: Hofmann, M.O. (ed.) TLCA 2003. LNCS, vol. 2701, pp. 105–119. Springer, Heidelberg (2003)
9. Cover - combining verification methods in software development, http://www.coverproject.org/
10. Dybjer, P.: Inductive families. Formal Aspects of Computing 6(4), 440–465 (1994)
11. Dybjer, P., Haiyan, Q., Takeyama, M.: Random generators for dependent types. In: Liu, Z., Araki, K. (eds.) ICTAC 2004. LNCS, vol. 3407, pp. 341–355. Springer, Heidelberg (2005)
12. Dybjer, P., Haiyan, Q., Takeyama, M.: Combining testing and proving in dependent type theory. In: Basin, D., Wolff, B. (eds.) TPHOLs 2003. LNCS, vol. 2758, Springer, Heidelberg (2003)
13. Dybjer, P., Setzer, A.: A finite axiomatization of inductive and inductive-recursive definitions. In: Girard, J.-Y. (ed.) TLCA 1999. LNCS, vol. 1581, pp. 129–146. Springer, Heidelberg (1999)
14. Dybjer, P., Setzer, A.: Indexed induction-recursion. In: Kahle, R., Schroeder-Heister, P., Stärk, R.F. (eds.) PTCS 2001. LNCS, vol. 2183, Springer, Heidelberg (2001)
15. Groote, J.F., Monin, F., van de Pol, J.: Checking verifications of protocols and distributed systems by computer. In: Sangiorgi, D., de Simone, R. (eds.) CONCUR 1998. LNCS, vol. 1466, pp. 629–655. Springer, Heidelberg (1998)
16. Hallgren, T.: The Alfa homepage, http://www.cs.chalmers.se/~hallgren/Alfa
17. Hayashi, S., Nakano, H.: PX, a Computational Logic. MIT Press, Cambridge (1988)
18. Hayashi, S., Sumitomo, R., Shii, K.-i.: Towards animation of proofs - testing proofs by examples. Theoretical Computer Science 272, 177–195 (2002)
19. Nordström, B., Petersson, K., Smith, J.M.: Programming in Martin-Löf type theory: an introduction. Oxford University Press, Oxford (1990)
20. Programatica: Integrating programming, properties, and validation, http://www.cse.ogi.edu/PacSoft/projects/programatica/
21. Vaandrager, F.W.: Verification of a distributed summation algorithm. In: Apt, K.R., Schrijver, A., Temme, N.M. (eds.) From Universal Morphisms to Megabytes – a Baayen Space Odyssey, Amsterdam, pp. 593–608. CWI (1994)

Automatic Testing from Formal Specifications*

Manoranjan Satpathy[1,**], Michael Butler[2], Michael Leuschel[3], and S. Ramesh[4]

[1] Department of Information Technologies, Abo Akademi University
Joukahaisenkatu 3-5, FIN-20520 Turku, Finland
[2] School of Electronic and Computer Science, University of Southampton
Highfield, Southampton, SO17 1BJ, UK
[3] Institute of Informatik, Heinrich-Heine Universitat Duesseldorf
Universitatsstr. 1, D-40225 Duesseldorf
[4] General Motors India Science Lab
International Tech Park, Whitefield Road, Bangalore – 560066
mannu.satpathy@abo.fi, mjb@ecs.soton.ac.uk,
leuschel@cs.uni-duesseldorf.de, s.ramesh@gm.com

Abstract. In this article, we consider model oriented formal specification languages. We generate test cases by performing symbolic execution
over a model, and from the test cases obtain a Java program. This Java
program acts as a test driver and when it is run in conjunction with the
implementation then testing is performed in an automatic manner. Our
approach makes the testing cycle fully automatic. The main contribution
of our work is that we perform automatic testing even when the models
are non-deterministic.

Keywords: Model Based Testing, B-Method, Non-determinism.

1 Introduction

Software models are usually built to reduce the complexity of the development
process and to ensure software quality. A model is usually a specification of the
system which is developed from the requirements early in the development cycle
[5]. In this paper, we consider model oriented formal specification languages like
Z [22], VDM [12] , B [1] and ASM [9]. By *model oriented* we mean that system
behaviour is described using an explicit model of the system state along with
operations on the state.

A formal model can be subjected to symbolic execution to obtain a coverage graph in which nodes represent instantiated states and edges are labeled
with operation applications. One can then select a finite set of finite behaviours
from the coverage graph and test if the implementation is consistent with these
behaviours. This approach is often termed as model based testing [6]. Model
based testing though is an incomplete activity; the selected behaviours could be

---

* Work done within the EU research project Rodin, IST 511599.
** Currently at the General Motors India Science Lab (ISL), Bangalore; part of this
work was done when the author was visiting GM ISL during Summar'05.

B. Meyer and Y. Gurevich (Eds.): TAP 2007, LNCS 4454, pp. 95–113, 2007.

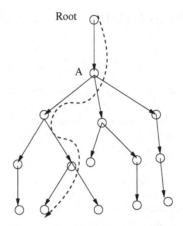

Fig. 1. Non-determinism Scenario

enriched to capture interesting aspects of the system and hence the success of their testing would give us confidence about the correctness of the system.

In this paper, we discuss automatic testing of an implementation or the system under test (SUT) written in accordance with a formal model in B [1]. Our method first generates a set of test cases from the model, and then from the test cases a test driver. The test driver is essentially a program in the target language. If this driver is plugged into the implementation, then testing can be performed automatically. It invokes all of the test cases generated from the model and reports about their success or failure. Our method does not require the implementation source to be available, and the entire testing cycle is automatic. The main contribution of our work is that our approach can perform automatic testing even if there is non-determinism in the model or in the implementation.

The basic idea behind the handling of non-determinism can be seen from Figure 1. Assume the solid lines in the figure show the full state space of a model in which branchings may be due to non-determinism. A correct implementation of this model must follow one of the paths in the figure, and for testing, we must know which path the SUT has taken. In our strategy, we maintain a generic representation of the possible paths that a model can take. Whenever the SUT makes a choice corresponding to a non-determinism in the model, we require that it makes this choice visible, and then this choice must satisfy a set of constraints which means that the implementation is not deviating from the model behaviour. Furthermore, the test driver uses the implementation choices to align the implementation trace with the appropriate trace of the model. Once this correspondence is established, additional properties could be checked with ease.

The organization of the paper is as follows. In Section 2, we discuss related work. Section 3 introduces the B notation with examples. In Section 4, we consider our approach to handle deterministic models, and in Section 5, we consider non-deterministic models. Section 6 discusses the implementation issues along with the current status of our implementation. In Section 7, we make an analysis of our method, and finally, Section 8 concludes the paper.

2   Related Work

A *testing criterion* is a set of requirements on test data which reflects a notion of adequacy on the testing of a system [19]. A test adequacy criterion determines whether sufficient testing has already been done, and in addition, it provides measurements to obtain the degree of adequacy obtained after testing stops [25]. A *test oracle* is a mechanism to determine correctness of test executions. A *test driver* is a tool which activates a system, provides test inputs and report test results [18]. *Representation mapping* is a mapping which maps the abstract name space of the model with the concrete name space of the SUT [7]. In this context, there are two kinds of mappings: control and data [19]. Control mappings are between control points in the implementation and locations in the specification; these are the points where the specification and the implementation states are to be matched. Data mappings are transformations between data structures in the implementation and those in the specification. A test sequence is called *preset* if the input sequence is fixed prior to the start of testing; it is called *adaptive* if at each step the choice of the next input symbol depends on the previous outputs [23]. The adaptive test cases are in the form of decision trees; the tester supplies an input and depending on the output, a branch is selected.

The work by Dick and Faivre [4] is a major contribution to the use of formal methods in software testing. A VDM [12] specification has state variables and an invariant (Inv) to restrict the variables. An operation, say OP, is specified by a pre-condition (OP_{pre}) and a post-condition (OP_{post}). The expression $OP_{pre} \wedge OP_{post} \wedge$ Inv is converted into its Disjunctive Normal Form (DNF); each disjunct, unless a contradiction itself, represents an input sub-domain of OP. Next, as many operation instances are created as the number of valid disjuncts in the DNF. An attempt is then made to create a FSA (Finite State Automaton) in which each node represents a possible machine state and an edge represents an application of an operation instance. A set of test cases is then generated by traversing the FSA, each test case being a sequence of operation instances. The authors discuss only the mechanism of the partitioning algorithm.

BZ-Testing Tool (BZ-TT) [2,3,14] generates functional test cases from B as well as Z specifications. BZ-TT assumes all sets in the B machine are finite enumerated sets. Each B operation is transformed to its *normal form* [1]. An operation is then partitioned into a set of operation instances; each partition usually corresponds to exactly one control path within the operation. The conjunction of all predicates in a control flow path and the postcondition is termed an *effect predicate* (EP). The free state variables in each EP are assigned to their maximum and minimum values – say, in terms of size – to obtain a set of *boundary goals*. *Boundary input values* are obtained by giving maximum and minimum values to the input variables in the EP. A Constraint Logic Programming (CLP) Solver tries to find a path through symbolic execution from the initial state to a boundary state, a state satisfying a given boundary goal. And then relevant operation instances are applied at the boundary state by giving them boundary input values. The results of the query operations become the oracle information. BZ-TT assumes that the B operations are deterministic. The authors point out that automatic verdict assignment is difficult because of non-determinism, and representation mappings [14,15].

Satpathy et al. [21] discuss the prototype of a tool called ProTest which performs testing of an implementation in relation to its B model. The tool performs partition analysis using a technique similar to that of Dick and Faivre. A finite coverage graph is created from a symbolic execution of the B model by a model checking tool called ProB [16]. Some paths starting from the initial state are taken as test cases. The ProTest tool can run Java programs. So the B model and its Java implementation are run simultaneously by the tool, and in relation to a test case, similar states are matched to assign a verdict.

Finite state machines have been used to model systems like sequential circuits, communication protocols and some types of programs such as lexical analysis and pattern matching [13]. Though the implementation of such systems is usually deterministic, some of the state parameters may be unspecified during the specification stage. In such cases, non-deterministic finite state machines (NDF-SMs) are used for modeling. Sometimes the code for the implementation (SUT) is not available and the problem then is to find if the SUT conforms to its finite state model; i.e. we need to show whether every i/o sequence that is possible in the SUT is also present in the specification. Solutions to this conformance testing problem when the specification is a NDFSM have been addressed by many authors including Hierons [10,11], Zhang and Cheung [24] and Nachmanson et al [17]. However, the models which we discuss in this paper are in general infinite state machines.

3   The B-Method and Examples

The B-method is a theory and methodology for formal development of computer systems [1]. The basic unit of specification in B is called a *B machine*. Larger specifications can be obtained by composing B machines in a hierarchical manner. An individual B machine consists of a set of variables, an invariant to restrict the variables, and a set of operations to modify the state. An operation has a precondition, and an operation invocation is defined only if the precondition holds. The initialization action and an operation body are written as atomic actions coded in a language called the *generalized substitution language* [1]. The language allows specification of deterministic and non-deterministic assignments and operations. An operation invocation transforms a machine state to a new state. The behaviour of a B machine can be described in terms of a sequence of operation invocations in which the first operation call originates from the initial state of the machine.

We consider two B machines. The B machine TAgency1.mch is deterministic (Table 1). It has two users ($u1$ and $u2$) and two rooms ($r1$ and $r2$). The model can

Table 1. A Deterministic B machine

Machine TAgency1
SETS USER = $\{u1, u2\}$; SESSION= $\{s1\}$; ROOM= $\{r1, r2\}$
VARIABLES
      sess, booking
INVARIANT
      sess $\in$ SESSION $+\rightarrow$USER /* $+\rightarrow$ means partial function */
      $\wedge$ booking $\in$ROOM $+\rightarrow$USER
INITIALISATION
      sess := $\emptyset$ || booking := $\emptyset$
OPERATIONS
login(u) = PRE $u \in$ USER $\wedge$ sess = $\emptyset$ THEN sess(s1) := u
      END;
alloc(s)= PRE $s \in$SESSION $\wedge$sess $\neq \emptyset \wedge dom(booking) \neq \{r1, r2\}$ THEN
      IF $r_1 \in dom(booking)$ THEN
            booking(r_2) := sess(s)
      ELSE booking(r1) := sess(s) END
      END;
logout(s) = PRE $s \in$SESSION$\wedge$sess $\neq \emptyset$ THEN sess := $\emptyset$ END
END

only handle a single session s1. sess and booking are the two variables, and the INVARIANT tells that both are partial functions. Both variables are initialized to empty. There are three operations in all. The login() operation assigns the single session to a user. Then alloc(ss) allocates a room in relation to the session ss, but preference is given to r1. The logout() operation terminates the session.

Appendix-A shows a skeleton of TAgency2.mch; it is a more complex version of TAgency1 and it involves non-determinism. The system can handle a number of parallel sessions given by the deferred set SESSION. A user can log into the system through the call login() to get an available session which is non-deterministically selected. He can then request to book or unbook a room (operations book() and unbook()), and makes (or receives) payment through a card (enterCard()). Next, the user can get a response from response_book() (or response_unbook()). Room allocation data is stored in the function booking. A user can book multiple rooms. The machine has five non-deterministic operations: login(), enterCard(), retryCard(), response_book() and response_unbook(). For the second and the third operations, when the card is entered or retried, a non-deterministic choice out of $\{valid, wrong\}$ is made. For the response_book(), any room out of the set of available rooms may be allocated. And in case of response_unbook(), any room out of the allocated rooms to the current user is cancelled.

4 The Method I: Deterministic Models

We assume flat B machines without any hierarchy and Java is the language of implementation. We now outline our method in the following steps.

Creation of Probe Operations: For each operation in the machine, a set of probe operations are manually created from the domain knowledge and the operation meaning. The probes will be used in matching similar specification and implementation states. For the operation `alloc(s)`, some possible queries to become its probe operations are:

- Which user made the allocation request? (`probe operation alloc_P1()`)
- How many rooms got allocated so far? (`probe operation alloc_P2()`)

These two probe operations can be encoded in B as follows:
uu ← alloc_P1(s) = PRE s ∈ SESSION THEN uu := sess(s) END
count ← alloc_P2 = BEGIN count := card(booking) END

Signature Generation: The SUT in Java must have a similar signature as the specification; i.e., the SUT will have the same operation names as those in the specification but their parameters would be similar in the following sense:

- If a model parameter type is either numeric or boolean it becomes `int` and `boolean` in the implementation respectively.
- For any other model parameter of type PP, we treat it as an object of a class PP in the implementation.

For instance, the login() will have the signature `'void login(USER uu)'`. We also create signatures of the probe operations; for instance, alloc_P1() will be of `'USER alloc_P1(SESSION s)'`. The SUT also implements SESSION, USER and ROOM as Java classes. It is expected that the developer while writing the SUT preserves the signatures of the B operations and their probes.

Generation of Operation Instances: We perform a DNF based analysis over the operation preconditions in order to obtain operation instances. However, operation preconditions in B are relatively simpler; therefore, in order to obtain interesting partitions, we add tautologies through conjunction to the precondition as per the following rules.

- If an operation has an IF like `'IF C THEN S1 ELSE S2'`, then add the tautology $(C \lor \neg C)$ to the precondition through conjunction. For `'IF C THEN (IF C1 THEN S1 ELSE S2) ELSE S2'`, we add $(C \land (C1 \lor \neg C1)) \lor \neg C$
- If the operation has a SELECT with branch conditions $C_1, \ldots, C_k$ then add to the precondition: $C_1 \lor C_2 \lor \ldots C_k \lor (\neg(C_1 \lor C_2 \lor \ldots C_k))$
- If set S occurs in the operation, then add to the precondition: $S = \emptyset \lor S \neq \emptyset$ (similar tautologies can also be added for other data constructs.)

Obtain the DNF of the modified precondition. The non-contradictory disjuncts are used for creating operation instances. Some instances of alloc() are shown below. From now onwards, by operations we will mean operation instances.

alloc₁(s): $s \in SESSION \land sess \neq \emptyset \land booking = \emptyset$
alloc₂(s): $s \in SESSION \land sess \neq \emptyset \land booking \neq \emptyset \land dom(booking) \neq \{r1, r2\}$
$\land booking(r_1) = sess(s)$
alloc₃(s): $s \in SESSION \land sess \neq \emptyset \land booking \neq \emptyset \land dom(booking) \neq \{r1, r2\}$
$\land booking(r_1) \neq sess(s)$

It is easy to see that for each control paths in an operation, we have an operation instance. This means that if are able to generate test cases for each of the operation instances, then the branches within the original operations are also covered.

Creation of a Coverage graph: Our testing criterion is to test each operation at least once; therefore, we try to generate a finite coverage graph so that each operation instance appears at least once. However, we may not be able to cover all operations because: (a) an operation may be infeasible, (b) a certain initialisation may prevent an operation from appearing or (c) an operation may not appear within the finite dimension of the graph. We now outline our construction process in the following steps. Figure 2 shows a coverage graph for TAgency1.mch. The probe calls and their results are shown within the dotted regions.

- **Step 1:** Create an initial node (the root) in which the variables of the B machine get the assignments of the INITIALISATION clause.
- **Step 2:** Take any node in the graph called `source` where all the state variables are already available as ground terms. If the precondition of a non-probe operation holds at source, apply this operation to obtain the target state. Create a new node for target state only if an identical state does not already exist. Label the edge (source,target) with the operation call.
- **Step 3:** For each probe operation `pop()` of OP(), make a call to it at the target state to obtain the result `res`. Attach to the edge just created the pair (`pop()`, `res`). If enough coverage has not been done then jump to Step 2.

Note that our method can be tuned to many other testing criteria; the graph creation process needs to be changed accordingly.

Generation of Test Sequences: We traverse the coverage graph to generate starting from the initial state a set of paths (or operation sequences) so that each operation is covered. We do not present such an algorithm here; one such algorithm has been given in [21]. It is important that while obtaining a test sequence, we do not go around a loop. And further, the problem being NP-complete [8], we only get a sub-optimal solution. In Figure 2, the path shown by the dashed lines is a test sequence.

Generation of a test driver: The test driver generator takes a set of test cases and generate a code fragment in Java. This code when executed in a testing context will infer whether the SUT has passed the test cases. At present we consider code for a single test case; multiple test cases can be executed by assuming an initialize() operation to take control back to the initial state. When a new test case is executed after re-initialization, the operation parameters are freshly created; therefore, they are not in conflict with the parameters of the previous runs. By testing context, we mean the following:

- If `MM.mch` is the B machine, then the SUT defines a class with name MM and creates an object of the same class, say `mmo`. It is expected that class MM has all operations of the machine as methods with similar signatures.

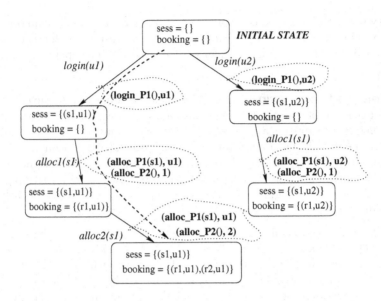

Fig. 2. A coverage graph for TAgency1.mch; dotted path shows one test case

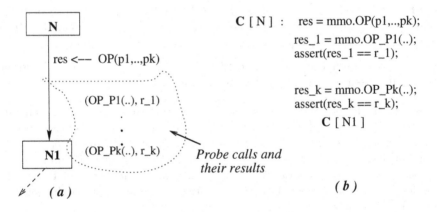

Fig. 3. Code generation from a test case

- In any test case, if an operation has a parameter **pp** as an element of set PP, then SUT must have the object **pp** of class PP.

Refer to Figure 3(a). (N, N') is an edge in the test sequence with $'res \leftarrow OP(..)'$ as the operation call. This edge has also k probe calls along with their results. The corresponding code in Java has been shown in Figure 3(b). $C[N]$ stand for the code generated at node N. First a call to mmo.OP(...) is made. Then we obtain the results of the probe operations from the SUT which are compared with the results of the same operations stored in the test case; this comparison is performed by Java assertions. In (b), `res_1,..., res_k` are the temporary variables to receive the probe results.

Table 2. Code for the test case in Figure 2

```
USER login_t1, alloc_t1; int alloc_t2;
TA1.login(u1); login_t1= TA1.login_P1();
        assert(login_t1==u1);
TA1.alloc(s1); alloc_t1= TA1.alloc_P1(s1);
        assert(alloc_t1==u1);
alloc_t2 = TA1.alloc_P2(s1);
        assert(alloc_t2== 1);
TA1.alloc(s1); alloc_t1= TA1.alloc_P1(s1);
        assert(alloc_t1==u1);
alloc_t2 = TA1.alloc_P2(s1);
        assert(alloc_t2== 2);
```

Table 2 shows the code fragment in relation to the test case shown in Figure 2. The testing context provides object TA1 of class TAgency1, objects u_1 and u_2 of class USER, objects r_1 and r_2 of class ROOM, and object s_1 of class SESSION. With these, the code in Table 2 if runs without any assertion violation it would mean that the SUT has passed the test case. Note that the generation of the code in Table 2 can easily be automated. It is to be further noted that the testing context must be provided by the implementor because it involves some design decisions like defining the constructors of various classes.

5   The Method II: Non-deterministic Models

The first three steps – generation of probe operations, signature file and the operation instances – of the method outlined in the last section, remain identical for non-deterministic B models. In addition, the process of attaching probe operation calls and their results to an edge in the coverage graph also remains the same. We will discuss the remaining steps here.

Table 3. Making internal choices observable: SELECT statement

OP(..)= ...	br ← OP(..)= ...
SELECT C1 THEN S_1	SELECT C1 THEN S_1 || br := 1
...	...
WHEN C_k THEN S_k END	WHEN C_k THEN S_k || br := k END

There are two primary categories of non-determinism in B [1]: unbounded choice through the ANY statement and bounded choice through the SELECT statement, both having the following syntax respectively.

ANY $x_1, \ldots, x_k$ WHERE   SELECT C_1 THEN S_1
  $P(x_1, \ldots, x_k)$ $\ldots$
THEN S END   WHEN C_k THEN S_k END

The ANY statement makes k non-deterministic choices satisfying the predicate $P(x_1, \ldots, x_k)$ which are used to perform the substitution S. For a non-deterministic SELECT, the branching conditions $C_1, \ldots C_k$ do overlap; and then one valid branch is selected in a non-deterministic way. In addition to SELECT and ANY, B supports non-deterministic assignments in initializations with the syntax $x :\in S$ meaning that x is given any element of S. However, this statement can always be converted to: ANY y WHERE $y \in S$ THEN $x := y$ END.

5.1   Pre-processing of the B Model

We make the internal choice – within an ANY statement or the branch selection in SELECT – visible by making the associated B operations more observable. This we do by introducing additional result parameters. Refer to the enterCard() in Appendix-A. We have added a result parameter to observe the internal choice made by the ANY statement. Similarly, we have also added a result parameter to login() to make its non-deterministic choice visible. We also make the branch choice that a non-deterministic SELECT makes observable by introducing an additional result parameter (refer to Table 3). We term the constraint under which a choice is made as *choice predicate*. For ANY, it is the constraint within the WHERE clause. For SELECT, we define it to be $br \in \{1, .., k\}$, where br is the output variable introduced to capture which branch the SUT would select (refer to Table 3), and k is the number of branches.

5.2   Coverage Graph for a Non-deterministic Model

Our convention is that whenever we make a call to a non-deterministic operation then we select a fresh variable in place of the choice and restrict it by the choice predicate. We will refer to this fresh variable as a `choice variable`. A choice variable once created can be used as a parameter in subsequent invocations as long as it satisfies the typing rules.

A node in the coverage graph is a tuple $< Vect, AC, AssP >$, where $Vect$ is the state vector to store the bindings of expressions to state variables; these expressions may contain choice variables as sub-terms. AC is the set of accumulated constraints which essentially restricts the choice variables occurring in the expressions in $Vect$. $AssP$ is an assertion which results from an application of a non-deterministic operation. For a node N, we refer to its fields by the dot notation such as $N.Vect, N.AC$ etc.

Figure 4 shows an edge in the coverage graph, where $< Vect, AC, AssP >$ constitute the source node. Let application of call OP(X) at the source would give us the target node $< Vect', AC', AssP' >$. The edge between the source and the target is labeled with $< P, y \leftarrow OP(X) >$. The derivation process is as follows:

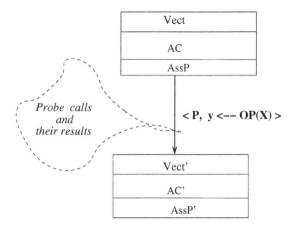

Fig. 4. Application of a non-deterministic operation

- P is a predicate to check that OP(X) is applicable at $< Vect, AC, AssP >$. If $pre(OP(X))$ is the precondition of OP(X) then P is an expression over the choice variables occurring in $Vect$ and is equivalent to $AC \wedge pre(OP(X))$ or its boolean simplification. We call it the Precondition Satisfaction Predicate (or PSP) which being **false** would mean that OP(X) is not applicable.
- If OP() is a non-deterministic operation, y stands for the choice variable selected in place of the internal non-deterministic choice. If cc is the internal choice in OP(), and $cpred$ is the choice predicate, then $AssP'$ is the reduced form of the constraint $cpred[y/cc]$; i.e., the substitution of y in place of the free occurrences of cc in $cpred$.
- $Vect'$ is the reduced form of $Vect[body(OP(X))]$ where $body(OP(X))$ is the substitution in relation to $OP(X)$.
- AC' is the accumulated constraint of the target node and is equivalent to the reduced form of $(AC \wedge P \wedge AssP')$. Note that AC' always includes $AssP'$. We maintain $AssP'$ separately to be referred to by the test case generator.

For the initial node, AC is initialized to the constraints made out of the set declarations and the constraints. Figure 5 shows a part of the coverage graph for the B machine TAgency2. The node marked '1' is the initial node. Its AC field is initialized to $AC0$ as given in the figure. The $Vect$ field here corresponds to the INITIALIZATION clause of the machine. $AssP$ is given the trivial value of $true$. In node 2, ZS_1 represents the non-deterministically selected session identifier. Now consider the call of responseBook$_1$(ZS1) at node 3. Observe how the choice variable $ZS1$ has been used as a parameter. Now consider the application of the following operation instance at node 3:

rstatus $\leftarrow$ responseBook$_1$(sid) =
PRE $sid \in SESSION \wedge sid \in dom(session) \wedge$
    $s\_req(sid) = book \wedge s\_state(sid) = s4 \wedge$
    $s\_card(sid) = valid \wedge dom(booking) \subset (ROOM - null_R)$

THEN
      ANY **rr** WHERE **rr**$\in (ROOM - null\_R) - dom(booking)$
      THEN booking(rr) := sess(sid) $\|$ rstatus := **rr** END $\| \ldots$
END

The predicate $AC3 \wedge pre(responseBook_1(ZS1))$ reduces to $ZC1 = valid$ to become the PSP of the current call. If $ZR1$ is the choice variable due to ANY, then $(rr \in (ROOM - null_R) - dom(booking)) [ZR1/rr]$ reduces to $ZR1 \in (ROOM - null_R)$ to becomes the AssP of the target node. Substitution of the operation body over the Vector of the source node, gives us the new Vector. Finally, $AC3$ augmented with the PSP and the AssP becomes the AC of the target node.

5.3   Test Cases from Non-deterministic Models

As in the case of deterministic models, the coverage graph could be traversed to generate a set of linear test cases. We will term those as basic test cases; they will be combined to form adaptive test cases. If we treat a basic test case as a test case proper, then consider the case when SUT control encounters an edge with a non-trivial PSP and it does not hold. For example, in Figure 5, if edge $(ZC1 = valid, ZC1 \leftarrow responseBook(ZS1))$ occurs in a basic test case, then $ZC1 = valid$ could be false, and then there is no point in following this edge any further. In the worst case scenario, we may not be able to test any of the basic test cases into completion. Adaptive test cases are introduced precisely for this purpose. An adaptive test case in the coverage graph is a subgraph in the form of a tree with the following properties:

- Its root is same as the root of the coverage graph.
- The paths from the root to the leaves are mutually exclusive in that at any non-leaf node, the PSPs of its outgoing edges are mutually contradictory. In this way we would be able to test all the paths of the test case by a single threaded test driver.

From this definition, it should be clear that given a set of basic test cases as paths in the coverage graph, we can carve out a set of adaptive test cases. One such algorithm is given in [20]. Refer to Figure 5. In this tree all paths from the root to leaves can be seen as basic test cases. Only the node marked 3 has outgoing edges with non-trivial PSPs. The PSPs of the two outgoing edges of this node are $ZC1 = valid$ and $ZC1 = wrong$, and hence mutually contradictory; so, the whole tree in the figure produces the single adaptive test case.

5.4   Test Driver Generation

Since the elements of an enumerated set is available in the model, the test driver can have control over its range. If there is a need to check the range of ROOM, it can be done explicitly. But the range of a deferred set like SESSION, cannot be checked. When the operation login() is called from SUT the system depending on availability may or may not be able to allocate a session for the user to

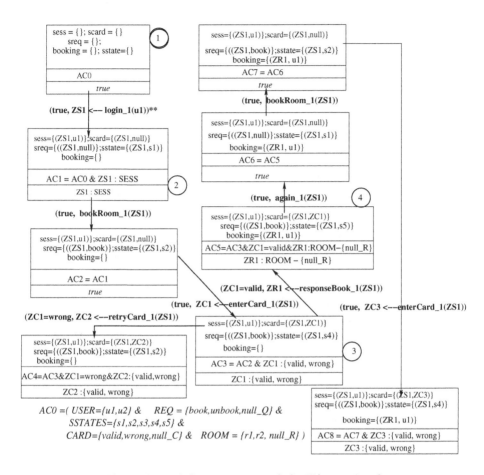

Fig. 5. Part of the coverage graph for TAgency2.mch

work with. When it allocates a session there is no need to check the model predicate $ZS1 \in SESSION$ because it would be trivially satisfied by the type checking rule of Java. But if a null object reference is returned then from the view point of testing there is no need to check the subsequent operation calls. In summary, when an element of a deferred set is obtained it must be checked for non-nullness. To signify that in the coverage graph of Figure 5, we have marked the edge joining nodes 1 and 2 with '**'.

B predicates to Java Assertions: While generating a coverage graph, we obtain predicates which involves choice variables. Let us call these *graph predicates*. They are different from model predicates, the predicates occurring in a B model. We require a Set Constraint Solver (SCS) to translate any graph predicate into Java assertions. The development of such a SCS in general is a challenging task. In this paper we consider a simple SCS and so we put restrictions on model predicates which in turn restrict the graph predicates. If x is an internal choice

Table 4. Schema Rules for reducing some B terms

term	Reduced Terms	condition
NULL	null	null object reference
$dom(R)$	$\{s_1, \ldots, s_k\}$	$R = \{(s_1, t_1), \ldots, (s_k, t_k)\}$
$ran(R)$	$\{t_1, \ldots, t_k\}$	$R = \{(s_1, t_1), \ldots, (s_k, t_k)\}$
R^{-1}	$\{(t_1, s_1) \ldots, (t_k, s_k)\}$	$R = \{(s_1, t_1), \ldots, (s_k, t_k)\}$
$F(s_i)$	t_i	$F = \{(s_1, t_1), \ldots, (s_k, t_k)\}$; F is a function

— like cc in enterCard() or rr in response_book() — the syntactic constraint on model predicates is that, it can be of the form: $x \in S \wedge P$, where S is either a deferred set or an enumerated set or a basic set (Bool or Int), and P includes finite number of (state) variables and constants. For instance, in login(), the model predicate $sid \in SESSION \wedge sid \notin dom(sess)$ is of this form.

SCS performs two main tasks: (a) to evaluate a graph predicate — involving choice variables, sets, relation, function etc. — to obtain PSPs; this can be done by extending Constraint Logic Programming (CLP) to sets, relations and functions; and (b) to reduce the PSPs and the AssPs into Java assertions.

Table 4 shows the reduction rules for some terms in graph predicates. Table 5 shows the rules to reduce some graph predicates to Java assertions by a translation function γ. Note that each s_i or t_i stands for a term occurring in graph predicates. We assume that the reduction of terms can be performed by syntactic checking only. For instance, the reduction of $\{(ZS1, u1), (ZS2, u2)\}(ZS2)$ can be done by syntax checking, whereas that of $\{(ZS1, u1), (ZS2, u2)\}(ZS8)$ given that $ZS8 \in \{ZS1, ZS2\}$ can not be performed by syntactic checking alone. Though the latter terms can be reduced to Java by defining more and more rules, we do not consider them here.

Table 5. Schema rules for transforming some B predicates

predicates	to Java	condition
$\gamma[TRUE]$	true	boolean constant in Java
$\gamma[FALSE]$	false	boolean constant in Java
$\gamma[(s_1, t_1) = (s_2, t_2)]$	$(s_1 == t_1) \,\&\&\, (s_2 == t_2)$	
$\gamma[X \in S]$	$(X == s_1) \,\|\| \ldots \|\| (X == s_k)$	$S = \{s_1, \ldots, s_k\}$
$\gamma[X \in S]$	$!(X == $ null$)$	S is a deferred set
$\gamma[X \in T_1 \cup T_2]$	$\gamma[(X \in T_1)] \,\|\|\, \gamma[(X \in T_2)]$	
$\gamma[X \in T_1 \cap T_2]$	$\gamma[X \in T_1] \,\&\&\, \gamma[X \in T_2]$	
$\gamma[A \subseteq B]$	$\gamma[s_1 \in B] \,\&\& \ldots \&\&\, \gamma[s_k \in B]$	$A = \{s_1, \ldots, s_k\}$
$\gamma[\forall x \in S.P(x)]$	$\gamma[P(s_1)] \,\&\& \ldots \&\&\, \gamma[P(s_k)]$	$S = \{s_1, \ldots, s_k\}$
$\gamma[\exists x \in S.P(x)]$	$\gamma[P(s_1)] \,\|\| \ldots \|\|\, \gamma[P(s_k)]$	$S = \{s_1, \ldots, s_k\}$

Test Driver Generation Algorithm: The test driver generation algorithm for adaptive test cases is trivial. An adaptive test case is in the form of a tree. A junction nodes gets transformed to an `if-elseif-else` statement, and the PSPs of the branches become the **if** (or **elseif**) conditions. In addition, there has to be an **else** clause because the set of the PSPs may not be exhaustive. If during testing, SUT control enters this **else branch**, this would mean that we cannot carry out testing any further; appropriate message can be given to the tester in this case. A detailed discussion on this situation has been given in [20]. Leaving aside the PSPs, in relation to a branch in the test case, we encounter a sequence of operation applications which may have assertions (AssPs) and they become Java assertions in the code. We show this by generating code for the single adaptive test case of Figure 5; the code has been shown below. Observe how the branching in the code corresponds to the branching in the adaptive test case. We do not show the testing context here since it remains the same as earlier.

```
SESSION ZS1; ROOM ZR1; CARD ZC1,ZC2;
USER temp_u; int temp_c;
ZS1 = TA2.login(u1); assert(ZS1 != null);
TA2.bookRoom(ZS1); ZC1 = TA2.enterCard(ZS1);
assert(ZC1 == valid || ZC1 == wrong);
if (ZC1 == wrong) { // PSP of 1st branch holds
     ZC2=TA2.retryCard(ZS1);
     assert(ZC5 == valid || ZC5 == wrong);
} else if (ZC1 == valid) { // PSP of next branch holds
     ZR1=TA2.responseRoom(ZS1);
     assert(ZR1 == u1 || ZR1 == u2 || ZR1 == u3);
     temp_u = TA2.whichUser(ZS1); assert(temp_u == u1);
     temp_c = TA2.numOfRoomsBooked(); assert(temp_c == 1);
} else {
     Sys.out.println("SUT control deviated; testing stops");
}
```

6   Implementation

ProB is a model checking and animation tool for B machines [16]. ProB includes a fully automatic animator written in SICStus prolog. An extension of ProB will be our implementation platform. As of now, we have implemented testing of a SUT written in accordance with a deterministic B model. We have made the following steps automatic so far.

- Given a B operation with its precondition enriched with tautologies (refer to Section 4) we generate a set of operation instances.
- Given a B model, we generate a Java signature template for all B operations.
- After restricting the sets to be finite, the current tool automatically creates a coverage graph (we do not yet support deferred sets).
- We traverse the coverage graph to generate a set of preset test cases; this is because we consider deterministic models only.
- Given a set of test cases, we generate a test driver which, when augmented with the testing context, performs automatic testing of a Java implementation.

Now the development of a SCS to handle a subset of B predicates is under progress. This will enable us in handling non-deterministic models.

7 Discussion

- Making the whole testing cycle automatic in presence of non-determinism is an important contribution of our work. It is often the case that non-determinism in B is gradually refined out in the B refinement process, but our strategy does not assume the implementation to be deterministic. In case the implementation is non-deterministic, our method would work without any change. Existing testing tools like BZ-TT [2] avoid the issues related to non-determinism.
- The tester (or the specifier) has to write a set of probe operations for each B operation. In this paper, we have kept this step outside of the scope of our testing cycle. However, we believe writing a set of probe operation from the domain knowledge and the intention of the operation is too ad-hoc an approach. Probe operations can be generated automatically from the model in a systematic manner. One possibility is to define abstract functions mapping the concrete states of the Java program to the abstraction level in the B machine. This issue requires further research.
- Our method can create a coverage graph in presence of deferred sets.
- The problem of obtaining a PSP out of a set of B constraints requires to solve a set of set constraints; this being a variant of the satisfiability problem is NP-complete [8]. Good specification practices recommend to write smaller and simpler operations. In this case, we expect the problem size would remain small and then a CLP solver can be used to do the job. This issue needs further investigation.
- For the development of a SCS, we took a simple subset of the B predicates. However, this is a useful subset since we have examined a number of examples and seen that this subset is sufficient. The examples include B models for a larger version of the travel agency example, the router component of a Network-on-Chip system and a component of a TV teletext system. The problem of implementing a robust SCS will require further research.

8 Conclusion

We have discussed how a test driver in the form of a Java program can be mechanically generated from a B model, possibly non-deterministic, to perform automatic testing. The constraints arising out of non-deterministic choices and oracle information matching become Java assertions in the test driver which if runs without any assertion violation would mean that the implementation has passed the test cases. Our approach can generate the test driver much before the implementation; however, it assumed that the implementation should adhere to the Java signature template obtained from the model. We have made comparisons of our research with existing work, the important contributions being the handling of non-determinism.

Acknowledgement. We would like to thank Linas Laibinis for going through an earlier version of this work and offering many a useful suggestion. The comments of the anonymous reviewers also helped us in improving the quality of this paper.

References

1. Abrial, J.-R.: The B–Book: Assigning Programs to Meanings. Cambridge University Press, Cambridge (1996)
2. Bernard, E., Legeard, B., Luck, X., Peureux, F.: Generation of test sequences from formal specifications: GSM 11-11 standard case study. Software Practice and Experience 34(10), 915–948 (2004)
3. Colin, S., Legeard, B., Peureux, F.: Preamble computation in automated test case generation using constraint logic programming. Software Testing Verification and Reliability, John Wiley 14, 213–235 (2004)
4. Dick, J., Faivre, A.: Automating the Generation and Sequencing of Test Cases from Model-based Specifications. In: Larsen, P.G., Woodcock, J.C.P. (eds.) FME 1993. LNCS, vol. 670, pp. 268–284. Springer, Heidelberg (1993)
5. Dalal, S.R., Jain, A., Karunanithi, N., Leaton, J.M., Lott, C.M., Patton, G.C., Horowitz, B.M.: Model Based Testing in Practice. In: Proc. of ICSE '99 (1999)
6. El-Far, I.K., Whittaker, J.A.: Model Based Software Testing. In: Marciniak, J.J. (ed.) Encyclopedia on Software Engineering, John Wiley, Chichester (2001)
7. Gannon, J.D., Hamlet, R.G., Mills, H.D.: Theory of modules. IEEE Transactions on Software Engineering 13(7), 820–829 (1987)
8. Garey, M.R., Johnson, D.S.: Computers and Intractability. W. H. Freeman and Company, New York (1979)
9. Gurevich, Y.: Sequential Abstract-State Machines Capture Sequential Programs. ACM Transaction on Computational Logic 1(1), 77–111 (2000)
10. Hierons, R.M.: Testing from a Non-deterministic Finite State Machine using Adaptive State Counting. IEEE Transactions on Computers 53(10), 1330–1342 (2004)
11. Hierons, R.M.: Applying Adaptive Test Cases to Non-deterministic Implementations. Information Processing Letters 98(2006), 56–60 (2006)
12. Jones, C.B.: Systematic Software Development using VDM, 2nd edn. Prentice-Hall, Englewood Cliffs (1990)
13. Lee, D., Yannakakis, M.: Principles and Methods of Testing Finite State Machines: A survey. Proc. of the IEEE 80(8), 1090–1123 (1996)
14. Legeard, B., Peureux, F., Utting, M.: Automatic Boundary Testing from Z and B. In: Eriksson, L.-H., Lindsay, P.A. (eds.) FME 2002. LNCS, vol. 2391, pp. 21–40. Springer, Heidelberg (2002)
15. Legeard, B., Peureux, F., Utting, M.: Controlling test case explosion in test generation from B formal models. In: Software Testing, Verification and Reliability, pp. 81–103. John Wiley, Chichester (2004)
16. Leuschel, M., Butler, M.: ProB: A Model Checker for B. In: Araki, K., Gnesi, S., Mandrioli, D. (eds.) FME 2003. LNCS, vol. 2805, pp. 855–874. Springer, Heidelberg (2003)
17. Nachmanson, L., Veanes, M., Schulte, W., Tillmann, N., Grieskamp, W.: Optimal Strategies for Testing Nondeterministic Systems. In: ACM ISSTA'04, Boston, ACM Press, New York (July 2004)
18. Panzl, D.J.: Automatic Software Test Drivers. IEEE Computer 11(4) (1978)

19. Richardson, D.J., Leif Aha, A., O'Malley, T.O.: Specification-based Test Oracles for Reactive Systems. In: Proc. of the 14th ICSE, Melbourne, pp. 105–118 (1992)
20. Satpathy, M., Butler, M., Ramesh, S., Leuschel, M.: Automatic Testing of Formal Specifications, Technical Report 792, Abo Akademi University, Turku, Finland (2006), available at: http://www.tucs.fi/publications
21. Satpathy, M., Leuschel, M., Butler, M.: ProTest: An Automatic Test Environment for B Specifications. Electronic Notes on TCS (ENTCS), vol. 111, pp. 113–136 (2005)
22. Spivey, J.M.: Understanding Z. Cambridge University Press, Cambridge (1988)
23. Yannakakis, M., Lee, D.: Testing Finite State Machines: Fault Detection. Journal of Computer and System Sciences 50, 209–277 (1995)
24. Zhang, F., Cheung, T.: Optimal Transfer Trees and Distinguishing Trees for Testing Observable Nondeterministic Finite State Machines. IEEE Transactions on Software Engineering 29(1), 1–14 (2003)
25. Zhu, H., Hall, P.A.V., May, J.H.R.: Software Unit Test Coverage and Adequacy. ACM Computing Surveys 29(4), 366–427 (1997)

Appendix–A

MACHINE TAgency2
SETS SESSION; /* A deferred set */
    USER $= \{u1, u2\}$; REQ$=\{book, unbook, null\_r\}$;
    SSTATES$= \{s1, s2, s3, s4, s5\}$;
    CARD $= \{valid, wrong, null\_C\}$; ROOM $= \{r1, r2, null\_R\}$
VARIABLES $sess, scard, sstate, sreq, booking$ /* all partial functions */
INVARIANT $sess \in SESSION \; +\!\!\rightarrow \; USER \wedge scard \in SESSION \; +\!\!\rightarrow \; CARD \wedge$
    $sstate \in SESSION \; +\!\!\rightarrow \; SSTATES \wedge sreq \in SESSION \; +\!\!\rightarrow \; REQ \wedge$
    $booking \in (ROOMS - \{null\_R\}) \; +\!\!\rightarrow \; USER \wedge \ldots$
INITIALISATION $sess, scard, sstate, sreq, booking := \emptyset, \emptyset, \emptyset, \emptyset, \emptyset$
OPERATIONS
    $id \longleftarrow login(uu) =$ PRE $uu \in USER$ THEN
        ANY sid WHERE $sid \in SESSION \wedge sid \notin dom(sess)$ THEN
            $sess(sid) := uu \;\|\; s\_card(sid) := null\_C \;\|$
            $s\_state(sid) := s1 \;\|\; s\_req(sid) := null\_r$
            $\|\; id := sid$
        END END;
    $bookRoom(sid) =$ PRE $sid \in SESSION \wedge sid \in dom(sess) \wedge$
        $s\_state(sid) = s1 \wedge s\_req(sid) = null_r$
        THEN $s\_state(sid) := s2 \;\|\; s\_req(sid) := book$
        END;
    $unbookRoom(sid) = \ldots$
    $cstatus \longleftarrow enterCard(sid) =$ PRE $sid \in SESSION \wedge sid \in dom(sess) \wedge$
        $s\_state(sid) \in \{s2, s3\}$
    THEN $s\_state(sid) := s4 \;\|$
        ANY cc WHERE $cc \in \{valid, wrong\}$
        THEN $s\_card(sid) := cc \;\|\; cstatus := cc$
    END END;

$cstatus \longleftarrow retryCard(sid) = $ PRE $sid \in SESSION \wedge sid \in dom(sess) \wedge$
$\qquad s\_state(sid) = s4 \wedge s\_card(sid) = wrong$
THEN ANY cc WHERE $cc \in \{valid, wrong\}$
$\qquad$ THEN $s\_card(sid) := cc \parallel cstatus := cc$
$\quad$ END END;
$rstatus \longleftarrow response\_book(sid) =$
$\quad$ PRE $sid \in SESSION \wedge sid \in dom(sess) \wedge s\_req(sid) = book \wedge$
$\qquad s\_state(sid) = s4 \wedge s\_card(sid) = valid$
$\quad$ THEN $s\_state(sid) := s5 \parallel$
$\quad$ IF $dom(booking) \subset (ROOM - \{null\_R\})$ THEN
$\qquad$ ANY rr WHERE $rr \in (ROOM - \{null\_R\}) - dom(booking)$
$\qquad$ THEN $booking(rr) := sess(sid) \parallel rstatus := rr$ END
$\quad$ ELSE $rstatus := null\_R$
$\quad$ END
$\quad$ END;
$rstatus \longleftarrow response\_unbook(sid) = \ldots$
$again(sid) = \ldots$
$logout(sid) = \ldots$
END

Using Contracts and Boolean Queries to Improve the Quality of Automatic Test Generation

Lisa (Ling) Liu, Bertrand Meyer, and Bernd Schoeller

Chair of Software Engineering,
ETH Zurich, Switzerland
{ling.liu,Bertrand.Meyer,bernd.schoeller}@inf.ethz.ch

Abstract. Since test cases cannot be exhaustive, any effective test case generation strategy must identify the execution states most likely to uncover bugs. The key issue is to define criteria for selecting such interesting states.

If the units being tested are classes in object-oriented programming, it seems attractive to rely on the *boolean queries* present in each class, which indeed define criteria on the states of the corresponding objects, and — in contract-equipped O-O software — figure prominently in preconditions, postconditions and invariants. As these queries are part of the class specification and hence relevant to its clients, one may conjecture that the resulting partition of the state space is also relevant for tests.

We explore this conjecture by examining whether relying on the boolean queries of a class to extract abstract states improves the results of black-box testing. The approach uses constraint-solving and proof techniques to generate objects that satisfy the class invariants, then performs testing by relying on postconditions as test oracles. The resulting strategy, in our experiments on library classes used in production software, finds significantly more bugs than random testing.

1 Overview

Unlike other approaches to improving program quality, in particular proofs, program testing focuses not on guaranteeing the absence of bugs but on uncovering bugs. This is by itself a very interesting goal since any bug removed is a significant improvement to a program.

The effectiveness of a testing strategy is, as a result, defined by how likely it is to uncover bugs. We present a testing strategy for classes — object-oriented program units — that takes advantage of two of their distinctive properties: the presence of *boolean queries* as part of the interface of a class, and in some programming formalisms, the use of *contracts* to specify abstract properties of classes.

The topic of this paper is, as a consequence, simple. We state a conjecture: that using contracts and queries will improve the effectiveness of testing strategies. Then we assess the validity of that conjecture by applying contract- and query-based testing through our automatic test environment, AutoTest [5], and measuring whether this improves AutoTest's effectiveness in finding bugs.

A characteristic of our testing work is that (rather than artificial examples, although one will be used to illustrate the concepts) it applies testing strategies and in particular the

B. Meyer and Y. Gurevich (Eds.): TAP 2007, LNCS 4454, pp. 114–130, 2007.

AutoTest tool to actual production software, in particular the EiffelBase library of fundamental data structures and algorithms, used daily in mission-critical production environments. Testing for us is then not just an academic pursuit but also a very practical attempt to find bugs in actual software. Along with the concepts we propose, the main concrete result of the study reported here is that it has enabled us to find and correct real bugs in software components that are in actual use, and hence provide a tangible benefit to the users of those components.

1.1 Correctness and Contracts

The correctness of a program element is not an absolute property but is always defined with respect to a certain specification. In the "Design by Contract" approach [18], the specification is present in the text of classes (the program units of object-oriented programming) in the form of invariants for classes, and preconditions and postconditions for routines[1]. Ascertaining the correctness of a class in languages that natively support such mechanisms —Eiffel [19] or Spec# [1] —, or in contract add-ons to Java (such as JML [13, 14], iContract [12]) or UML (Object Constraint Language [23, 8]), means ascertaining that the implementations are consistent with the contracts: specifically, that every creation procedure (constructor) yields an object satisfying the invariant of its class, and that every exported routine, started in a state satisfying the invariant and the precondition, terminates in a state satisfying the invariant and the postcondition.

Using testing we cannot prove such correctness for any realistic program, but we can uncover correctness violations — bugs — by finding inputs that will cause routine executions to violate an invariant or postcondition.

1.2 Testing and Program States

Because the set of possible program execution states is inexhaustible, any practical testing strategy must identify a subset of interesting states, where "interest" is defined — in the negative mindset that characterizes the work of the tester, whose reward is to prove software *in*correct — as likelihood to uncover bugs. Usually this is achieved through a *partitioning* approach which, using appropriate criteria, divides the state space into disjoint parts, then picks one state (or a few) from each such part, with the expectation that each selected state is somehow representative of that part.

A common approach for such partitioning is to use white-box tests, based on an analysis of the implementation's control flow, such as "path coverage" and "branch coverage". This has two disadvantages. First, the tester needs access to the implementation, which may be an unrealistic requirement in the presence of information hiding. Second, the approach requires possibly complex computation to exercise specific branches or paths.

1.3 Query-Based Testing

The approach described here relies instead on a black-box testing strategy, based on contracts. Specifically:

---

[1] "Routines" are called "methods" in Java and C++. This paper uses Eiffel terminology and notation.

- Instead of relying on the implementation of a class, it uses its contracts and its boolean queries to partition the state space.
- The partitioning is aided by an insight into the structure of good contracts, the *Boolean Query Conjecture*, defined below.
- Techniques from boolean constraint solving and program proving help reduce the resulting state space further.
- Then we develop a test strategy - boolean query coverage to achieve complete test coverage based on the outcomes of this reasoning.

The main contributions of this paper are the following:

1. New application of Design by Contract techniques to improve the testing process.
2. A new method for partitioning program state, applied here to testing but (we think) with potential applications elsewhere, for example in model checking.
3. The experimental validation of that method on concrete examples.
4. New techniques for improving test coverage.
5. The integration of constraint-solving and program-proving techniques in a testing framework.
6. A technique for taking advantage of test results to improve not only test coverage but also class designs (through stronger invariants).
7. Concretely, as noted, the detection through an automatic procedure (and subsequent correction), in actual production libraries, of real bugs, until now unsuspected and not found by any previous technique, manual or automatic.

Section 2 presents the notion of boolean query and introduces the conjecture behind this work's approach to testing, as well as the method for assessing the conjecture. Section 3 explains the overall strategy based on contracts, the notion of abstract state space, constraint satisfaction techniques, proof techniques, and the AutoTest framework. Section 4 describes the experimental study applying this strategy to a set of actual classes, and analyzes the result. Section 5 discusses related work, and section 6 discusses future work.

2   The Role of Boolean Queries

The central issue of test case generation is, as noted above, to maximize the likelihood of uncovering bugs. If we are testing object-oriented software we should take advantage of the distinctive structure of O-O programs.

2.1   Classes and Object States

A class is often an implementation of an abstract data type, providing all the operations, or "features", on a certain type of run-time objects. These features are of two kinds [18]:

- **Commands.** modify the corresponding object: withdraw money (for a class representing bank accounts), open (for a class representing files), increase indent (for a class representing paragraphs in a text).
- **Queries.** return information about an object: current balance, number of characters, margin size.

Both commands and queries can be exercised on a particular object through a "feature call" written, in most object-oriented languages, through dot notation, as in

> *my_account.withdraw* (500)
>
> *b* := *my_account.balance*

2.2 Argumentless Boolean Queries

Among queries, *boolean* queries are of particular interest, especially boolean queries without arguments. Examination of object-oriented libraries such as EiffelBase [17] and others indicates that 90% classes are equipped argumentless boolean queries. Examples include:

- In a bank account class, *is_overdraft*.
- In a paragraph class, *is_justified*.
- In data structure classes, *is_empty* and (if the representation has limited capacity) *is_full*.
- In a list class where lists have cursors indicating a current position of interest, *is_before*, *is_after*, *off*, *is_first*.

The recommended Eiffel convention, whose very existence reflects the ubiquity and importance of such queries, is to give them names starting with *is_*.

Such argumentless queries are generally part of the official interface of the corresponding classes. They intuitively seem, for a well-designed class, to reflect fundamental, *qualitative* properties of the state. For example a list may, or not, be empty; and it may, or not, have twenty-five elements. While the corresponding classes will typically have a query *is_empty* they will not, in general, offer *has_twenty_five_elements*. This is because the designer of the class intuitively thought of the second property (if he considered it at all) to reflect a circumstantial possibility for the state of a list, but understood the distinction between empty and non-empty lists as a critical division of the set of possible list states.

Observation of well-written O-O software reinforces this intuition about the importance of argumentless queries, both externally (as part of the interface of classes) and internally (as part of their implementation):

- Externally, boolean queries often serve as preconditions and appear in invariants. For example, the precondition of a routine to remove an item from a list is **not** *is_empty*; and the invariant will include properties such as *is_before* **implies** *off*.
- Internally, the implementation of a routine to add an item to a list will proceed differently depending on whether the list is initially empty or not and (in an implementation based on an array but dynamically resizable) whether the current implementation is full or not.

All this suggests that the distinction may also be useful when it comes to dividing the state space for purposes of testing the software.

In particular, it follows from the last comment — about features being internally relevant to the implementation — that argumentless boolean queries may be our best bet when we are doing black-box testing and trying to guess the kind of properties actually used in decision branches of the implementation. A query such as *is_empty* is, in the end, nothing else than a predicate — a boolean expression — as used by the control structure of programs to select between branches of conditional expressions and to decide whether to terminate loops. Since testing strategies must partition the state space into representative categories, they use such predicates for the partitioning; for example white-box testing relies on predicates used in tests, such as c in **if** c **then** a **else** b **end**, to generate a test with c true to exercise a and one with c false to exercise b. If our intuition is correct that boolean queries reflect qualitatively important properties of the object state, then it may be useful to use them, rather than arbitrary predicates, to partition the state space. This possibility is particularly attractive in black-box testing, where we don't have access to the internal structure of the code, and cannot, as a result, directly know which boolean expressions, such as c above, actually appear in tests governing the control structure. In light of the above observations, argumentless queries are our best bet.

2.3 The Conjecture

The preceding observations lead to the conjecture behind the present work:

> *Boolean Query Conjecture:* The argumentless boolean queries of a well-written class yield a partition of the corresponding object state space that helps the effectiveness of testing strategies.

"Well-written" is a subjective term, but we will assume the following:

- The class indeed includes boolean queries reflecting important abstract properties of the corresponding objects.
- Routines are equipped with contracts, in particular preconditions. Our main experimentation target is the EiffelBase libraries [17], which indeed is equipped with contracts.
- The contracting style is on the "demanding" side [18]: routines try to limit their functionality to the required minimum by enforcing reasonableness conditions on their clients.

2.4 Assessing the Conjecture

The Boolean Query Conjecture is of a heuristic nature and, as such, not amenable to a formal proof. To assess its validity, we simply:

- Extend an existing tool for automatic test generation, AutoTest, to take advantage of partitioning based on argumentless boolean queries.

- Compare the effectiveness of the resulting testing strategy — how many buggy routines it finds, and the quality of its routine coverage — with the effectiveness of the original AutoTest using a random strategy for black-box testing.

3 Using Contracts and Proof Techniques

3.1 Basic Definitions

In the rest of this discussion the term **query** will be used as a shorthand for "exported argumentless boolean query", since these are the only kinds of queries of interest for the discussion. The following definitions will be useful.

Boolean abstraction function: A *boolean abstraction function* is a vector $<q_1, q_2, ..., q_n>$ of queries.

Abstract object state: An *abstract object state* is the vector $<v_1, v_2, ..., v_n>$ containing the result of evaluating the queries of a boolean abstraction function $<q_1, q_2, ..., q_n>$ in a concrete state s of a particular object, with $v_i = q_i(s)$ for all $i \in 1..n$.

If a class has n queries, the number of abstract object states for an instance of the class is 2^n. Note that usually only a subset of these possible abstract states makes sense, since a useful state should satisfy the class invariant.

As a simple example of these concepts, consider the following Eiffel class, adapted from actual (generic) stack classes in EiffelBase:

Listing 1. Class *INT_STACK*

```
class
    INT_STACK
create
    make                                    feature  -- Modifier
feature -- Initialization                       pop is
    make (n : INTEGER ) is                          -- Pop top integer from stack  .
        -- Create empty stack .                     require
        require                                         not_empty : not is _empty
            n > 0                               do
        do                                          ...
            ...                                     ensure
        ensure                                          popped : count = old count - 1
            empty : count =0                    end
            capacity_ set: capacity = n     push (n: INTEGER) is
        end                                         -- Push `n' on top of stack  .
feature -- Queries                                  require
    capacity : INTEGER                                  not_full : not is _full
    count : INTEGER                             do
    top: INTEGER is                                 ...
        -- Top item of stack                    ensure
        require                                         pushed : top = n
            not_empty: not is _empty                    count_increased : count = old count +1
        do                                      end
            ...                             feature  {NONE} -- Implementation
        end                                     s: FIXED_LIST [INTEGER ]
    is_empty : BOOLEAN is                   invariant
        --                                      is _empty: is _empty = count = 0
        do                                      is _full: is_full = count = capacity
            Result := count = 0                 count_small_enough : count <= capacity
        end                                     count _big _enough : count >= 0
                                                capacity_big _ enough : capacity > 0
    is_full : BOOLEAN is                        not _empty_full: is_empty => not is_full
        --                                      s_not_void: s /= Void
        do                                  end
            Result := count = capacity
        end
```

The features "*is_empty*" and "*is_full*" are queries. The vector $<is\_empty, is\_full>$ makes up the boolean abstraction function for the class. The set of abstract object states is $\{<0, 0>, <0, 1>, <1, 0>, <1, 1>\}$) (using 0 for False and 1 for True).

Such an abstract state space will usually be too large to be practically tractable. With a language supporting the inclusion of class invariants, and classes that take advantage of this mechanism, we can reduce that size significantly by excluding states that do not satisfy the invariant. For example a stack cannot (with *capacity*> 0, as also ensured by the invariant) be both empty and full, so we can remove <1, 1> from the above state space. The following definition generalizes this observation:

Reachable abstract object state. An abstract object state is *reachable* if it satisfies the class invariant.

3.2 Query-Based Testing

The general strategy for query-based testing, represented by figure 1, will involve the following elements, detailed in subsequent sections:

- Find the exported argumentless boolean queries.
- (Section 3.3 below.) Use a boolean constraint solver (SICStus) to generate all possible abstract object states that satisfy the clauses of the class invariant involving only these queries — ignoring any invariant clauses involving other features of the class, such as the integer attributes *count* and *capacity* in the above example, since this is beyond the reach of a boolean constraint solver.
- (3.4) Use a theorem prover (Simplify) to prune abstract object states that do not satisfy the invariant (including the previously ignored clauses, such as those involving *count* and *capacity* in the example.

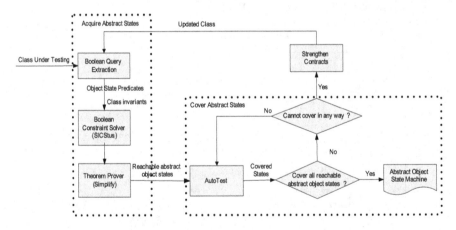

Fig. 1. Overview of class testing procedure

- (3.5) Use a forward testing approach (part of the AutoTest tool), attempt to cover all the resulting abstract object states. In this process, any routine execution that violates a contract element uncovers a bug and hence marks a success of the strategy.
- (3.6) All the previous steps are automatic. After they have been run, it is useful to perform a manual inspection to determine how many of the abstract object states have been covered. For each state that has *not* been covered, you

should inspect the specification to determine whether each uncovered state makes sense or not. If not, this may lead, if you have access to the original class or may make suggestions to its developers, to strengthening its invariant. On the other hand if you find out that the state is logically meaningful, you may have to adapt the testing strategy, adding manual tests if necessary, to extend coverage.

3.3 Generating Abstract State Through Boolean Constraint Solving

Acquiring all reachable abstract object states requires the support of a boolean constraint solver and theorem prover. As noted above, the first step is to collect all the exported, argumentless boolean queries from the class interface; this can be done in several ways (parsing of the class of just its official interface documentation, reflection, or data from the IDE). The next step is to strip down the class invariant to those clauses that only involve these queries, temporarily dropping any other clauses, for example those involving *count* or *capacity*.

This allows feeding the resulting simplified invariant into a boolean constraint solver. We have chosen the SCIStus solver [24] for that purpose. The result is to obtain all possible abstract object states; in the simple example above, after feeding SICStus variant clause "*is_empty* => not *is_full*", we would get { <0, 1>, <1, 0>, <0, 0>}. Note that <1, 1> is not a member of that set since the constraint solver takes advantage of the invariant clause **not** *is_empty* **or not** *is_full* to remove it as inconsistent.

For an actual class, *FIXED_LIST*, the number of applicable queries is 9, resulting in an abstract state space with 512 elements. Contraint solving reduces this number considerably, to 224.

3.4 Pruning the State Space Through Theorem Proving

The resulting abstract state space may still includes states that do not make sense. This is not the case in the simple *INT_STACK* example, since the three states that survive the previous step are all reachable, but often happens in larger cases; for example, in the *FIXED_LIST* class of EiffelBase, boolean constraint solving does not eliminate a state in which "**not** *before* **and not** *after* **and** *off*" holds.

To prune the state space from such spurious cases violating the invariant, the strategy next applies theorem proving. The theorem prover reintroduces the invariant clauses ignored by the previous step to reduce the state of the state space. The proof tool we use is **Simplify** [6]. **Simplify** accepts a sequence of first order formulas as input, and attempts to prove each one. **Simplify** does not implement a decision procedure for its inputs: it can sometimes fail to prove a valid formula. But it is conservative in that it never claims that an invalid formula is valid. As a result, the invariant clauses are encoded as facts and definitions in Simplify; the acquired abstract states are encoded as formulas. Then **Simplify** is used to prove the negation of each formula is valid. If **Simplify** can prove it, the corresponding abstract state is unreachable and can be removed from the abstract state sets that should be covered by the testing procedure. For the *INT_STACK* example, the facts, definitions and formulas fed to Simplify are as follows:

facts:

> (BG_PUSH   (>= *count* 0))
> (BG_PUSH   (<= *count capacity*))
> (BG_PUSH   (> *capacity* 0))

definitions:

> (DEFPRED (*is_empty*) (EQ *count* 0))
> (DEFPRED (is_full) (EQ count capacity))

formulas:

> 1. (NOT (AND (NOT (is_empty)) (NOT (is_full))))
> 2. (NOT (AND (NOT (is_empty)) (is_full)))
> 3. (NOT (AND (is_empty) (NOT (is_full))))

These three formulas cannot be proved valid by **Simplify**, hence they may be reachable and should be covered by the test cases.

Adding this step is quite effective: for example, in the *FIXED_LIST* case, it reduces the state space from 224 elements to 64.

3.5   Forward Testing

The previous steps give us a set of abstract states that can be used as a criterion for test coverage according to the following definition:

> **Boolean query coverage.** A set of tests for a class satisfies *boolean query coverage* if and only if the execution of these tests can cover all the reachable abstract object states for that class.

This sets the stage for the testing effort: try to achieve boolean query coverage by covering as many as possible of the abstract object states determined through application of the preceding techniques.

For the testing effort we rely on AutoTest [5], a testing tool that uses contracts to perform automatic test generation and bug detection. AutoTest uses a *forward testing* [16] process.

The forward testing process attempts to explore all abstract object states. The process first creates some objects via different creation procedures and acquires a set of abstract object states of these objects. Starting from these initially acquired abstract object states, it executes all exported routines in these abstract object states to explore more abstract states. It repeats this step until it either finds no new abstract object states or reaches a predefined threshold (of number of calls, or testing time). Listing 2 describes the procedure more precisely.

To formalize this process it is useful to rely on the following notion (adapted from [15]):

> **Object state machine.** Consider a class C; let EC be its set of exported commands and S be the set of corresponding object states. The *object state machine* for C is defined by the subset $I \subseteq S$ of initial object states (as produced by creation procedures) and the transition function t: $S \times EC \rightarrow S$ describing the effect of C's commands.

Listing 2. Forward Testing

```
forward_testing (threshold : INTEGER) : ABSTRACT_STATE_SET is
    local
        S, T : ABSTRACT_STATE_SET
        a, b: ABSTRACT_STATE
        length : INTEGER
        r : ROUTINE
        R: ROUTINE_SET
        i: INTEGER
    do
        T := Initial abstract object states
        S := { }
        length := 0
        R := All exported routines
        from
        until
            T = { } or length > threshold
        loop
            a := T.remove_one_state
            S := S + a
            length := length + 1
            from
                i := 1
            until
                i > R.count
            loop
                r := R.get(i)
                execute r in a to get abstract object state b
                if b not in S and b not in T then
                    T := T + b
                i := i + 1
            end
        end
        Result := S
    end
```

We can talk of abstract or concrete object state machines, based on this definition, by choosing S to be the set of abstract or concrete states.

The class testing procedure records all exercised abstract object states and transitions. This means that developers can examine the result of a test campaign to determine if the class under testing exhibits unexpected behavior, or to assess the completeness of a test suite.

For INT_STACK, the extracted abstract object state machine is as follows.

Queries:
1. is_empty
2. is_full

Set of states S:
{<1, 0>, <0, 0> , <0, 1>}

Initial states I:
<1, 0>

Command set EC:
pop, push

Transition function t:

<1, 0>	push	<0, 0>
<0, 0>	pop	<1, 0>
<0, 0>	push	<0, 1>
<0, 1>	pop	<0, 0>
<0, 0>	pop	<0, 0>
<0, 0>	push	<0, 0>

Applying AutoTest's forward testing to class *INT_STACK* will cover all reachable abstract object states. This may seem to be because of the simple nature of this academic example, but in fact a very encouraging result of our experiments is that AutoTest's automated strategy yields a very high initial coverage, 80% or higher, of the abstract object state space for all the actual (production) library classes we have tried. As described in the next section, we then perform a manual inspection of the results to examine uncovered states, and improve the invariants as a result of this inspection; in all of our experiments so far this has enabled us in the end to reach 100% boolean query coverage.

3.6 Inspecting the Specification

At the end of the process it is useful to inspect the results, in particular to examine boolean query coverage. If an abstract state has not been covered, possible actions are:

- Add manual tests that will exercise the corresponding states. (AutoTest has the possibility of including manual tests along the automatically generated ones.)
- If it appears that the states are not possible, reinforce the class invariants to exclude them.

As noted earlier, our experiments so far have yielded excellent coverage of the abstract state. But as an example of the second case, we found that in class *FIXED_LIST* 32 states, out of the 64 remaining from previous reductions of the abstract state space, seemed unreachable because a particular property relative to the query *extendible* seems to be missing. Adding the corresponding invariant clause achieves total coverage.

4 Experimental Setup and Study Results

4.1 Choice of Library

To examine the Boolean Query Conjecture with the above strategy, we performed a number of tests of classes from the EiffelBase library. EiffelBase is particularly interesting in several respects:

- It is not an academic example but a production library, used — in its successive incarnations since its first version almost twenty years ago — in numerous applications, in particular, currently, in large, mission-critical systems handling billions of dollars of investments or large-scale missile simulations.
- In spite of this background it still has bugs.
- These bugs arise only in remote, uncommon cases, and are only found through systematic testing by AutoTest, which has taken EiffelBase as one of its primary experimental targets. Obviously, all EiffelBase bugs found so far by AutoTest, including the ones uncovered by present study, have now been corrected.
- EiffelBase is a showcase of object-oriented techniques and in particular makes extensive use of contracts.

4.2 Choice of Target Classes

For the present study, we used *INT_STACK*, our toy example (for reference purposes), and four important classes of the EiffelBase library: *LINKED_LIST*, *BINARY_TREE* , *ARRAYED_SET* and *FIXED_LIST*.

The size of these classes, in terms of number of routines (and ignoring attributes) is as follows:

- *LINKED_LIST*: 89 routines.
- *BINARY_TREE*: 93 routines.
- *ARRAYED_SET*: 70 routines.
- *FIXED_LIST*: 82 routines.

Of these, 27 come from the top-level class *ANY*, which is the one of the ancestors of the classes given. (All Eiffel classes inherit from *ANY*). AutoTest tests all routines, whether defined in the class itself or inherited. Indeed, as the classes given are pretty deep in the inheritance hierarchy, many of their routines are inherited.

4.3 The Testing Environment

The AutoTest tool, the centerpiece of our testing work and responsible for the forward testing step (3.5), is a testing environment which takes care of both test case generation and test oracles. Test cases are generated by systematically calling all the routines of the selected classes and any classes on which they rely; test oracles (the mechanisms to determine whether a test is successful) are entirely provided by routine postconditions and invariants. More precisely:

- A precondition violation for a routine directly called by AutoTest indicates that the test is not interesting; AutoTest minimizes such occurrences through constraint solving and proof techniques as used in this article.
- If a routine gets executed (its precondition was satisfied), any violation of the class invariant, the routine's postcondition, or the precondition of another routine that it calls indicates a buggy routine to be added to the output of the AutoTest run.

In the last case, AutoTest performs a *minimization* step that finds, if possible, a shorter sequence leading to the same incorrect result; this enables using the shorter sequence, and hence maximizing efficiency, for debugging, and for later regression testing.

AutoTest has a sophisticated testing architecture making it possible to perform a large number of such automatic routine executions, recovering if any of them fails, and presenting the test results in convenient HTML format. When detecting a bug — a sequence of execution that leads to a violation of a postcondition or other contract element.

Although primarily an automatic testing tool, AutoTest is also a general testing environment supporting the addition of manually selected test cases, and automating the testing process, in particular regression testing. AutoTest is being more closely integrated with the EiffelStudio environment so that in the future, for example, users will have the choice, when an execution fails, of having the faulty call sequence automatically integrated, after minimization, in the regression test suite.

4.4 Study Results

We applied AutoTest to the result of performing the constraint solving and theorem proving steps described above on the selected classes. We also applied plain

Table 1. Comparison of boolean query testing with random testing

Tested Class	Boolean queries	Testin time (mins.)	LOC	Routine coverage		Buggy routines	
				BQT	RT	BQT	RT
INT_STACK	2	2	444	100%	100%	1	0
LINKED_LIST	14	20	1909	97%	87%	3	2
BINARY_TREE	20	14	1507	97%	91%	10	6
ARRAYED_SET	11	9	2565	100%	96%	3	1
FIXED_LIST	9	45	1856	99%	94%	5	5

AutoTest, not taking advantage of these steps, to the same class, and compared the results for *number of routines that contain bugs* and *routine coverage* (the number of routines exercised). The following table shows the results.

Where LOC denotes "lines of code", BQT denotes "boolean query testing" and RT denotes "random testing". Boolean query testing denotes the testing procedure that satisfies boolean query coverage.

4.5 Evaluation

The number of classes to which we have applied the strategy is still too small to warrant statistically significant conclusions, but the number of buggy routines found and the high routine cover show the worth of boolean query testing. The high routine coverage of boolean query testing show that it is effective in constructing interesting target object states. For example, for the LINKED_LIST class, the routines item, last, replace that are covered by boolean query testing but not random testing require target object states "not off", "not is_empty" and "writable" separately. The higher buggy routines discovered by boolean query testing also provide an evidence for its effectiveness in computing interesting object states. For example, in class *ARRATED_SET*, the buggy routine that is discovered by boolean query testing not random testing require an target object state "not off unless after". To get this object state a routine call sequence <make (n), put (o), forth> should be execute, where n >0, o is any object that is not Void.

Since we are studying production-grade software; any buggy routine identified is a major result. In this respect the techniques described here have already proved their worth by enabling us to detect and correct heretofore unsuspected bugs, and hence improve the reliability of real software systems.

5 Related Work

The following work is relevant to the discussion of the testing strategy presented in this paper.

5.1 Construction of Abstract States

Queries and boolean predicates have been used to generalize concrete states [2, 26, 27]. Xie et al. gave a black-box abstraction method that uses public observers that return non-void values to generalize concrete object state machine into observable object state machine and infer this abstract machine through unit testing [26]. This approach cannot bound concrete object states to a finite abstract object states, as a result, cannot achieve abstract state coverage in testing. Ball et al. presented a white-box boolean predicate abstraction approach that uses all predicates appearing in program to generalize concrete program states into a set of abstract program states, and gave the upper bound and lower bound of these abstract states. This approach cannot infer all abstract states of a program that satisfy its specification since it is a white-box method. Therefore, it cannot statically decide the exact bound of satisfiable abstract states. Yorsh et al. make use of the boolean predicate abstraction approach to find a proof for a program rather than detecting real errors.

Our object state abstraction approach is a black-box method and uses contracts and proof techniques to infer all abstract object states that satisfy class contracts. This abstraction process is independent of testing and can be done statically. Moreover, it also provides a way to inspect class contracts. Because our abstraction approach maps concrete object states to finite reachable abstract states, we can direct our class testing procedure to completely explore these states.

5.2 Black-Box Test Coverage Criteria

Category-Partition (CP) [22] is a common black-box test strategy. Each category defines a major property of the parameter or condition of a function/routine and partitioned into a series of distinct choices. A set of choices from all the categories is combined into a test frame, where each category contributes with, at most, one choice. These test frames are templates used to derive test cases. To apply CP, we need to consider the approach to combining choices. There are three combing approaches: *all combination*, *base choice* and *each choice*, where *all combination* derives all combinations of choices as test frame. Hence *all combination* partitions the whole input domain and is the most expensive and effective combining approach. boolean query coverage is essentially a Category-Partition strategy used for generating object states. This strategy takes every boolean query as a category and defines all possible combinations among the values of these boolean queries. Therefore, it partitions the whole object sate space and is a most effective CP strategy for generating object states.

Because of the easiness of automation, random testing [7, 9, 10] is practically widely adopted black-box test strategy. The studies in [7, 9] show that random testing could be more cost-effective than partition testing (assuming that its cost is lower than that of partition testing) with respect to the probability of detecting at least one failure. Comparing to random testing, boolean query coverage can also be implemented automatically and detects more object state related bugs.

5.3 Test Case Generation and Automatic Testing

To cover all reachable abstract object state space, we mainly use the forward testing and complement this process with random testing and manual testing. All of these testing strategies have been implemented in Eiffel automatic unit testing tool AutoTest.

Automatic class testing is more practical when class specification are embedded into the program as formal or semi-formal contracts. TestEra[20] is a contract-based software test tool targeting Java source code and specification written in Alloy [11] (a structural modeling language based on first-order logic). Due to the impedance mismatch between the specification and the implementation language the testing process is not fully automatic and there is a higher barrier for the developer to provide the specification since he has to learn a new language. This automatic testing tool does not adopt object state abstraction approach, while uses model checking technique to generate the test inputs that satisfy a function's precondition.

The Korat tool [3] uses a function's precondition on its input to automatically generate all (nonisomorphic) test cases up to a given small size. Korat constructs test cases by setting the field values directly not by invoking routines as done in our forward testing strategy.

Another tool, Check'n'Crash [4], does not use specifications but uses an external static verifier (ESC/Java2) to calculate a precondition to describe the conditions that might result in a failure. It then uses a constraint solver to generate instances that satisfy this precondition. Since their approach assumes no specifications, they use a heuristic to filter expected failures from unexpected ones.

AutoTest [5] implements fully automatic class testing based on contracts. Without intervention from a user, AutoTest generates tests, executes tests and verifies test results. This testing tool is configurable. Testers can configure the testing strategies (random, forward and manual), then AutoTest can execute these selected testing strategies automatically.

Our testing procedure includes two fully automatic testing processes. The first is using forward testing to explore most abstract object states. If there are some abstract object states that cannot be covered then tester complement some test cases encoded in manual test case form and execute AutoTest to cover all abstract object states and construct abstract object state machine. The second is an automatic test oracle that uses contracts embedded in the class under test.

6 Future Work

The results presented here are particularly promising but require further work, in particular:

- Application to many more example classes. Potentially we should process all EiffelBase classes.
- Application to software that is more representative of user programs: EiffelBase is a general-purpose library, but we must also apply the approach to typical commercial software in various application areas.
- Closer evaluation of the results, in particular with respect to the time needed to find bugs (for the whole strategy, including testing but also the preparatory stages of constraint solving and proof), not just the number of bugs eventually found.
- Integration of the techniques, to the extent that will appear justified, in the AutoTest framework, so that it can take advantage of the best combination of various software reliability techniques, from constraint solving and model checking to proofs as well as tests.

Acknowledgements

We thank Joseph N. Ruskiewicz for his help with Simplify and constructive comments. We also thank Stephanie Balzer, Andreas Leitner, Ilinca Ciupa and Manuel Oriol for their feedback and many invaluable technical discussions. We also thank Eric Bezault for providing Gobo Eiffel which served us as a great platform to build our tools on.

References

[1] Barnettl, M., Rustan, K., Leinol, M., Schultel, W.: The Spec# programming system: An overview. In: Barthe, G., Burdy, L., Huisman, M., Lanet, J.-L., Muntean, T. (eds.) CASSIS 2004. LNCS, vol. 3362, Springer, Heidelberg (2005)

[2] Ball, T.: A theory of predicate-complete test coverage and generation. In: 3rd Interna tional Symposium on Formal Methods for Components and Objects, pp. 1–22 (2004)

[3] Boyapati, C., Khurshid, S., Marinov, D.: Korat: Automated testing based on Java predicates. In: ISSTA'02. Proceedings of the ACM SIGSOFT International Symposium on Software Testing and Analysis, pp. 123–133. ACM Press, New York (2002)

[4] Csallner, C., Smaragdakis, Y.: Check 'n' crash: combining static checking and testing. In: Inverardi, P., Jazayeri, M. (eds.) ICSE 2005. LNCS, vol. 4309, pp. 422–431. Springer, Heidelberg (2006)

[5] Ciupa, I., Leitner, A.: Automatic testing based on design by contract. In: Proceedings of Net.ObjectDays 2005 (6th Annual International Conference on Object-Oriented and Internet-based Technologies, Concepts and Applications for a Networked World), pp. 545–557 (2005)

[6] Detlefs, D., Nelson, G., Saxe, J.B.: Simplify: A theorem prover for program checking. Technical Report HPL-2003-148, HP Labs (2003), http:// research.compaq.com/ SRC/ esc/Simplify.html

[7] Duran, J., Ntafos, S.: An evaluation of random testing. IEEE Transactions on Software Engineering SE-10, 438–444 (1984)

[8] Hamie, A.: Towards verifying Java realization of OCL-constrained design models using JML. In: Proceedings of 6th IASTED International Conference on Software Engineering and Applications, ACTA Press, MIT, Cambridge, MA, USA (2002)

[9] Hamlet, D., Taylor, R.: Partition testing does not inspire confidence. IEEE Transactions on Software Engineering 16(12), 1402–1411 (1990)

[10] Hamlet, R.: Random testing. In: Marciniak, J. (ed.) Encyclopedia of Software Engineering, pp. 970–978. Wiley, Chichester (1994)

[11] Jackson, D.: Alloy: Alightweight object modeling notation. ACM Trans. Soft. Eng. Methodology 11(2), 256–290 (2002)

[12] Kramer, R.: iContract - the Java ™ design by contract ™ tool. In: Proceedings of Object-Oriented Language and Systems, pp. 295-307. IEEE Computer Society, Washington, DC, USA (1998)

[13] Leavens, G.T., Baker, A.L.: Enhancing the pre- and postcondition technique for more expressive specifications. In: World Congress on Formal Methods, pp. 1087–1106 (1999)

[14] Leavens, G.T., Cheon, Y., Clifton, C., Ruby, C., Cok, D.R.: How the design of jml accommodates both runtime assertion checking and formal verification. In: de Boer, F.S., Bonsangue, M.M., Graf, S., de Roever, W.-P. (eds.) FMCO 2002. LNCS, vol. 2852, pp. 262–284. Springer, Heidelberg (2003)

[15] Lee, D., Yannakakis, M.: Principles and methods of testing finite state machines - A survey. In: Proc. The IEEE, pp. 1090–1123. IEEE Computer Society Press, Los Alamitos (1996)

[16] Liu, L., Leitner, A., Offutt, J.: Using contracts to automate forward class testing. Journal of System and Software (submitted)

[17] Meyer, B.: Reusable Software: The Base Object-Oriented Libraries. Prentice Hall, Englewood Cliffs (1994)

[18] Meyer, B.: Object-Oriented Software Construction, 2nd edn. Prentice-Hall, Englewood Cliffs (1997)

[19] Meyer, B.: Eiffel: The Language, Prentice Hall, 1991, revised edn. in progress at (2006), http://se.ethz.ch/ meyer/ongoing/etl/

[20] Marinov, D., Khurshid, S.: TestEra: A novel framework for automated testing of Java programs. In: ASE. Proc. 16th IEEE International Conference on Automated Software Engineering, pp. 22–34. IEEE Computer Society Press, Los Alamitos (2001)

[21] Nimmer, J.W., Ernst, M.D.: Invariant inference for static checking: An empirical evaluation, in: FSE 2002. In: Daemen, J., Rijmen, V. (eds.) FSE 2002. LNCS, vol. 2365, pp. 11–20. Springer, Heidelberg (2002)

[22] Ostrand, T.J., Balcer, M.J.: The Category-Partition method for specifying and generating functional test. Comm. ACM 31(6), 676–686 (1988)

[23] Richtersl, M., Gogolla, M.: On formalizing the UML object constraint language OCL. In: Ling, T.-W., Ram, S., Lee, M.L. (eds.) Conceptual Modeling – ER '98. LNCS, vol. 1507, Springer, Heidelberg, Singapore (1998)

[24] SICStus Prolog User's Manual, http://www.sics.se/sicstus/docs/latest/pdf/sicstus.pdf

[25] Whaley, J., Martin, M.C., Lam, M.S.: Automatic extraction of object-oriented component interface. In: ISSTA 2002, pp. 218–228 (2002)

[26] Xie, T., Notkin, D.: Automatic extraction of object-oriented observer abstractions from unit-test executions. In: Davies, J., Schulte, W., Barnett, M. (eds.) ICFEM 2004. LNCS, vol. 3308, pp. 290–305. Springer, Heidelberg (2004)

[27] Yorsh, G., Ball, T., Sagiv, M.: Testing, abstraction, theorem proving: better together! In: ISSTA 2006, pp. 145-156 (2006)

Symbolic Execution Techniques for Refinement Testing*

Pascale Le Gall[1], Nicolas Rapin[2], and Assia Touil[1]

[1] Université d'Évry, IBISC - FRE CNRS 2873,
523 pl. des Terrasses F-91000 Évry
{pascale.legall,assia.touil}@ibisc.univ-evry.fr
[2] CEA/LIST Saclay
F-91191 Gif sur Yvette
{nicolas.rapin}@cea.fr

Abstract. We propose an approach to test whether an abstract specification is refined or not by a more concrete one. The specifications are input / output symbolic transition systems (IOSTS). The refinement relation requires that all traces of the abstract system are also traces of the concrete system, up to some signature inclusion. Our work takes inspiration from the conformance testing area. Symbolic execution techniques allow us to select traces of the abstract system and to submit them on the concrete specification. Each trace execution leads to a verdict *Fail*, *Pass* or *Warning*. The verdict *Pass* is provided with a formula which has to be verified by the values only manipulated at the level of the concrete specification in order to ensure the refinement relation. The verdict *Warning* reports that the concrete specification has not been sufficiently explored to give a reliable verdict. This is thus a partial verification process, related to the quality of the set of selected traces and of the exploration of the concrete specification. Our approach has been implemented and is demonstrated on a simple example.

Keywords: refinement, conformance testing, symbolic execution, symbolic transition system.

1 Introduction

Formal specifications serve as references for the rigorous definition of correct implementations. Implementation correctness is usually based on some hypotheses stating that implementations can be modelled as a formal model. For example, specifications can be used to generate test cases in order to verify whether an implementation conforms or not to its specification. However, it is widely recognised that it is often difficult to write the right formal specifications in adequacy to the informal requirements given by the users. To overcome this difficulty, refinement techniques are often advocated to help the designers to incrementally design a detailed specification. Implementation design choices (non-determinism

---

* This work was partially supported by the RNRT French project STACS.

B. Meyer and Y. Gurevich (Eds.): TAP 2007, LNCS 4454, pp. 131–148, 2007.

elimination, data types concretisation) are progressively introduced in specifications such that the specification design becomes a general stepwise refinement process from the more abstract specification to the more concrete specification [24]. Then, the executable implementation may be simply derived, by handwriting code or by automatic code generation techniques. Intuitively, a concrete specification Sp_2 refines another abstract one Sp_1 if it has the same behaviours, up to some formal refinement relation. According to the considered underlying formalism, the refinement process is more or less equipped with verification techniques and tools. For example, model-oriented frameworks like the B method [2] or property-oriented frameworks like algebraic specifications [13] are provided with a theory of specification refinement, mainly based on proof-based verification : proof obligations are associated to each refinement step. For formalisms based on transition systems (labelled transition systems, input/output transition systems, Petri Net, etc), the refinement relation is generally expressed using some relations of simulation or notions of trace containment (see for example [3,23]). In this paper, we focus on specifications described with symbolic transitions systems (STS). They are finite state transition automata including first-order data used both to characterise internal states and to guard transitions by means of first-order conditions. They provide us with an appropriate level of abstraction and are useful to avoid the classical state explosion problem. We find these symbolic models under different names STG [14], STS [5,6] or IOSTS [16,10,11]. We use IOSTS formalism defined in [12,20] that is very similar to the systems used in [16,10]. The aim of the paper is to verify a refinement step following the reasoning of conformance testing. Thus, the key idea is to extract from the abstract specification Sp_1 some representative behaviours, or test cases, and then to submit them to the concrete specification Sp_2 in order to get a verdict. Symbolic execution techniques will be used not only to select test cases from Sp_1 as in [12] but also to execute test cases on Sp_2. Indeed, unlike conformance testing for which verdicts come from the execution of the system under test with test cases as input data, refinement testing requires to be able to analyse Sp_2 with respect to the abstract requirements. Symbolic execution techniques precisely allow us to explore Sp_2 according to the selected abstract behavior given as a trace. The verdict depends on the satisfiability of the associated path condition computed on Sp_2. Related works (e.g. [15]) on verification of STS mainly concern symbolic bisimulation relations. They involve an algebra of regions over the data type part provided with operations supposed to be decidable. Unlike such works, we take into account the fact that generally, Sp_2 has often a larger interface than Sp_1, and thus, the signature of Sp_2 may strictly contain the one of Sp_1. Thus, refinement verification precisely requires to automatically compute data emitted and received at the concrete level ensuring the abstract requirements. Symbolic execution provided with some constraint solving mechanisms allows us to perform such computations on Sp_2. Moreover, from a practical point of view, our testing-based approach allows us to more easily debug the concrete specification Sp_2 when a verdict $Fail$ is emitted. Indeed, the corresponding unsatisfiable path condition gives some clues to modify Sp_2 in order to ensure the refinement relation with Sp_1. Testing and refinement have already been linked in previous works. Most of them [9,22] study the relationship between abstract tests selected from an abstract specification and concrete tests which are submitted to the implementation under test (IUT). Generally, the IUT interface is such that an abstract action (or function) of the specification may be decomposed into elementary actions making explicit how the abstract action is concretely achieved by the IUT. We are not interested in this problem but we rather focus on the testing-based method for the partial verification of a refinement step between two specifications.

The paper is structured as follows. In Section 2 we present IOSTS, their syntax and semantics. The refinement relation is introduced in Section 3. A theorem relates the refinement relation with all symbolic executions of a concrete specification with respect to all traces of the abstract specification. This result will found our method given in Section 4 which aims at testing whether a concrete specification verifies or not an abstract one. Our approach is illustrated by an example and some details on algorithms and implementations are given. Finally, Section 5 contains concluding remarks.

2   Input Output Symbolic Transition Systems

Reactive systems are open systems interacting with their environment. Such systems can be modeled by using Input/Output Symbolic Transition Systems (IOSTS). Communications consist of sending or receiving messages represented by first-order terms through communication channels. IOSTS specify dynamic aspects of reactive systems by describing possible evolutions of system states. This is done by modifying values associated to some variables, called *attribute variables*, in order to denote system state modifications. Each elementary modification is given by a transition labelled by a communication action (sending or receipt of messages, or an internal action), guards expressed with first-order properties, and assignments of attribute variables.

2.1   Data Types

Let us first introduce the data part of the IOSTS formalism. Data types are specified with a many-sorted first-order equational logic.

Syntax. A data type signature is a couple $\Omega = (S, Op)$ where S is a set of type names, Op is a set of operation names, each one provided with a profile $s_1 \cdots s_{n-1} \to s_n$ (for $i \leq n$, $s_i \in S$). Let $V = \bigcup_{s \in S} V_s$ be a set of typed variable names. The set of Ω-*terms* with variables in V is denoted $T_\Omega(V) = \bigcup_{s \in S} T_\Omega(V)_s$ and is inductively defined as usual over Op and V. $T_\Omega(\emptyset)$, simply denoted T_Ω, is the set of all ground terms that have no occurrences of variables. A Ω-*substitution* is a function $\sigma : V \to T_\Omega(V)$ preserving types. In the following, we denote by

$T_{\Omega}(V)^V$ the set of all Ω-substitutions of the variables V. Any substitution σ may be canonically extended to terms (and will be also noted σ). The set $Sen_{\Omega}(V)$ of all typed equational Ω-*formulae* contains the constant symbols $\top$, $\bot$ (denoting the usual truth values *truth* and *false*) and all formulae built using the equality predicates $t = t'$ for $t, t' \in T_{\Omega}(V)_s$, and the usual connectives $\neg, \vee, \wedge, \Rightarrow$.

Semantics. A Ω-*model* is a family $M = \{M_s\}_{s \in S}$ with, for each $f : s_1 \cdots s_n \to s \in Op$, a function $f_M : M_{s_1} \times \cdots \times M_{s_n} \to M_s$. We define Ω-*interpretations* as applications ν from V to M preserving types, extended to terms in $T_{\Omega}(V)$. A model M satisfies a formula φ, denoted by $M \models \varphi$, iff, for all interpretations ν, $M \models_{\nu} \varphi$, where $M \models_{\nu} t = t'$ is defined by $\nu(t) = \nu(t')$, and where the constant symbols $\top$ and $\bot$ and the connectives are handled as usual. M^V is the set of all Ω-interpretations from V to M. Given a model M and a formula φ, φ is said *satisfiable* in M, if there exists an interpretation ν s.t. $M \models_{\nu} \varphi$.

In the sequel, we suppose that data types of all IOSTS correspond to an arbitrary common data signature $\Omega = (S, Op)$ and are interpreted in a fixed model M. So, the data type signature Ω will be left implicit in the sequel. Moreover, elements of M will be called *concrete data* and denoted by ground terms in T_{Ω}. The examples illustrating our approach will be built on data types issued from Presburger arithmetics and from some enumerated types. So, concrete data will be natural numbers or boolean values provided with some usual operations as addition, comparison operators, etc. Moreover, expressions such as $\leq (5, x) = \top$ will be simply denoted $5 \leq x$.

2.2 Syntax

Definition 1 (IOSTS-signature). *An IOSTS-signature Σ is a couple (A, C) where $A = \bigcup_{s \in S} A_s$ is a set of variable names, called attribute variables, over the signature Ω and where C is a set of communication channel names.*

Let $\Sigma_1 = (A_1, C_1)$ and $\Sigma_2 = (A_2, C_2)$ two IOSTS-signatures. Σ_1 is said to be included in Σ_2, denoted by $\Sigma_1 \subseteq \Sigma_2$, iff $C_1 \subseteq C_2$.

For a given IOSTS-signature $\Sigma = (A, C)$, the set C of communication channels represents the interface of the corresponding IOSTS while the set A of attribute variables is used to characterize the different states of the IOSTS, and thus are internal information of the IOSTS. It explains why signatures are only compared with respect to their respective sets of communication channels. In the sequel, signature inclusions will be denoted[1] as $\rho : \Sigma_1 \subseteq \Sigma_2$ or simply ρ.

Example 1. Let us introduce a IOSTS-signature $\Sigma_1 = (A_1, C_1)$ to specify a drink machine:

- $A_1 = \{coin, m, price, B\}$ where the $coin$ variable will denote the value of the coin introduced by the user, m the value of the available amount to be spent, $price$ the price of the beverages, B the selected beverage.

---

[1] Clearly, signatures and signature inclusions constitute a category.

- $C_1 = \{introduce, select, screen, refund, serve, take\_cup\}$ where *introduce* allows the user to introduce coins, *select* denotes the button used to select a beverage, *screen* the place where some messages are displayed, *refund* the way to give back money in excess, *serve* the fact that the cup is filled with the beverage and lastly, *take_cup* the fact that the user is taking off his beverage.

An *IOSTS* communicates through communication actions consisting in receipts (inputs) and emissions (outputs) of values through channels.

Definition 2 (Actions). *The* set of communication actions, *denoted* $Act_\Sigma = Input(\Sigma) \cup Output(\Sigma)$ *where:*
$$Input(\Sigma) = \{(c, ?, y) \mid c \in C, y \in A\} \quad Output(\Sigma) = \{(c, !, t) \mid c \in C, t \in T_\Sigma(A)\}$$

In the sequel we will note $c?y$ for $(c, ?, x)$ and $c!t$ for $(c, !, t)$. Actions are interactions with the environment: $c?x$ represents a receipt of a value from its environment which will be assigned to the attribute variable x. $c!t$ represents the emission of the value t through the channel c. Interactions with no exchange of values (i.e. pure signals) on a channel c are conventionally modelled by $c!\top$ or $c?x_\top$ with $x_\top$ a variable reserved for that purpose, and simply written resp. as $c!$ or $c?$ in the sequel.

Definition 3 (Observable traces). *An observable trace r over Σ is a finite sequence of observations belonging to $Obs_\Sigma = (C \times \{?, !\} \times M)$. We note $ObsTr(\Sigma)$ the set of observable traces[2] over Σ.*

Let us consider the signature inclusion $\rho : \Sigma_1 \subseteq \Sigma_2$. Given an observable trace r over Σ_2, the projection of r on Σ_1, denoted $r_{|\rho}$, or simply $r_{|\Sigma_1}$, is the observable trace over Σ_1 obtained by removing from r observations not belonging to Obs_{Σ_1}: thus, if r is decomposed as "$e\ r'$" with e an observation of Obs_{Σ_2} and r' the ending trace, then $r_{|\rho} = e\ r'_{|\rho}$ if e belongs to Obs_{Σ_1}, else $r'_{|\rho}$.

Observable traces represent observations which can be done on a IOSTS: they give which values are exchanged, as emissions or receipts, with the environment, and according to which order. Projections of traces on a subsignature allow us to restrict the signature to be considered as exported, and thus as observable.

Definition 4 (*IOSTS*). *An IOSTS over a signature $\Sigma = (A, C)$ is a 4-tuple $(Q, q_0, Trans, \iota)$ where Q is a set of state names, $q_0 \in Q$ is the initial state, $Trans \subseteq Q \times Act_\Sigma \times Sen_\Omega(A) \times T_\Omega(A)^A \times Q$ and ι is a substitution associating to each attribute of A a term in[3] $T_\Omega(V \cup A)$. A transition $tr = (q, act, \varphi, \rho, q')$ of Trans is composed of a source state q denoted by source(tr), an action act denoted by act(tr), a guard φ, a substitution of variables ρ and a target state q' denoted by target(tr). For each state $q \in Q$, there is a finite number of transitions of source state q.*

An IOSTS over the signature Σ is said to be initialized if for every attribute variable v in A, $\iota(v)$ is a ground term of T_Ω.

---

[2] In the sequel, for an observable trace r, we will denote $r[n]$ the nth element of the trace when it exists.

[3] V is any set of variables disjoint with the set A.

Using initialized $IOSTS$ allows to precisely specify initial values of the attribute variables in order to restrict the set of admissible initial states. On the contrary, non initialized $IOSTS$ admit several (or maybe all) initial conditions for the attribute variables : in this case, the first communications are often used to restrict the set of acceptable states which are reachable from the initial states.

Example 2. We present an $IOSTS$, denoted Sp_1, in Figure 1. It represents an abstract coffee machine over Σ_1. That machine accepts coins as input from the environment (*introduce?coin*). After inserting coins, there is two possibilities, either the machine is out of order (*screen!"out of order"*) then, the user is refunded (*refund!m*), or the user selects the drink (*select?B*). Here, there is again three possibilities: there is no cups (*screen!"no cups"*) and the user is refunded, or there is no enough money, then the machine asks more coins (*screen!(price − m)*) with *price* the price of the drink and *m* the total amount that has been already introduced by the user), or the machine serves the drink (*serve!B*). Lastly, if the amount introduced is more than the price of the drink, the user receives the difference back.

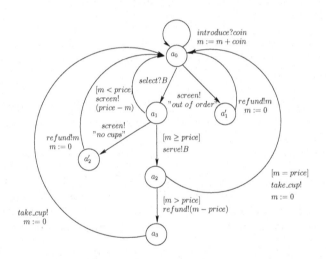

Fig. 1. Specification Sp_1

2.3   Semantics

Definition 5 (Runs of a transition). *Let $tr = (q, act, \varphi, \rho, q') \in Trans$. The set $Run(tr) \subseteq M^A \times Obs_\Sigma \times M^A$ of runs of tr is s.t. $(\nu^i, act_M, \nu^f) \in Run(tr)$ iff:*

- *if act is of the form c!t then $M \models_{\nu^i} \varphi$, $\nu^f = \nu^i \circ \rho$ and $act_M = c!\nu^i(t)$,*
- *if act is of the form c?y then $M \models_{\nu^i} \varphi$, there exists ν^a such that $\nu^a(z) = \nu^i(z)$ for all $z \neq y$, $\nu^f = \nu^a \circ \rho$ and $act_M = c?\nu^a(y)$.*

For a run $r = (\nu^i, act_M, \nu^f)$, we denote source($r$), obs($r$) and target($r$) respectively ν^i, act_M and ν^f.

Definition 6 (Finite Paths of an $IOSTS$). *Let $G = (Q, q_0, Trans, \iota)$ be an IOSTS over Σ. The set of finite paths in G, denoted $FP(G)$ contains all finite sequences $tr_1 \ldots tr_n$ of transitions in $Trans$ s.t. source(tr_1) $= q_0$ and for all $i < n$, target(tr_i) $=$ source(tr_{i+1}).*

The runs of a finite path $tr_1 \ldots tr_n$ in $FP(G)$ are sequences $r_1 \ldots r_n$ such that for all $i \leq n$, r_i is a run of tr_i, there exists an Ω-interpretation ν_1 such that source(r_1) $= \nu_1 \circ \iota$ and for all $i < n$, target(r_i) $=$ source(r_{i+1}). The set of observable traces of a finite path $p = tr_1 \ldots tr_n$, denoted $ObsTr(p)$ is the set of finite observation sequences obs(r_1) $\ldots$ obs(r_n) for any run $r_1 \cdots r_n$ of p.

Definition 7. *Let G be an IOSTS over Σ. The semantics of G is $ObsTr(G) =$*

$$\bigcup_{p \in FP(G)} ObsTr(p).$$

Let $\rho : \Sigma_1 \subseteq \Sigma_2$ be an inclusion signature and G an IOSTS over Σ_2. The semantics of G with respect to ρ is $ObsTr_{|\rho}(G) = \{r_{|\rho} \mid r \in ObsTr(G)\}$.

3 Refinement

3.1 Definition

The refinement relation between IOSTS allows the specifier to relate an IOSTS specification Sp_1 defined over a signature Σ_1 to a more concrete one, Sp_2, in a formal way. Intuitively, Sp_2 should not only include all behaviors of the abstract specification Sp_1, but also may incorporate some specific behaviors that the specifier could not have anticipated at the abstract level. In particular, Sp_2 may involve some concrete actions, emissions or receipts on some new channels, that are not previously known at the abstract level. Such a point of view is similar to the refinement relation given in [8] in the framework of interface automata: the set of legal inputs of the concrete specification (or implementation) may strictly contain the one of the abstract specification. In our setting, we require that all the behaviors of Sp_1 are preserved by SP_2. Obviously, all the behaviors of Sp_1 are given by its semantics: they simply correspond to the set of observable traces of Sp_1. Thus, to refine Sp_1, a specification Sp_2 should be defined over a signature Σ_2 including Σ_1, and should preserve the semantics of Sp_1 in the sense that semantics of Sp_2 w.r.t. Σ_1 contain the one of Sp_1.

Definition 8 (Refinement). *Let $\rho : \Sigma_1 \subseteq \Sigma_2$ be a signature inclusion. Let Sp_1 and Sp_2 be two IOSTS over Σ_1 and Σ_2 respectively. Sp_2 is a refinement of Sp_1, denoted by $Sp_1 \overset{\rho}{\rightsquigarrow} Sp_2$ iff*

$$ObsTr(Sp_1) \subseteq ObsTr_{|\rho}(Sp_2)$$

In the sequel, in the context of a refinement relation $Sp_1 \overset{\rho}{\leadsto} Sp_2$, the elements of Act_{Σ_2} (resp. Obs_{Σ_2}) expressed on a channel in[4] $C_2 \backslash C_1$ are said to be concrete actions (resp. observations).

3.2   Our Approach for Refinement Testing

As presented in the Introduction, we propose to check if a specification refines another one by following a testing approach. The underlying principle is quite simple. First, we extract an observable trace θ from Sp_1 and then we execute it on Sp_2. During the execution, we check if Sp_2 accepts all observations specified by θ. However, since Sp_2 may involve concrete actions, we have to take them into account during the execution of θ. The difficulty is to manipulate intermediate concrete actions of Sp_2 in a generic way so that we can avoid evaluating concrete actions too early. Indeed, this could limit the execution of θ on Sp_2, or even worse, could forbid its execution though it would be possible with other values. Indeed, blindly choosing some arbitrary values for these intermediate concrete actions can clearly eliminate some possibilities of executing θ on Sp_2 since these particular values can unnecessarily constraint the next execution steps. A convenient way to handle this problem is to use, as inputs, some symbols instead of values to represent any of them. The symbolic execution technique [7] is well adapted to perform this. Such a point of view has already been applied for parameterized unit tests [21]: symbolic execution and constraint solving are advocated to instantiate parameter data according to some unit coverage issues.

3.3   Symbolic Execution

In previous papers [20,12], we have shown that *symbolic execution* [7] is a powerful technique in order to explore the semantics of IOSTS models. As stated in those papers a symbolic execution path can be considered as an *intensional* definition for many concrete executions (or runs): a symbolic execution introduces new fresh variables, also called symbolic inputs, and is characterized by its so-called *path condition* which defines the possible interpretation of the terms involved in the execution path. Obviously, interpretations of all execution paths preserve the IOSTS semantics.

Such symbolic execution paths may be systematically built, or at least with respect to any given arbitrary path length. We can also look for building only symbolic execution paths satisfying some constraint. In particular, we are interested by defining symbolic execution paths matching some particular patterns given as observable traces. As previously explained, for refinement testing, symbolic execution will be exercised on the concrete specification with traces selected from the abstract specification. We will say that such a symbolic execution is constrained by an observable trace. As usual, the main idea is to replace concrete input values and initialization values of attribute variables by symbols and to execute transitions. Substitutions are executed in a natural way. At a given

---

[4] Given E and F two sets, $E \backslash F$ denotes the set $\{x \in E \mid x \notin F\}$.

step of the execution, encountered guards induce an accessibility constraint on the last constructed state. This constraint is stored in this state as its so-called *path condition*. In the sequel we assume that symbols used as inputs are fresh variables chosen in a set $F = \bigcup_{s \in S} F_s$ disjoint from the set of attribute variables A.

We first give the intermediate definition of *symbolic extended state* which is a structure allowing to store information about a symbolic behaviour: the IOSTS current location (target state of the last transition of the symbolic behaviour), the path condition, the symbolic values associated to attribute variables and a mark given as a natural number.

Definition 9 (Symbolic extended state). *A symbolic extended state over F for an IOSTS $G = (Q, q_0, Trans)$ is a quadruple $\eta = (q, \pi, \sigma, n)$ where $q \in Q$, $\pi \in Sen_\Omega(F)$ is called a* path condition, *$\sigma \in T_\Omega(F)^A$ and n is a natural number. $\eta = (q, \pi, \sigma, n)$ is said to be satisfiable if π is satisfiable[5]. One notes S (resp. S_{sat}) the set of all the (resp. satisfiable) symbolic extended states over F.*

The natural number associated to each symbolic state will serve us to mark them with respect to some external information. In particular, we will use them to synchronise the reading of an abstract observable trace θ over Σ_1 given as a parameter of the symbolic execution of an IOSTS Sp_2 defined over Σ_2 with $\Sigma_1 \subseteq \Sigma_2$. Constraining the symbolic execution of Sp_2 by θ consists in developing all the symbolic executions compatible with θ. For that, all the states will be labelled by a natural number less or equal than k, the length of the trace θ: if a symbolic extended state η is labelled by n, it will simply mean that the n first observations of θ have already been recognized before reaching η and that all other transitions of the corresponding symbolic path concern concrete actions.

Definition 10 (Symbolic execution of an IOSTS constrained by an observable trace). *Let $\Sigma_1 \subseteq \Sigma_2$ an inclusion signature. We assume that $\Sigma_1 = (A_1, C_1)$ and $\Sigma_2 = (A_2, C_2)$. Let $G = (Q, q_0, Trans, \iota)$ an IOSTS over Σ_2. Let us note $\Sigma_F = (F, C_2)$. Let $\theta \in ObsTr(\Sigma_1)$ an observable trace of length k. The full symbolic execution of G constrained by θ is a triple $(S, init, R)$ with $init = (q_0, true, \sigma_0, 0)$ where σ_0 is an injective substitution in F^A and $R \subseteq S \times Act(\Sigma_F) \times S$ such that for any two transitions in R respectively of the form $(\eta^i, c?x, \eta^f)$ and $(\eta'^i, d?y, \eta'^f)$, the variables x and y are distinct and $\forall a \in A, \sigma_0(a) \neq x$. For any $\eta \in S$ of the form (q, π, σ, n), for all $tr \in Trans$ of the form $(q, act, \varphi, \rho, q')$, then there exists a symbolic transition $st = (\eta, sa, \eta')$ in R iff one of the following conditions detailed below is satisfied:*

– *if $act = c!t$ and $c \notin \Sigma_1$ then $sa = c!\sigma(t)$ and $\eta' = (q', \pi \wedge \sigma(\varphi), \sigma \circ \rho, n)$,*
– *if $act = c?x$ with x in A_2 and $c \notin \Sigma_1$ then $sa = c?z$ with z in F, and $\eta' = (q', \pi \wedge \sigma(\varphi), \sigma \circ (x \mapsto z) \circ \rho, n)$,*

---

[5] Let us recall that here, π is *satisfiable* if and only if there exists $\nu \in M^F$ such that $M \models_\nu \pi$ since variables of π are by construction in F.

- if $act = c!t$ and $c \in \Sigma_1$ and $\theta[n] = c!u$ then[6] $sa = c!t_u$ and $\eta' = (q', \pi \wedge \sigma(\varphi) \wedge (t = t_u), \sigma \circ \rho), n + 1)$.
- if $act = c?x$ with x in A_2 and $c \in \Sigma_1$ and $\theta[n] = c?u$, then $sa = c?t_u$ and $\eta' = (q', \pi \wedge \sigma(\varphi), \sigma \circ (x \mapsto t_u) \circ \rho, n + 1)$,

The symbolic execution of G over F is the triple $SE(G) = (\mathcal{S}_{sat}, init, R_{sat})$ where R_{sat} is the restriction of R to $\mathcal{S}_{sat} \times Act(\Sigma_F) \times \mathcal{S}_{sat}$. It is said consistent if there exits at least a symbolic state of the form (q, π, σ, k). Such states are called terminal.

Let us point out that in the above construction, for the case $act = c!t$ (resp. $c?x$) with $c \in \Sigma_1$, if $\theta[n]$ can be written as $d!u$ with $d \neq c$ or $d'?u$ (resp. $d?y$ with $d \neq c$ or $d'!t$), then no transition is built. It means that when a non compatible observation is encountered, the observable trace θ over Σ_1 cannot be pursued beyond its nth observation.

As previously indicated, the integer constituting the fourth parameter of a symbolic state is used to synchronise observable actions deduced from the symbolic execution with the ones involved in the observable trace θ constraining the execution. From state $(q, \pi, \sigma, n - 1)$, if a transition uses the channel involved in the nth element of the trace, we require the compatibility by reinforcing the path condition at the next state. Consequently, if there exists a consistent symbolic state η with the number k, this means that θ as been totally *matched* over a symbolic execution path from the initial state to η. In particular, the symbolic execution only involving concrete actions allows us to retrieve the usual symbolic execution as given in [12], all symbolic states being marked with the natural number 0. Since the natural numbers associated to the symbolic states have been introduced for technical reasons, in the sequel, they are left implicit in the examples. Now we can state the main theorem:

Theorem 1. *Let us consider Sp_2 an IOSTS over Σ_2 and Sp_1 an IOSTS over Σ_1 with $\Sigma_1 \subseteq \Sigma_2$. $Sp_1 \overset{\rho}{\leadsto} Sp_2 \iff \forall \theta \in ObsTr(Sp_1)$ the symbolic execution of Sp_2 constrained by θ is consistent.*

Example 3. Figure 2 illustrates a part of the symbolic execution of the abstract drink machine Sp_1 presented in Figure 1 constrained with the empty path.

4   Refinement Verification by Testing

4.1   Our Approach

Just as for conformance testing our approach consists in executing some observable traces extracted from a specification, Sp_1 on an entity which is supposed to be a realization of this specification. Here the entity under test is also a specification, Sp_2, called the concrete specification. The execution will be naturally performed by means of the symbolic execution constrained by an observable

---

[6] For a value u of M, t_u denotes a ground term of T_Ω of value u.

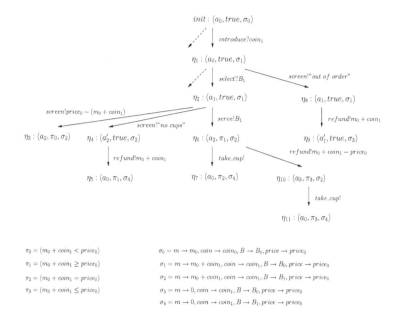

$$\pi_0 = (m_0 + coin_1 < price_0)$$
$$\pi_1 = (m_0 + coin_1 \geq price_0)$$
$$\pi_2 = (m_0 + coin_1 = price_0)$$
$$\pi_3 = (m_0 + coin_1 \leq price_0)$$

$$\sigma_0 = m \to m_0, coin \to coin_0, B \to B_0, price \to price_0$$
$$\sigma_1 = m \to m_0 + coin_1, coin \to coin_1, B \to B_0, price \to price_0$$
$$\sigma_2 = m \to m_0 + coin_1, coin \to coin_1, B \to B_1, price \to price_0$$
$$\sigma_3 = m \to 0, coin \to coin_1, B \to B_0, price \to price_0$$
$$\sigma_4 = m \to 0, coin \to coin_1, B \to B_1, price \to price_0$$

Fig. 2. Symbolic execution of Sp_1

trace. Our approach could be then qualified as *half-symbolic*. One could ask: why not being full symbolic, since Definition 10 could be slightly modified to deal with a full symbolic trace? The main reason for this choice is that industrial users are more familiar with explicit state approaches[7]. Moreover, by choosing to only take observable traces from Sp_1, we ensure that the computed path conditions are expressed on variables of Sp_2 instead of mixing variables of both specifications in the formula. Such mixed formulas would be difficult to analyse.

Now let us notice that Sp_2 may contain loops, involving only concrete actions: the unfolding of those loops during execution may lead to produce paths of an huge size, maybe of an infinite size. To ensure that the computation terminates, we need to define a bound to limit the unfolding of those loops. We decide to allow at most $N(N \in \mathbb{N}^*)$ consecutive occurrences of concrete actions in any path of the symbolic execution tree. Consequently three verdicts, *Warning*, *Fail*, and *Pass*, are necessary to represent the possible conclusions of the execution of a trace θ of Sp_1. The verdict *Warning* occurs when the execution ends before reaching any terminal state, the bound N has been reached in some paths and all the other states are (implicitly) maximal[8]. In this case we do not know if θ belongs or not to Sp_2. Perhaps with a larger bound we could have found it. The verdict *Fail* occurs when the execution ends before reaching any terminal state and when all paths are maximal. This means that we are sure that the

---

[7] "explicit state" means here that variables are instantiated by values.

[8] A path is said to be maximal when any extension has a non satisfiable path condition.

refinement relation is not satisfied since θ does not belong to Sp_2. The verdict *Pass* occurs when at least a terminal state has been reached. This means that the trace under test belongs to Sp_2 up to the inclusion ρ.

Our algorithm can be described informally as follows. It admits three inputs: an observable trace θ derived from Sp_1, the concrete specification Sp_2 and the bound N. It is a bread-first algorithm which instantiates Definition 10. To take into account the bound N, a parameter, called the distance, denoted by d, is added in the definition of a symbolic extended state. We also add a label $l \in \{stop, go, wrg, rch\}$ (*wrg* is for *warning* and *rch* for *reached*). So a symbolic extended state is now of the form $(q, \pi, \sigma, n, d, l)$ with $d = 0$, $l = go$ in the initial state. In an execution step, we consider all states whose label is *go*. We execute all their outgoing transitions. For a state such that no transition can be executed (because all targets would have an un-satisfiable path condition) its label becomes *stop*. Now a target state obtained by execution satisfies those requirements: if its incoming transition carries an abstract action, its distance parameter is set to 0; if it is a concrete action, the distance is the distance of the source state plus one; if this distance is N then its label is *wrg*; if $n = length(\theta)$ then its label is *rch*. The algorithm stops when the set of states labelled by *go* is empty. If there is at least a state labelled *rch* the verdict is *Pass*. If leaves of the execution tree are all labelled by *stop* the verdict is *Fail*. If those leaves are all labelled by *wrg*, or some by *wrg* or and others by *stop* then the verdict is *Warning*. The corresponding path conditions are collected to help the tester to analyse the situation: under which conditions on the concrete variables Sp_2 refines Sp_1 ? Is there a loop in Sp_2 to justify the *Warning* verdict ?

Example 4. We illustrate the process described above with the following example. Figure 3 represents a concrete coffee machine on Σ_2 where $\Sigma_2 = (A_2, C_2)$ with $A_2 = \{coin, m, price, B, G, ok\}$ and $C_2 = \{introduce, select, screen, refund, serve, take\_cup, error, agent\_put\_cups\}$.

In this drink machine, the attribute variable G represents the number of goblets available in the machine. When a drink is served, one withdraws 1 to the value of the variable G. When G becomes equal to 0, the machine can no more serve a drink and the attribute variable ok is put at *false* to mean that the machine is out of order (*screen!"out of order"*). An agent of maintenance can put goblets in the machine (*agent_puts_cups?NewG*), or repair the machine. Then he puts the variable ok at *true* (to mean that the machine is ready again). The number $NewG$ of introduced goblets is added to the variable G.

Let us choose an arbitrary observable trace, denoted t_1, from Sp_1 given in Figure 1), defined on $\Sigma_1 \subseteq \Sigma_2$, introduced in Example 1. The selected observable trace t_1 is the following: *introduce?20 select?coffee screen!"no cups" refund!20 introduce?20 select?coffee serve!coffee take_cup!*

Figure 4 gives the symbolic execution of Sp_2 constrained by t_1. For lack of space, this tree is still partial and does not contain the whole branches : cut branches are represented by dotted transitions.

The first state is *init*. The first observation *introduce?20* of t_1 is matching with a symbolic transition of Sp_2 issued from *init*, annotated with the symbolic

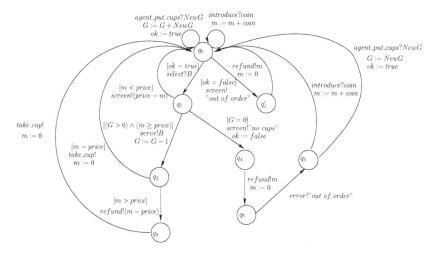

Fig. 3. Concrete specification Sp_2

action $introduce?coin$. The matching with the observable trace is required by considering the transition of action $introduce?20$ and adding the constraint $m = m_0 + 20$ in the path condition of the target state η_1. From $init$, there is also a transition (dotted in Figure 4) labelled by $agent\_put\_cups?NewG$ because the action is in Σ_2 and not in Σ_1. Indeed, this represents a hidden concrete action, not observable at the abstract level. The tree construction is pursued and we can recognize two traces including the observable trace t_1, and possibly adding some intermediate concrete actions (as $agent\_put\_cup?NewG_1$ in the right-hand side trace). We can remark that the symbolic state η_5 gives rise two transitions stemming from η_5, respectively with the actions $introduce?20$ and $agent\_put\_cups?NewG_1$. Both branches should be considered in order to search for symbolic states labelled by 8, the length of t_1, meaning that the last action of t_1 has been recognized. For the right-hand side trace, the state η_{12} is labelled by 8, and the associated path condition π_4 gives some sufficient conditions (on the initial values of the attribute variables, denoted by symbolic variables indexed by 0, and on intermediate interaction variables used for hidden concrete actions, here $NewG_1$ for example) under which Sp_2 may refine Sp_1. When applying our algorithm, two cases are thus possible depending on whether the chosen bound N is less or equal to 2 or is strictly greater than 2.

- In the first case, the exploration is stopped before encountering the second $introduce?20$ action of t_1. Indeed, there are two consecutive non observable actions $error!"outoforder"$ and $agent\_puts\_cup?NewG_1$ preceding the next required observable action $introduce?20$. Since the exploration is unfortunately stopped too early, we only get a $Warning$ verdict.
- On the contrary, in the second case (N is strictly greater than 2), we can observe the second $introduce?20$ action of the trace t_1 and pursue the reading of the observable trace in Sp_2 until the last state η_{12} is reached. So, when

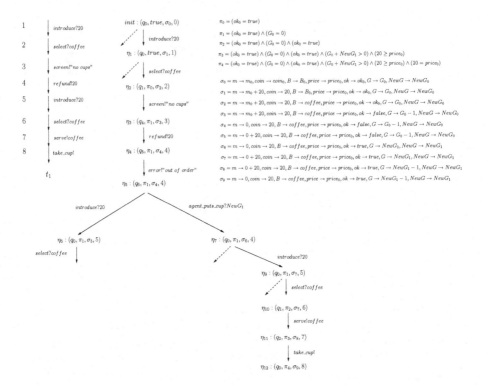

Fig. 4. Symbolic execution of Sp_2 constrained by the observable trace t_1

the bound is strictly greater than 2, for the observable trace t_1 selected from Sp_1, we get a *Pass* verdict for Sp_2 since the path condition π_4 associated to the symbolic state η_{12} is satisfiable.

Example 5. Let us suppose that $t_2 = introduce?20 \; select?coffee \; take\_cup!$ would be a second observable trace of Sp_1. In fact, t_2 is not an observable trace of Sp_1 as one may verify it on Figure 1. Let us introduce in Figure 5 the (partial) symbolic execution of Sp_2 constrained by t_2.

The two first actions of t_2 are recognized since the symbolic state η_2 is labelled by the natural number 2. When building the following symbolic states, there are three possible transitions given by Sp_2 respectively with the actions $screen!(price - m)$, $screen!"no \; cups"$ and $serve!B$, but there is no $take\_cup!$ action like in the trace t_2. All the three actions are observable since they are expressed on the signature Σ_1. But they are not compatible with the next action of t_2 to be recognized. Thus, the symbolic execution of Sp_2 constrained by t_2 reveals that t_2 is not an observable trace of Sp_2, up to the inclusion morphism $\Sigma_1 \subseteq \Sigma_2$. So, we get a *Fail* verdict. Finally, provided that t_2 would be really an observable trace of Sp_1, such a scenario would mean that Sp_2 does not refine Sp_1.

Fig. 5. Symbolic execution of Sp_2 constrained by t_2

4.2   Trace Selection and Implementation Issues

In order to test whether Sp_2 refines Sp_1, the first step is to select some observable traces from Sp_1 to be symbolically executed on Sp_2. Algorithms implementing some classical coverage criteria [25] can be applied to extract traces from Sp_1. Here we propose, like in [17,7], to select among symbolic execution paths. The idea is to compute a finite sub-tree of the symbolic execution of Sp_1 (without being constrained by a given trace). Afterwards, a constraint solver is used at each leaf of this sub-tree to extract an observable trace from the symbolic path ended by the considered leaf. All these observable traces will be executed on Sp_2. The question is how to define this finite sub-tree. In a previous paper [12], we have proposed the so-called *k-inclusion* criterion. The idea is to perform a symbolic execution such that each path carries $k.n$ symbolic transitions[9]. Clearly, this definition depends on a deepness parameter $k.n$. k is a non null integer arbitrarily chosen by the user while n is the result of a calculus. It is the length of the longest path of a symbolic execution reduced by the *inclusion criterion* which, as explained in [12,20], eliminates redundancy in the symbolic execution tree.

The work presented here has been implemented as an extension of the AGATHA tool set [18,20] which as been designed to perform symbolic execution of IOSTS. Presburger arithmetics [19] constitutes the data part of IOSTS treated by AGATHA. The Omega Library [1] has been chosen to handle this data part and is used for two purposes.

5   Conclusion

In this paper, we propose a testing based approach to check whether a concrete specification is a legitimate refinement of an abstract specification. Our approach is based on a combination of concrete and symbolic execution of the specifications. These specifications are described using a first order automata based formalism, namely IOSTS. Our method is strongly inspired from the well-known framework of conformance testing based on the use of test purposes for test case selection. Like conformance testing, some behaviours (observable traces) are selected from the abstract specification Sp_1 by solving a path constraint over

---

[9] When a path carries less actions, this is because it cannot be extended with non-consistent states.

every execution path of a bounded length from Sp_1. For each observable selected trace θ, the concrete specification Sp_2 is symbolically executed in a way that is constrained by the observable trace θ. This symbolic execution is parameterized by a bound given by the user which controls the number of loop unrollings in Sp_2. It allows us to get a verdict about the refinement relation. Either a counter example is found (verdict $Fail$), a proof is found (verdict $Pass$) or the result remains inconclusive because only a bounded number of loop unrollings has been considered (verdict $Warning$). Contrarily to conformance testing techniques, the execution of selected behaviours is not a black box procedure but a white box procedure based on static analysis of the specification to be tested. The involved static analysis is based on symbolic execution techniques associated to a constraints solver. This white box approach brings the advantage that there is no more the inconclusive verdict related to non-determinism of reactive systems, even if for some cases, the algorithmic limitations do not allow us to fully conclude about the verdict. Moreover, some path conditions are associated to the verdict $Pass$, given information about the appropriate initialisations of the attribute variables of the concrete specification, and about intermediate interaction variables used at the concrete level, and not observable at the abstract level. Such kind of information allows us either to debug a concrete specification detected as not refining the abstract specification or to analyse design choices made by the specifier, for example for reverse-engineering purposes.

In this paper, we perform a blinded exploration of the concrete specification Sp_2 with respect to an observable trace extracted from the abstract specification Sp_1. The given of a bound allows us to arbitrarily stop the exploration between two consecutive observable actions of the trace. Obviously, by making some static analysis of Sp_2, we could get some additional indications on how to appropriately compute a bound of exploration or on how to adapt our algorithm in order to do without a bound. In particular, following the approach developed for Bounded Model Checking in [4], we could try to detect the presence of loops in Sp_2 in order to compute verdicts in the same way bounded model checking is performed. Indeed, the verification process for bounded model checking can terminate when considering finite paths including loops and existential properties. As we look for the existence of a path in Sp_2 with respect to an abstract property (the observable trace), it would be interesting to study if such a finite technique can be transposed in our context in the goal of having less $Warning$ verdicts.

References

1. Omega 1.2. The Omega Project: Algorithms and Frameworks for Analyzing and Transforming Scientific Programs (1994)
2. Abrial, J.-R.: The B book - Assigning Programs to Meanings. Cambridge University Press, Cambridge (1996)
3. Alur, R., Henzinger, T.A., Kupferman, O., Vardi, M.Y.: Alternating refinement relations. In: Sangiorgi, D., de Simone, R. (eds.) CONCUR 1998. LNCS, vol. 1466, pp. 163–178. Springer, Heidelberg (1998)

4. Biere, A., Cimatti, A., Clarke, E., Strichman, O., Zhu, Y.: Bounded model checking. In: Highly Dependable Software, vol. 58 of Advances in Computers (2003)
5. Calder, M., Maharaj, S., Shankland, C.: An adequate logic for full lotos. In: Oliveira, J.N., Zave, P. (eds.) FME 2001. LNCS, vol. 2021, pp. 384–395. Springer, Heidelberg (2001)
6. Choppy, C., Poizat, P., Royer, J.-C.: A global semantics for views. In: Rus, T. (ed.) AMAST 2000. LNCS, vol. 1816, pp. 165–180. Springer, Heidelberg (2000)
7. Clarke, L.-A.: A system to generate test data and symbolically execute programs. IEEE Transactions on software engineering 2(3), 215–222 (1976)
8. de Alfaro, L., Henzinger, T.A.: Interface automata. In: ESEC/FSE-9. Proceedings of the 8th European software engineering conference held jointly with 9th ACM SIGSOFT international symposium on Foundations of software engineering, pp. 109–120. ACM Press, New York, USA (2001)
9. Derrick, J., Boiten, E.A.: Testing refinements by refining tests. In: Bowen, J.P., Fett, A., Hinchey, M.G. (eds.) ZUM 1998. LNCS, vol. 1493, pp. 265–283. Springer, Heidelberg (1998)
10. Frantzen, L., Tretmans, J., Willemse, T.A.C.: Test generation based on symbolic specifications. In: Grabowski, J., Nielsen, B. (eds.) FATES 2004. LNCS, vol. 3395, pp. 1–15. Springer, Heidelberg (2005)
11. Frantzen, L., Tretmans, J., Willemse, T.A.C.: A symbolic framework for model-based testing. In: Havelund, K., Núñez, M., Roşu, G., Wolff, B. (eds.) Formal Approaches to Software Testing and Runtime Verification. LNCS, vol. 4262, Springer, Heidelberg (2006)
12. Gaston, C., Le Gall, P., Rapin, N., Touil, A.: Symbolic execution techniques for test purpose definition. In: Uyar, M.Ü., Duale, A.Y., Fecko, M.A. (eds.) TestCom 2006. LNCS, vol. 3964, Springer, Heidelberg (2006)
13. Gaudel, M.-C., Bernot, G.: The role of formal specifications. In: Astesiano, E., Kreowski, H.-J., Krieg-Brckner, B. (eds.) Algebraic Foundations of Systems Specification, IFIP State-of-the-Art Report, pp. 1–12. Springer, Heidelberg (1999)
14. Hennessy, M., Lin, H.: Symbolic bisimulations. In: MFPS '92. Selected papers of the meeting on Mathematical foundations of programming semantics, Amsterdam, The Netherlands, pp. 353–389. Elsevier Science Publishers B.V., Amsterdam (1995)
15. Henzinger, T.A., Majumbar, R., Raskin, J.-F.: A classification of symbolic transition systems. ACM Transactions on Computational Logic V, 1–31 (2006)
16. Jeannet, B., Jéron, T., Rusu, V., Zinovieva, E.: Symbolic test selection based on approximate analysis. In: Halbwachs, N., Zuck, L.D. (eds.) TACAS 2005. LNCS, vol. 3440, Springer, Heidelberg (2005)
17. King, J.-C.: A new approach to program testing. In: Proceedings of the international conference on Reliable software, Los Angeles, California, vol. 21-23, pp. 228–233 (April 1975)
18. Lugato, D., Rapin, N., Gallois, J.-P.: Verification and tests generation for SDL industrial specifications with the AGATHA toolset. In: Petterson, P., Yovine, S. (eds.) Proceedings of the Workshop on Real-Time Tools affiliated to CONCUR01. Department of Information Technology UPPSALA UNIVERSITY Box 337, August 2001, Sweden, vol. SE-751 05 (2001)
19. Presburger, M.: Über die Vollständigkeit eines gewissen Systems der Arithmetic. Comptes rendus du premier Congres des Math. des Pays Slaves 395, 92–101 (1929)
20. Rapin, N., Gaston, C., Lapitre, A., Gallois, J.-P.: Behavioural unfolding of formal specifications based on communicating automata. In: Proceedings of first Workshop on Automated technology for verification and analysis, Taiwan (2003)

21. Tillman, N., Schulte, W.: Parameterized unit tests. In: 10th European Software Engineering Conference, pp. 253–262. ACM Press, New York (2005)
22. van der Bijl, M., Rensink, A., Tretmans, J.: Action refinement in conformance testing. In: Khendek, F., Dssouli, R. (eds.) TestCom 2005. LNCS, vol. 3502, Springer, Heidelberg (2005)
23. van Glabbeek, R.J., Goltz, U.: Refinement of actions and equivalence notions for concurrent systems. Acta Informatica 37(4/5), 229–327 (2001)
24. Wirth, N.: Program development by stepwise refinement. Commun. ACM 14(4), 221–227 (1971)
25. Zhu, H., Hall, P.A.V., May, J.H.R.: Software unit test coverage and adequacy. ACM Comput. Surv. 29(4), 366–427 (1997)

Test-Sequence Generation with Hol-TestGen with an Application to Firewall Testing

Achim D. Brucker and Burkhart Wolff

Information Security, ETH Zurich, ETH Zentrum, CH-8092 Zürich, Switzerland
{brucker,bwolff}@inf.ethz.ch

Abstract. HOL-TESTGEN is a specification and test case generation environment extending the interactive theorem prover Isabelle/HOL. Its method is two-staged: first, the original formula is partitioned into *test cases* by transformation into a normal form called *test theorem*. Second, the test cases are analyzed for ground instances (the *test data*) satisfying the constraints of the test cases. Particular emphasis is put on the control of explicit test hypotheses which can be proven over concrete programs.

Although originally designed for black-box unit-tests, HOL-TESTGEN's underlying logic and deduction engine is powerful enough to be used in test-sequence generation, too.

We develop the theory for test-sequence generation with HOL-TESTGEN and describe its use in a substantial case-study in the field of computer security, namely the black-box test of configured firewalls.

Keywords: symbolic test case generations, test sequence generation, black box testing, theorem proving, Isabelle/HOL, computer security.

1 Introduction

Today, essentially two software validation techniques are used: *software verification* and *software testing*. As far as symbolic verification methods and model-based testing techniques are concerned, the interest among researchers in the mutual fertilization of these fields is growing.

From the verification perspective, testing offers:

- experiences on test-adequacy criteria [12], which can be viewed as *new abstraction techniques* reducing infinite models to finite and checkable ones,
- new approaches to generate *counter-examples*, and
- new application scenarios for verification, since black-box testing can be used as a systematic experimentation method for *reverse engineering specifications* for legacy systems.

From the testing perspective, symbolic verification offers:

- ways to cope with the *state space explosions* inherent to test case generation techniques, and
- ways to log the implicit *testing hypothesis* underlying a test and to make them explicit.

B. Meyer and Y. Gurevich (Eds.): TAP 2007, LNCS 4454, pp. 149–168, 2007.

The HOL-TESTGEN system [5, 4, 3] is designed to explore and exploit these complementary assets. Built on top of a widely-used interactive theorem prover, it provides automatic procedures for test case generation and test-data selection as well as interactive means to perform logical massages of the intermediate results by derived rules. The core of HOL-TESTGEN is a test case generation procedure that decomposes a *test specification* (TS), i.e., test-property over a program under test, into a semantically equivalent *test theorem* of the form:

$$[\![\mathrm{TC}_1; \ldots; \mathrm{TC}_n; \mathrm{THYP}\ H_1; \ldots; \mathrm{THYP}\ H_m]\!] \Longrightarrow \mathrm{TS}$$

where the TC_i are the *test cases* and THYP is a constant (semantically defined as identity) used to mark the explicit *test hypotheses* H_j that are underlying this test. Thus, a test theorem has the following meaning:

> If the program under test passes the tests with a witness for all TC_i successfully, and if it satisfies all test hypothesis, it is correct with respect to TS.

In this sense, the test theorem bridges the gap between test and verification. Testing can be viewed as systematic weakening of specifications.

HOL-TESTGEN has been applied to unit-tests; for example, [5] discusses tests of insert and delete operations for library implementations of red-black trees. In this paper, however, we show that the procedure can also be used for sequence testing of locally non-deterministic reactive systems as well: instead of using an automaton, we build a test-specification based on its input traces. We apply this technique to a substantial case study in the field of computer security, namely the black-box test of a *configured network firewall*. As firewalls are part of today's IT security infrastructure, testing their correct behavior is a rewarding task and, and as we will see, a challenging application for specification based testing.

This paper consists of two parts: In part one, we introduce HOL-TESTGEN, its explicit test hypothesis generation and its potential for sequence test generation conceptually. In part two, we outline the firewall problem domain, present formal test plans based on these concepts for a concrete configuration, and evaluate them by some empirical data.

2   Foundations

2.1   Isabelle

Isabelle [10] is a *generic* theorem prover. New object logics can be introduced by specifying their syntax and natural deduction inference rules. Among other logics, Isabelle supports first-order logic, Zermelo-Fraenkel set theory and HOL, which we choose as framework for HOL-TESTGEN.

While Isabelle/HOL is usually coined as "proof assistant," we use it as symbolic computation environment. Implementations on Isabelle/HOL can re-use existing powerful deduction mechanisms such as higher-order resolution and rewriting, and the overall environment provides a large collection of components ranging from documentation generators and code-generators to (generic) decision procedures for datatypes and Presburger Arithmetic.

Isabelle can easily be controlled by a programming interface on its implementation level in SML in a logically safe way, as well as in the Isar level, i. e., a tactic proof language in which interactive and automated proofs can be mixed arbitrarily. Documents in the Isar format, enriched by the commands provided by HOL-TESTGEN, can be processed incrementally within Proof General (see section 3) as well as in batch mode. These documents can be seen as formal and technically checked test plan of a program under test.

Isabelle processes rules and theorems of the form $A_1 \implies \ldots \implies A_n \implies A_{n+1}$, also denoted as $[\![A_1; \ldots; A_n]\!] \implies A_{n+1}$. They can be understood as a rule of the form "from assumptions A_1 to A_n, infer conclusion A_{n+1}." Further, Isabelle provides a built-in meta-quantifier: $\bigwedge x_1, \ldots, x_m. \ [\![A_1; \ldots; A_n]\!] \implies A_{n+1}$ for representing "fresh free variables not occurring elsewhere" thus avoiding the usual provisos on logical rules. In particular, the presentation of sub-goals uses this format. We will refer to assumptions A_i also as *constraints* in this paper.

2.2 Higher-Order Logic

Higher-order logic (HOL) [6, 2] is a classical logic with equality enriched by total polymorphic[1] higher-order functions. It is more expressive than first-order logic, since e. g., induction schemes can be expressed inside the logic. Pragmatically, HOL can be viewed as a combination of a typed functional programming language like SML or Haskell extended by logical quantifiers. Thus, it often allows a very natural way of specification.

Isabelle/HOL provides also a large collection of theories like sets, lists, multisets, orderings, and various arithmetic theories. Furthermore, it provides the means for defining data types and recursive function definitions over them in a style similar to a functional programming language.

3   The HOL-TestGen System: An Overview

HOL-TESTGEN is an *interactive* (semi-automated) test tool for specification based tests. Its theory and implementation has been described elsewhere [5, 3]; here, we briefly review main concepts and outline the standard workflow. The latter is divided into four phases: writing the *test specification* TS, generation of *test cases* TC along with a *test theorem* for TS, generation of *test data* TD, i. e., constraint-free instances of TC, and the *test execution* (*result verification*) phase involving runs of the "real code" of the program under test. (See Figure 1 for the overall workflow.) Once a test theory is completed, documents can be generated that represent a formal test plan. The test plan containing test theory, test specifications, configurations of the test data and test script generation commands, possibly extended by proofs for rules that support the overall process,

---

[1] To be more specific: *parametric polymorphism*.

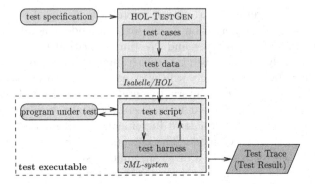

Fig. 1. Overview of the Standard Workflow of HOL-TESTGEN

is written in an extension of the Isar language [11]. It can be processed in batch mode, but also using the Proof General interface interactively, see Figure 2. This interface allows for interactively stepping through a test theory in the upper sub-window while the sub-window below shows the corresponding system state. This may be a proof state in a test theorem development, a list of generated test data or a list of test hypothesis. After test data generation, HOL-TESTGEN produces

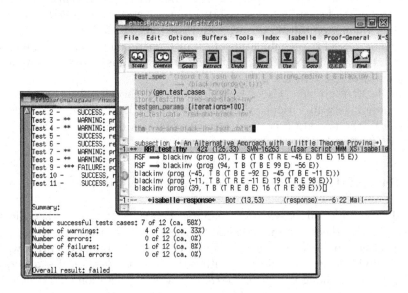

Fig. 2. A HOL-TESTGEN Session Using Proof General

a *test script* driving the test using the provided *test harness*. The test script together with the test harness stimulate the code for the program under test built into the *test executable*. Executing the *test executable* runs the test and yields a *test trace* showing errors in the implementation (see lower window in Figure 2).

4 Test Case Generation with Explicit Test-Hypothesis

In this section, we describe the test case generation procedure of HOL-TESTGEN. It is driven by an exhaustive backward-application of the tableaux calculus presented in section A combined with certain normal-form computations eliminating certain forms of redundancy. Interleaved with this partitioning process (similar to the DNF of Dick and Faivre [7]), test hypothesis rules are generated on the fly and applied to certain subgoals in a backward manner. In the following, we only present two well-known kinds of test hypothesis. Following the terminology of Gaudel [9], these are called *uniformity* and *regularity* hypothesis.

4.1 Inserting Uniformity Hypothesis

Uniformity hypothesis have the form:

$$\text{THYP}(\exists x_1 \ldots x_n.\ P\ x_1, \ldots, x_n \to \forall x_1 \ldots x_n.\ P\ x_1 \ldots x_n)$$

where THYP is a constant defined as the identity; this constant is used as marker to protect this type of formulae from other decomposition steps in the generation procedure. Semantically, this kind of hypothesis expresses that whenever there is a successful test for a test case, it is assumed that the program will behave correctly for *all* data of this test case.

The derived rule in natural deduction format expressing this kind of test theorem transformation reads as follows:

$$\frac{P\ ?x_1 \ldots ?x_n \quad \text{THYP}(\exists x_1 \ldots x_n.\ P\ x_1 \ldots x_n \to \forall x_1 \ldots x_n.\ P\ x_1 \ldots x_n)}{\forall x_1 \ldots x_n.\ P\ x_1 \ldots x_n}$$

where the $?x_i$ are just meta variables, i.e., place-holders for arbitrary terms. This rule can also be applied for arbitrary formulae just containing free variables since universal quantifiers may be introduced for them aforehand.

Tactically, these hypothesis were introduced *at the end* of the test case generation process, i.e., when all other rules can no longer be applied. Using a uniformity hypothesis for each (non-THYP) clause allows for the replacement of free variables by meta-variables which can be instantiated by ground terms during the test data selection phase later. This transformation is logically sound. For example, for a test specification if $x \leq 0$ then *ioprg* x else *ioprg* $-x$, the test case generation produces for the program *ioprg* under test the test theorem:

$test :$ if $0 \leq x$ then *ioprg* x else *ioprg* $-x$

    1. $0 \leq ?x \implies$ *ioprg* $?x$

    2. $\text{THYP}((\exists x.0 \leq x \to ioprg\ x) \to (\forall x.0 \leq x \to ioprg\ x))$

    3. $?y < 0 \implies$ *ioprg* $-?y$

    4. $\text{THYP}((\exists x.\ x < 0 \to ioprg\ -x) \to (\forall x.\ x < 0 \to ioprg\ -x))$

The test-data selection phase will easily generate the instances of the test cases *ioprg* 3 and *ioprg* $(-(-4))$ (satisfying the constraints) to be used in a black-box test. If we have the implementation of *ioprg* in our hands, we could also verify the test-hypothesis; provided that execution paths in the concrete program correspond to test classes, we gain knowledge from the test for the verification.

4.2 Inserting Regularity Hypothesis

In the following, we address the problem of test case generation for quantifiers (or, equivalently: free variables) ranging over recursive datatypes such as lists or trees. As an introductory example, we consider the membership predicate of an element in a list defined by the following recursive rules:

$$
\begin{aligned}
x \ \text{mem} \ [] &= \text{false} \\
x \ \text{mem} \ (y\#ys) &= \text{if } y = x \text{ then true else } x \ \text{mem} \ ys
\end{aligned}
\tag{1}
$$

which occurs as "precondition" in the example test specification:

$$x \ \text{mem} \ S \rightarrow ioprg \ x \ S$$

For testing recursive data structures, Gaudels [9] suggested the introduction of a *regularity hypothesis* as one possible form of a test hypothesis:

$$
\frac{\begin{array}{c}[|x| < k]\\ \vdots \\ P\,x\end{array}}{P\,x}
$$

This rule formalizes the hypothesis: assuming that a predicate P is true for all data x whose *size* (denoted by $|x|$) is less than a given depth k, P is always true. The original rule can be viewed as a meta-notation: In a rule for a concrete datatype, the premises $|x| < k$ can be expanded to several premises enumerating constructor terms.

Instead of this unsound rule, HOL-TESTGEN derives on-the-fly a special datatype exhaustion theorem; its form depends on k and the structure of the datatype of x. For the user-defined value $k = 3$ and for the type α *list*, we have:

$$
\frac{\begin{array}{c}[x = []]\\ \vdots \\ P(x)\end{array} \quad \bigwedge a. \quad \begin{array}{c}[x = [a]]\\ \vdots \\ P(x)\end{array} \quad \bigwedge a\ b. \quad \begin{array}{c}[x = [a,b]]\\ \vdots \\ P(x)\end{array} \quad \text{THYP}\big(3 \le |x| \rightarrow P(x)\big)}{P(x)}
$$

The equalities introduced by this rule lead together with the simplification rules shown in Equation 1 of the predicate mem to the following result of the test case generation (we omit the uniformity hypothesis insertion here):

$test :$ x mem $S \rightarrow ioprg \ x \ S$

1. $ioprg \ x \ [x]$

2. $\bigwedge b.\ ioprg \ x \ [x, b]$

3. $\bigwedge a.\ a \neq x \Longrightarrow ioprg \ x \ [a, x]$

4. $\text{THYP}(3 \le |S| \rightarrow x \ \text{mem} \ S \rightarrow ioprg \ x \ S)$

and, again, it is an easy game for a random-based test-data-selection method to provide constraint free instances of the test cases.

4.3   Principles of Test-Sequence-Generation in HOL-TestGen

Considering the previous subsection more closely, one easily recognizes that it also holds the key for the principles of test sequence generation in HOL-TestGen: since a finite automaton can be converted into (mutual) recursive acceptance predicate accept on input lists, this scheme of a test specification can also be used for specifying the test of a transition function $ioprg :: \alpha \Rightarrow \sigma \Rightarrow \sigma$ option under test, which takes some input of type α and some state of type σ and can produce a successor state (the α option type contains the constructors Some a and None). Together with the recursively defined Mfold-combinator:

$$\text{Mfold } [] \ \sigma \ ioprg = \text{Some } \sigma$$

$$\text{Mfold } (in\#H) \ \sigma \ ioprg = \begin{cases} \text{Mfold } H \ \sigma' \ ioprg & \text{if } ioprg(in,\sigma) = \text{Some } \sigma', \\ \text{None} & \text{otherwise.} \end{cases}$$

it is now possible to lift an individual (partial) function $ioprg$ to be run in a complete sequence by using the following scheme of a test specification:

$$\text{accept } S \rightarrow P(\text{Mfold } S \ \sigma_0 \ ioprg)$$

where σ_0 is the initial state. After HOL-TestGen synthesized a trace S and suitable input for variables occurring in P, a test driver running the test sequence can be generated. Note that the function $ioprg$ can in particular log the complete run of a system and make the test verdict depending on this log, i.e., the complete history of inputs and outputs in the real system trace.

4.4   An Infra-structure for Reactive Sequence Test

This concept is also powerful enough to cover situations where the program under test produces output that changes the input of later runs of $ioprg$, i.e., in situations where the test-driver and the external program under test represent a communicating system.

In the following, we describe a special instance of the overall scheme discussed in subsection 4.3. As fundamental modeling assumption of this instance, we require that the test-driver can be built upon an "i/o stepping function" $ioprg :: \iota \Rightarrow \sigma' \Rightarrow (o \times \sigma')$ option. This function takes an input of type ι, an internal state of type σ' only managed by itself, and returns the observable output of type o plus the result state of one step of the system under test. We allow $ioprg$ to fail, depending on the concrete realization inside the test harness. This could represent timeouts or other forms of misbehavior of the system under test. Further, we assume a function: $post :: \sigma \times \sigma' \Rightarrow \iota \Rightarrow o \Rightarrow$ bool that, depending on the observer state, the $ioprg$ state, the (concrete) input and the (concrete) output decides that the behavior of $ioprg$ conforms to the specification in this step. We assume *ioprg* to be a function in the mathematical sense, so identical runs with the same inputs will produce the same outputs; *which* outputs were chosen is unimportant as long as *post* remains satisfied. The choice of the output and the successor state is non-deterministic in this sense, and even the stimulation sequence automaton may be non-deterministic. We call these assumptions on non-determinism occurring in the system under test *local non-determinism*, in contrast to *deep non-determism* occurring in testing theories such as [8] and at least partially in their test system implementation.

The key element for the instantiation of the scheme of subsection 4.3 lies in the generic definition of an adapter function that builds a stepping function from this i/o stepping function. As a suitable abstraction over a history log, we integrate into this adapter an environment of type σ that keeps track of values exchanged at runtime of a test which were bound to symbolic variables occurring in *abstract traces*. The latter were gained from standard protocols by replacing values which were only known at runtime; thus, we will be able to tackle with a quite common class of reactive systems.

As a prerequisite, we need the two functions *rebind* :: $\sigma \Rightarrow o \Rightarrow \sigma$ and *subst* :: $\sigma \Rightarrow \iota \Rightarrow \iota$. The former extracts from a concrete output a new binding for corresponding variables occurring in abstract output; the latter replaces variables occurring in abstract input to the corresponding values exchanged in the previous system run. Wiring everything together, we get the following definition:

$$\text{observer } \textit{rebind subst post ioprg in } (\sigma, \sigma') \equiv \text{let } in' = \textit{subst } \sigma \textit{ in } in$$
$$\text{case } \textit{ioprg ioprg}' \ \sigma' \text{ of None} \Rightarrow \text{None}$$
$$| \ \text{Some}(out, \sigma''') \Rightarrow \text{let } \sigma'' = \textit{rebind } \sigma \textit{ out } \text{in}$$
$$\text{if } post(\sigma'', \sigma''') \ in' \ out$$
$$\text{then Some}(\sigma'', \sigma''') \text{ else None}$$

The adapter function observer essentially runs *ioprg* on its state and on the *in* resulting from *subst*; the resulting *out* leads to an update of the observer state. Occurring errors were propagated. The function observer is fully executable and is compiled to a part of the test driver.

4.5   An Example

As an example of a reactive system, we assume a client/server situation where the client sends a server a communication request and specifies a "port-range" X (for simplicity, just an upper bound). The server non-deterministically chooses a port Y which is within the specified range. The client sends a sequence of data (abstracted away in our example to just one constant Data) on the port allocated by the server. The communication is terminated by the client with a stop event. Figure 3 shows the abstract protocol (containing variables and constraints over them) and its sub-protocol containing just the input stimulation sequence.

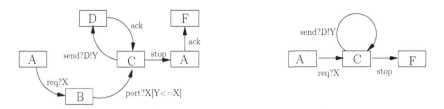

Fig. 3. An abstract protocol automaton and the resulting stimulation sequence automaton

In the following, we describe the necessary infra-structure of our model in HOL-TESTGEN. We define the explicit variables occurring in this protocol:

$$\text{vars} = X \mid Y$$

and specify the combined type of abstract and concrete input and output events:

$$\text{InEvent} = \text{req chan} \mid \text{reqA vars} \mid \text{send data chan} \mid \text{sendA data vars} \mid \text{stop}$$
$$\text{OutEvent} = \text{port chan} \mid \text{portA vars} \mid \text{ack}$$

The definition of subst is now straight-forward:

$$
\begin{aligned}
\text{subst } env \;(\text{req } n) \quad &= \text{req } n \\
\text{subst } env \;(\text{reqA } v) \quad &= \text{req}(\text{lookup } env \; v) \\
\text{subst } env \;(\text{send } d\, n) \quad &= \text{send } d\, n \\
\text{subst } env \;(\text{sendA } d\, v) &= \text{send } d(\text{lookup } env \; v) \\
\text{subst } env \text{ stop} \quad &= \text{stop}
\end{aligned}
$$

as well as defining rebind

$$
\begin{aligned}
\text{rebind } env(\text{port } n) &= env(Y \mapsto n) \\
\text{rebind } env \text{ ack} \quad &= env
\end{aligned}
$$

and the definition of the post-condition:

$$
\begin{aligned}
\text{post}' \;(env, x, \text{req } n, \text{port } m) &= (n \leq m) \\
\text{post}' \;(env, x, \text{send } z\, n, \text{ack}) &= \text{true} \\
\text{post}' \;(env, x, \text{stop}, \text{ack}) \quad &= \text{true} \\
\text{post}' \;(env, x, y, z) \quad &= \text{false}
\end{aligned}
$$

$$
\begin{aligned}
\text{post} \quad &:: (\text{vars} \rightharpoonup \text{int}) \times \text{unit} \Rightarrow \text{InEvent} \Rightarrow \text{OutEvent} \Rightarrow \text{bool} \\
\text{post } x \; y \; z &\equiv \text{post}'(\text{fst } x, \text{snd } x, y, z)
\end{aligned}
$$

Here, $\alpha \rightharpoonup \beta$ denotes partial functions and is just a synonym for $\alpha \Rightarrow \beta$ option.

The predicate post checks the constraint that the server must return a port within a previously communicated range. The abstract inputs like sendA Data X will be converted to concrete input send Data 23 if 23 has been communicated previously by the server under test; the explicit variable management is done once-and-for-all in the observer adapter.

The automaton for the set of stimulation traces results from a direct translation of the diagram above:

$$
\begin{aligned}
\text{stimTrace}'\ (A, (\text{reqA}\ X)\#S) &= \text{stimTrace}'(C, S) \\
\text{stimTrace}'\ (C, (\text{sendA}\ d\,Y)\#S) &= \text{stimTrace}'(C, S) \\
\text{stimTrace}'\ (C, [\text{stop}]) &= \text{true} \\
\text{stimTrace}'\ (x, y) &= \text{false}
\end{aligned}
$$

$$
\begin{aligned}
\text{stimTrace} &\ ::\ \text{InEvent} \Rightarrow \text{listbool} \\
\text{stimTrace}\ s &\equiv \text{stimTrace}'(A, s)
\end{aligned}
$$

Finally, we state the test specification for a reactive sequence test. Note that its pattern is an instance of the sequence test (see subsection 4.3) which is again an instance of the pattern post $x \rightarrow$ post x (*ioprg x*) in subsection 4.2:

$$
\boxed{
\begin{aligned}
\text{stimTrace}\ trace &\longrightarrow \\
\text{success}(\text{Mfold}\ trace((X &\mapsto init), ())(\text{observer rebind subst post}\ ioprog))
\end{aligned}
}
$$

where success :: α option $\Rightarrow$ bool is an auxiliary function that yields true for values of the form Some E. Applying our test case generation and test data generation procedures takes only a few seconds, including the generation of the test script containing the abstract input sequences plus the test program run over them; this test program also contains the compiled versions of observer, subst, rebind, etc.

For the test depth $k = 4$ of the test case-generation procedure we already reach path coverage in the stimulation protocol automaton and therefore implicitly on the protocol automaton shown in Figure 3.

5   Case-Study: Testing Firewall Configurations

In many institutions, an unrestricted connection of the internal network to he Internet is classified as a security risk. *Firewalls* as means to restrict network traffic are therefore widely used in todays IT infrastructures. As security infrastructure crucially depend on them, testing their correct behavior is an important and rewarding task. As we will see, it is also an interesting application for specification based testing. The complete specification is part of the HOL-TESTGEN distribution [1].

If we have the implementation of *ioprg* in our hands, we could also verify that it represents an automaton; the minimal path length covering all vertexes in this automaton gives a bound for k.

5.1   A Bluffers Guide to Firewalls

In a computer network, e. g., based on TCP/IP, a message from A to B is encapsulated in one or more *packets* which contains the content of the message and routing information. The routing information of a packet mainly contains its source address (where does the packet come from), its destination address (where should the packet go to) and the protocol (e. g., http, smtp) used on top of transport layer (e. g., TCP/IP).

In its simplest form, a firewall is just a *stateless packet filter* which just filters (i. e., rejects or accepts it) traffic from one network to another based on the destination address, source address and the protocol, the *policy* used. The policy is the specification (or configuration) of the firewall which describes which packets should be denied and which should be rejected. In some cases, stateless filtering is not enough, some application protocols, like ftp or most of the protocols used for Internet telephony such as Voice over IP (VoIP) have an internal state of which the firewall must be aware of. For example, some connections are only allowed within a specific state of the protocol.

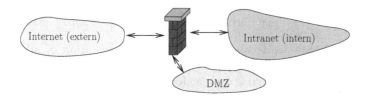

Fig. 4. A simple firewalling scenario

Figure 4 illustrates a simple and common setup of a firewall, separating three networks: the external (potentially dangerous) Internet, the internal network that has to be protected (intranet) and a network that is somewhat in-between, the demilitarized zone (DMZ). The DMZ is usually used for servers (e. g., the Web server and the Mail server) that should be accessible both from the outside (Internet) and the internal network (Intranet) and thus underlie, a more relaxed policy than the intranet. An example for a simple firewall policy is shown in Table 1 in an informal way. Such a policy uses a first-fit pattern matching strategy, i.e., the first match overrides later ones. For example, a packet from the Internet to the intranet is rejected (it only matches the last line of the table)

Table 1. A simple Firewall Policy

source	destination	protocol	action
DMZ	Intranet	any	deny
Intranet	Webserver	http	accept
Internet	Webserver	https	accept
Intranet	Mailserver	smtp	accept
Intranet	Mailserver	imap	accept
Intranet	Mailserver	imaps	accept
any	any	any	deny

whereas a http-packet from the Intranet to the Web server is accepted (second line of the table. The lines of such a table are also called *rules*; together, they build the *policy* of a firewall.

In the remainder of this section, we will briefly introduce a formal HOL model of networks and policies; it will turn out that these concepts can be used uniformly both for stateless packet filters and statefull application level firewalls. This model forms the basis for several test case generation scenarios that validate a firewall implementation against its specified policy.

5.2 A Formal Firewall Model

Packets and Networks. As a prerequisite, we need a formal models of protocols, packets and nets. We model protocols as an abstract data types, e. g., the most common ones are declared by:

$$\text{protocol} := \text{ftp} \mid \text{http} \mid \text{https} \mid \text{voip} \mid \text{smtp} \mid \text{imap} \mid \text{imaps} \mid \text{unknown} \ .$$

As we do not want to depend on a specific representation of addresses and package content, we introduce the abstract types α src and α dest for the source and destination address and β content for the content. Moreover, we introduce an unique identifier id for each packet. Thus, the type of a package defined straight-forward as:

$$(\alpha, \beta) \, \text{packet} := \text{id} \times \text{protocol} \times \alpha \, \text{src} \times \alpha \, \text{dest} \times \beta \, \text{content}$$

Further, we define projectors, e. g., getId, getSrc, for accessing the different components of packet directly.

As a next step, we model networks, or just *nets*, and parts thereof (*subnets*). To be as abstract as possible at this stage, we model nets as an axiomatic type class [10]. For the purpose of this paper, it suffices to know that a net is a set of sets of addresses, i. e.,

$$\alpha \, \text{subnet} = (\alpha :: \text{net}) \, \text{set set}$$

where $(\alpha :: \text{net})$ requires that the types we use to instantiate α are members of the type class net. This definition allows us to model firewall policies that restrict the traffic between sub-networks and also between single hosts (addresses). For checking, if a given address is part of a subnet, we define the following operator:

$$a \sqsubset S \equiv \exists s \in S. \, (a \in s) \qquad \text{with type } \alpha \, \text{adr} \Rightarrow \alpha \, \text{subnet} \Rightarrow \text{bool}.$$

The Firewall Policy. From an abstract point of view, a policy is a partial mapping of packets to decisions, e. g., deny or accept. The datatype:

$$\alpha \, \text{out} := r \, \text{accept} \, \alpha \mid \text{deny}$$

for decisions allows for modeling the modifications of return packages; Thus, our model can capture address-translation techniques (network address translation

(NAT)) realized by some firewalls as well.[2] The type of a policy follows directly from this:

$$(\alpha, \beta)\, policy := (\alpha, \beta)\, packet \rightharpoonup ((\alpha, \beta)\, packet)\, out$$

where $\alpha \rightharpoonup \beta$ denotes the partial mapping (i. e., type synonyms to $\alpha \Rightarrow \beta$ option; cf. subsection 4.2). In our model, rules and policies have the same type, i. e., we can introduce a type synonym:

$$(\alpha, \beta)\, policy := (\alpha, \beta)\, rule$$

for rules. Moreover, the override operator for partial mappings ($\_ ++ \_$) allows for nicely combining several rules to a policy. For example, $r_2 ++ r_1$ combines the rules r_1 and r_2 where r_1 overrides (has higher precedence) r_2. We can define several *generic rules combinators* at this abstract level (without concrete format of addresses) that substantially simplify the formalization of a concrete policies. For example, the usual two "catch-all" rules for accepting or denying all traffic were expressed as:

$$allowAll\, p \equiv Some(accept\, p) \qquad \text{with type } (\alpha, \beta)\, rule, \text{ and}$$
$$denyAll\, p \equiv Some(deny) \qquad \text{with type } (\alpha, \beta)\, rule.$$

Many other combinators for restricting traffic based on its source, destination or protocol can already be defined on this abstraction level. A rule restriction all packets coming from subnet s can be defined as

$$allowAllFrom\, s \equiv Some\, allowAll \restriction_{\{p | (getSrc\, p) \sqsubseteq s\}}$$

with type $(\alpha :: net)\, subnet \Rightarrow (\alpha, \beta)\, rule$, and where $\_ \restriction \_$ is the restriction operator on partial mappings.

IPv4. At this point, we make the packet address format more concrete. We specify the underlying transport protocol, e. g., IPv4 or IPv6. For our example, we use tcp combined with ip version 4. In this setting, an address consists out of an unique 32 bit number, represented as four-tuple and a port:

$$ipv4Ip := int \times int \times int \times int$$
$$port := int$$
$$ipv4 := ipv4Ip \times port$$

Based on these definitions, we can define further combinators (rules) that are specific to tcp/ip addresses, i. e., they can accept or reject packages based on an ip address and a port.

---

[2] However, in reality, a firewall policy can describe more fine-grained how packets are denied, e. g., some packages could be silently discarded (this is often called *drop*) or the packet could be rejected, causing an error message is send to the origin.

5.3   Testing Stateless Firewalls

Our abstract firewall model, presented in the last section, allows for the direct formalization of the informal policy given in Table 1. First we have to define the subnets of type ipv4 subnet, based on their ip address ranges, e. g.:

$$\text{intranet} \equiv \left\{\left\{((a, b, c, d), p)\,\middle|\,(a = 192) \wedge (b = 168)\right\}\right\}$$

$$\text{webserver} \equiv \left\{\left\{((a, b, c, d), p)\,\middle|\,(a = 172) \wedge (b = 16) \wedge (c = 70) \wedge (d = 4)\right\}\right\}$$

Grouping the rules of our informal policy with the same source and same destination, define:

$$\text{DmzIntranet} \equiv \text{denyAllFromTo dmz intranet}$$
$$\text{toWebserver} \equiv \text{allowProtFromTo http intranet webserver}$$
$$\text{toMailserver} \equiv \text{allowProtFromTo smtp intranet mailserver}$$
$$+\!+\,\text{allowProtTo imap mailserver}$$
$$+\!+\,\text{allowProtTo imaps mailserver}$$

The *test specification* for the stateless firewall case is now within reach: we just state that the *firewall under test (fut)* has the same filtering function behavior as our given combined policy:

$$fut(x) = (\text{denyAll} +\!+ \text{DmzIntranet} +\!+ \text{toWebserver} +\!+ \text{toMailserver})(x)$$

Applying our test case generation and test data generation procedures results, after 72 hours running time on a modest equipped workstation, in 828 test cases, among them:

$$fut(9, \text{smtp}, ((6, 2, 8, 5), 0), ((7, 3, 8, 1), 1), \text{content}) = \text{Some deny}$$
$$fut(8, \text{http}, ((6, 6, 10, 3), 6), ((4, 7, 5, 9), 1), \text{content}) = \text{Some deny}$$
$$fut(2, \text{imaps}, ((6, 2, 10, 7), 9), ((172, 16, 70, 5), 3), \text{content})$$
$$= \text{Some}(\text{accept}(2, \text{imaps}, ((6, 2, 10, 7), 9), ((172, 16, 70, 5), 3), \text{content}))$$
$$fut(6, \text{imaps}, ((9, 7, 9, 10), 9), ((172, 16, 70, 5), 0), \text{content})$$
$$= \text{Some}(\text{accept}(6, \text{imaps}, ((9, 7, 9, 10), 9), ((172, 16, 70, 5), 0), \text{content}))$$

Overall, testing stateless packet filters is quite similar to classical unit testing of stateless software. The test-data selection is trivial in this example.

5.4   Testing Statefull Firewalls

The well-known file-transfer protocol file transfer protocol (ftp) is based on a dynamic negotiation of a port number which is then used as channel to communicate the file content between the sender and the receiver. Thus, a stateless firewall can only provide a very limited form of network protection if ftp is involved, whereas a statefull firewall that observes the inner state of the ftp session can open the negotiated port dynamically. Testing statefull firewalls, where the filter functions change over time, requires test-sequence generation.

A Statefull Firewall Model. First we model the internal state of a statefull firewall as a tuple of a store and the current policy (that can change during a transition):

$$(\alpha, \beta, \gamma)\, \text{FwState} = \alpha \times (\beta, \gamma)\, \text{Policy}$$

One possibility is, to model the store as the list of accepted packages:

$$(\beta, \gamma)\, \text{history} = (\beta, \gamma)\, \text{packet list}$$

A transition from state to state is a mapping from the packet that fired the transition, the current state to the new state:

$$(\alpha, \beta, \gamma)\, \text{FwStateTrans} = (\beta, \gamma)\, \text{packet} \times (\alpha, \beta, \gamma)\, \text{FwState} \rightharpoonup (\alpha, \beta, \gamma)\, \text{FwState}$$

Moreover, for combining state transitions, we define two combinators: orelse takes the first defined transitions

$$f \text{ orelse } g \equiv \begin{cases} \text{Some } y & \text{if } f\, x = \text{Some } y, \\ \text{None} & \text{otherwise,} \end{cases}$$

and repeat repeats as long as the transitions is defined:

$$f \text{ repeat } g \equiv \begin{cases} \text{Some } z & \text{if } f\, x = \text{Some } y \text{ and } f\, y = \text{Some } z \\ \text{None} & \text{otherwise.} \end{cases}$$

Modeling the file transfer protocol (ftp). During an ftp session, the server (normally located in the Internet) opens a data connection to the client (e. g., located in the intranet) using a port that is negotiated: Figure 5 shows an abstract trace of an ftp session: the client initializes the session by sending a init message to the server, the client answers with a port request containing a dynamic port

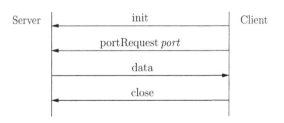

Fig. 5. A sample trace of an file transfer protocol (ftp) run

for the data connection and then the server sends the data to the client using this dynamic port. Eventually, the client will close the connection and the firewall has to close the data port. We model the communication as follows:

$$\text{ftpMsg} = \text{init} \mid \text{portRequest } port \mid \text{data} \mid \text{close} \mid \text{other}$$

Further, we will use the id part of a package to distinguish several ftp-sessions. We model state transitions of the ftp protocol as recursive predicates. First we define a generic state transition for messages that do not change the policy and special transition for the portRequest (that opens the data port) and close (that closes the data port). As an example, we present the simple generic transition (see [1] for the remaining details) that is defined recursively based on the definitions:

$$\text{ftpSt}_f((a, \text{ftp}, c, d, e), (in, policy)) \equiv \text{if accept}(a, \text{ftp}, c, d, e)policy$$
$$\text{then Some}((a, \text{ftp}, c, d, e)\#in, policy)$$
$$\text{else Some}(in, policy)$$
$$\text{ftpSt}_f(x, (in, policy)) \equiv \text{None}$$

The state machine modeling ftp can be defined using the orelse combinator for combining the singe transitions:

$$\text{ftpSt} \equiv \text{ftpSt}_{\text{portRequest}} \text{ orelse ftpSt}_{\text{close}} \text{ orelse ftpSt}_f$$

Using the repeat combinator, we can easily model arbitrary runs of the protocol.

Testing ftp. We have to clarify the test purpose first: for example, one could aim for testing one or more correct protocol runs (with or without interleavings), or for illegal protocol runs. Here, we show a test for single, legal protocol runs. We define a recursive acceptance predicate isFtp testing for legal ftp traces. We assume a simple test scenario with a initial policy only allowing ftp sessions (initiated using port 21, the control port of the ftp protocol) from the intranet to the Internet:

$$\text{ftpPolicy} \equiv \text{allowAll} + + \text{allowProtFromToPort ftp intranet internet } 21$$

The accept-predicate for traces in the sense of subsection 4.3 is defined on the basis of the ftp protocol machine together with some additional constraints:

$$\text{accept}(t) = t \in \{x \mid \text{isFtp } c \ s \ i \ x\}$$
$$\wedge \text{ isInIntranet } c \wedge \text{ isInInternet } s \wedge \text{ getPort } s = 21$$

using predicates (isInIntranet and isInInternet) for checking if an address is within a specific subnet. The key stone of our test section is the test specification:

$$\text{accept}(t) \rightarrow \textit{fut } t = \text{Mfold (rev } t) \ ([], \text{ftpPolicy) ftpSt}$$

which is an instance of the test specification scheme discussed in subsection 4.3. Using our test method, we receive four test cases which each represent different ftp traces. The test case generation took about 5 minutes. For space reasons, we omit the quite involved code of the generated test script here; the interested reader is referred to [1]).

6   Conclusion

It comes perhaps as a surprise that conceptually—viewed from a strict datatype centric angle and using a powerful logic—sequence testing is just a special case of unit testing. Instead of one input to be send to the system under test to receive one output, a *list* of input is generated to receive a *list* of outputs; the rest is the usual monadic trickery to represent *i/o* in a functional setting and the use of abstract test traces instead of concrete ones.

One might question the practical relevance of this observation since the length of the considered sequences is fairly small in the firewall study ($k = 4$ in our ftp example, and $k = 8$ in experiments with VoIP protocols, where the slow-down was already considerable). However, the example in subsection 4.5 can easily be blown up to protocol-lengths of 100; test case generation including test script generation still takes less than a minute (see HOL-TESTGEN example suite). It is therefore the combination between richness of data-structures, the branching-factor in the automaton, *and* the length of the protocol, which may represent a fundamental barrier to our approach, not the length alone. So far, we do not see that this is different from any other tool-supported test case generation approach.

The combination of theorem proving and test data generation is a fruitful one, in particular to control the state-space explosion which is in our case an explosion of test cases for testing the filter-function of firewalls. Using theorem proving techniques for simplifying firewall policies can reduce dramatically both, the overall time for generating test cases as well as the number of generated test data. For example, within HOL-TESTGEN, we can formally prove the following equality which formalizes the fact, that a global allow-all rule will override a direct predecessor with the more specific allow rule:

$$(\text{allowAll} ++ \text{allowAllFromTo } x\, y) = \text{allowAll}$$

Thus, proving equalities and using them for the "logical massage" of policies in test-specifications will eliminate redundant test cases by computing a semantically equivalent, but "simpler" policy with respect to time and space consumption.

Our integrated approach to unit and sequence testing also paves the way for combined scenarios: it is straight-forward to formulate test specifications that "guide" a statefull firewall in a specific state and to compute test cases that test the specific filter-function in this state.

Finally, there is the possibility to verify test-hypothesis generated throughout the test theorem generation phase. In our view, a specification-based test is clearly an approximation to verification. A test has the advantage to be potentially based on more abstract data than the concrete program. Once generated, test data can be used for fast checks that a (complex, black-box) program conforms to the test specification. Such fast checks can be of crucial importance in a software development process, e. g., when checking in a new version of a program into the version management system of a development project. In later stages, a full review and even a verification of the test hypothesis might be in order; depending on the degree of abstraction of the test specification with respect to the concrete program, the test cases can help to structure and simplify this code-verification task.

Acknowledgment

We thank Lukas Brügger for valuable discussions on the subject of firewall testing and the work he did during his semester thesis.

References

[1] The HOL-TestGen Website, http://www.brucker.ch/projects/hol-testgen/
[2] Andrews, P.B.: An Introduction to Mathematical Logic and Type Theory: To Truth Through Proof. Academic Press, Orlando (May 1986)
[3] Brucker, A.D., Wolff, B.: HOL-TestGen 1.0.0 user guide. Technical Report 482, ETH Zürich (April 2005)
[4] Brucker, A.D., Wolff, B.: Interactive testing using HOL-TestGen. In: Grieskamp, W., Weise, C. (eds.) FATES 2005. LNCS, vol. 3997, pp. 87–102. Springer, Heidelberg (2006)
[5] Brucker, A.D., Wolff, B.: Symbolic test case generation for primitive recursive functions. In: Grabowski, J., Nielsen, B. (eds.) FATES 2004. LNCS, vol. 3395, pp. 16–32. Springer, Heidelberg (2005)
[6] Church, A.: A formulation of the simple theory of types. Journal of Symbolic Logic 5, 56–68 (1940)
[7] Dick, J., Faivre, A.: Automating the generation and sequencing of test cases from model-based specications. In: Larsen, P.G., Woodcock, J.C.P. (eds.) FME 1993. LNCS, vol. 670, pp. 268–284. Springer, Heidelberg (1993)
[8] Frantzen, L., Tretmans, J., Willemse, T.A.C.: A symbolic framework for model-based testing. In: Havelund, K., Núñez, M., Roşu, G., Wolff, B. (eds.) Formal Approaches to Software Testing and Runtime Verification. LNCS, vol. 4262, Springer, Heidelberg (2006)
[9] Gaudel, M.-C.: Testing can be formal, too. In: Mosses, P.D., Schwartzbach, M.I., Nielsen, M. (eds.) CAAP 1995, FASE 1995, and TAPSOFT 1995. LNCS, vol. 915, pp. 82–96. Springer, Heidelberg (1995)
[10] Nipkow, T., Paulson, L.C., Wenzel, M. (eds.): Isabelle/HOL. LNCS, vol. 2283. Springer, Heidelberg (2002)
[11] Wenzel, M.M.: Isabelle/Isar — a versatile environment for human-readable formal proof documents. PhD thesis, TU München, München (February 2002)
[12] Zhu, H., Hall, P.A., May, J.H.R.: Software unit test coverage and adequacy. ACM Computing Surveys 29(4), 366–427 (1997)

A   Tableaux Calculus for HOL

Table 2. The Standard Tableaux Calculus for HOL

$$\frac{P \; ?x}{\exists x. \, P \; x} \qquad \frac{\bigwedge x. \, P \; x}{\forall x. \, P \; x}$$

(a) Quantifier Introduction Rules

$$\frac{}{t = t} \qquad \frac{}{\text{true}} \qquad \frac{P \quad Q}{P \wedge Q} \qquad \frac{\begin{array}{c}[\neg Q]\\ \vdots\\ P\end{array}}{P \vee Q} \qquad \frac{\begin{array}{c}[P]\\ \vdots\\ Q\end{array}}{P \to Q} \qquad \frac{\begin{array}{c}[P]\\ \vdots\\ \text{false}\end{array}}{\neg P} \qquad \frac{\begin{array}{cc}[P] & [Q]\\ \vdots & \vdots\\ Q & P\end{array}}{P = Q}$$

(b) Safe Introduction Rules

$$\frac{\forall x. \, P \; x \quad \begin{array}{c}[P \; ?x]\\ \vdots\\ R\end{array}}{R} \qquad \frac{\forall x. \, P \; x \quad \begin{array}{c}[\forall x. \, P \; x, \; P \; ?x]\\ \vdots\\ R\end{array}}{R}$$

(c) Unsafe Elimination Rules

$$\frac{\text{false}}{P} \qquad \frac{P \wedge Q \quad \begin{array}{c}[P, Q]\\ \vdots\\ R\end{array}}{R} \qquad \frac{P \vee Q \quad \begin{array}{cc}[P] & [Q]\\ \vdots & \vdots\\ R & R\end{array}}{R} \qquad \frac{P \to Q \quad \begin{array}{cc}[\neg P] & [Q]\\ \vdots & \vdots\\ R & R\end{array}}{R}$$

$$\frac{\exists x. \, P \; x \quad \bigwedge x. \begin{array}{c}[P \; x]\\ \vdots\\ Q\end{array}}{Q} \qquad \frac{P = Q \quad \begin{array}{cc}[P, Q] & [\neg P, \neg Q]\\ \vdots & \vdots\\ R & R\end{array}}{R}$$

(d) Safe Elimination Rules

$$\text{if } P \text{ then } A \text{ else } B = (P \to A) \wedge (\neg P \to B)$$

(e) Rewrites

B   A Sample Derivation

In the following, we show, how the test case generation procedure inside HOL-TESTGEN synthesizes input data by a fully automatic symbolic constraint solution process. We pick the example of subsection 4.2:

$$x \ \text{mem} \ S \rightarrow ioprg \ x \ S$$

Since S is the only free variable of list type, the procedure picks it, derives a datatype exhaustion theorem (as shown in subsection 4.2) on the fly and applies it. The following proof-state is the result:

1. $S = [] \Longrightarrow x \ \text{mem} \ S \rightarrow ioprg \ x \ S$

2. $\bigwedge a. \ S = [a] \Longrightarrow x \ \text{mem} \ S \rightarrow ioprg \ x \ S$

3. $\bigwedge a \ b. \ S = [a, b] \Longrightarrow x \ \text{mem} \ S \rightarrow ioprg \ x \ S$

4. $\text{THYP}(3 \leq |S| \rightarrow x \ \text{mem} \ S \rightarrow ioprg \ x \ S)$

Variable propagation, simplification with the rules of (1) in subsection 4.2 and the implication introduction rule from 3b yield the following state:

1. $\text{false} \Longrightarrow ioprg \ x \ []$

2. $\bigwedge a. \ \text{if} \ a = x \ \text{then} \ \text{true} \ \text{else} \ \text{false} \Longrightarrow ioprg \ x \ [a]$

3. $\bigwedge a \ b. \ \text{if} \ a = x \ \text{then} \ \text{true} \ \text{else if} \ b = x \ \text{then} \ \text{true} \ \text{else} \ \text{false}$
   $\Longrightarrow ioprg \ x \ [a, b]$

4. $\text{THYP}(3 \leq |S| \rightarrow x \ \text{mem} \ S \rightarrow ioprg \ x \ S)$

Thus, the constraints for the first test case are not satisfiable anymore and it can be erased. In the sequel, we apply the simplification of the conditional of 3e and the safe elimination rule for conjunction 3c.

1. $\bigwedge a. \ ioprg \ x \ [x]$

2. $\bigwedge a \ b. \ [\![a = x \rightarrow \text{true}; a \neq x \rightarrow (x = b \rightarrow \text{true} \wedge x \neq b \rightarrow \text{false})]\!]$
   $\Longrightarrow ioprg \ x \ [a, b]$

3. $\text{THYP}(3 \leq |S| \rightarrow x \ \text{mem} \ S \rightarrow ioprg \ x \ S)$

Now, the safe elimination rule for implication in 3c effectively produces a series of case splits; variable propagation and elimination of contradictory clauses simplify the proof state again. Thus, cascades of conditionals were eliminated.

Finally, the elimination of superfluous quantifiers result in the proof state shown in subsection 4.2.

Generating Unit Tests from Formal Proofs

Christian Engel and Reiner Hähnle

Department of Computer Science and Engineering, Chalmers University of Technology
412 96 Göteborg, Sweden
engelc@ira.uka.de, reiner@chalmers.se

Abstract. We present a new automatic test generation method for JAVA CARD based on attempts at formal verification of the implementation under test (IUT). Self-contained unit tests in JUnit format are generated automatically. The advantages of the approach are: (i) it exploits the full information available in the IUT and in its formal model giving very good hybrid coverage; (ii) a non-trivial formal model of the IUT is unnecessary; (iii) it is adaptable to the skills that users may possess in formal methods.

Keywords: model-based testing, program verification, symbolic execution, test coverage, theorem proving, unit testing, white-box testing.

1 Introduction

We present a new automatic test case generation (ATCG) method for object-oriented software based on formal verification technology, accordingly called *verification-based test generation* (VBT). It combines features from white and black box test generation methods. VBT uses the full information contained in a formal specification *and* the underlying implementation under test (IUT). The main advantages over model-based test generation are: a detailed formal model of the IUT is not needed, in fact, test cases can be generated even from trivial specifications; in addition, it is possible to generate test cases that exhibit bugs contained only in the code and not in the specification. Such errors cannot reliably be detected with model-based test generation. As test generation is based on *systematic* attempts to verify the IUT against its specification, the resulting test cases satisfy rather strong *hybrid*, i.e., model-based as well as code-based coverage criteria.

Like other test generation approaches we concentrate on creating self-contained unit test cases including fixtures and test oracles. The intended application domain are safety- and security-critical JAVA and JAVA CARD programs running on small embedded devices such as smart cards or mobile phones. Unit testing is an essential technique for ensuring quality of industrial software. Writing unit tests by hand is labour intensive and leaves significant uncertainties concerning the quality of the produced tests in terms of achieved test coverage and of correctness of the test oracle relative to the specification of the tested code. To remedy this situation, various ATCG approaches have been suggested. The most common are specification- or model-based test generation (commonly referred to as black box techniques) [1,4,5,9,10,11] and white box approaches [8,26,27,28] that are based on code-driven state exploration by symbolic execution. A

B. Meyer and Y. Gurevich (Eds.): TAP 2007, LNCS 4454, pp. 169–188, 2007.

detailed comparison of our method to these and to other ATCG approaches is done in Section 8.

Our own approach contains features from both white and black box techniques, but adds a new ingredient: the starting point of the VBT process is a systematic attempt, based on symbolic execution, to formally verify correctness of a given JAVA CARD program p relative to a precondition *pre* and postcondition *post*. In our concrete setting we use the KeY verification system [2] that provides appropriate (attempted) proofs based on symbolic execution of the target program p, interleaved with first-order simplification. It returns tree-shaped proof objects where the nodes can be interpreted as symbolic execution states and the branches as symbolic execution paths through p. The presentation in this paper is based on the implementation in the KeY system, but in principle, it would be possible to use any other JAVA verification system that works with symbolic execution, for example, the KIV system [25].

The proof object on which test case generation is based does not need to constitute a complete proof, for example, loops may have been approximated by executing them symbolically a fixed number of times. This has the advantage that the proof construction phase and, therefore, test generation is fully automatic. The information contained in a proof is used to extract test data from the path conditions that characterize certain symbolic execution paths (or all of them, depending on the desired test coverage). From the postcondition *post* test oracles are generated.

A complete functional specification of the implementation under test p is not required, because test generation is based on symbolic execution of the *code* p, while the *specification pre, post* is only needed to synthesize the test oracle. Meaningful test cases are obtained already for trivial specifications. For example, the precondition *pre* could just express that object references in p are non-null and the postcondition *post* is merely *true*. For the generation of test oracles, somewhat more extensive specifications are required, even though they can be far from complete (as will be shown below).

For specification our implementation supports the popular high-level Java Modeling Language (JML) [23] whose compatibility with JAVA syntax reduces the extent of formal methods knowledge that JAVA developers need to come up with formal specifications. For example, it enables the programmer to write the postcondition as a JAVA expression using query methods. In essence, the test oracle is then directly provided as a JAVA method.

In summary, the main advantages of the VBT methodology are: (i) it is fully automatic, but since coverage and quality of tests can be improved by more complete proofs it is adaptable to the skill of users; (ii) test generation is possible already with a trivial specification—again, since test oracles and relevance of generated test cases are improved by fuller specifications, the method is adaptable to the skill of users; (iii) rather strong hybrid code- and model-based coverage criteria are met; (iv) test generation and verification happen in a uniform framework and tool; (v) the full JAVA CARD programming language is covered.

In the next section we provide background on test coverage, JAVA CARD, formal verification, program logics, and symbolic execution. In Sect. 3 we outline a basic version of our method guided by an example. In Sect. 4 we extend it to code with unbounded loops and recursion. We also discuss when various code-based coverage criteria are reached. In Sect. 5 we present some measures that ensure high automation of our method and in Sect. 6 we show that the tests obtained from our approach satisfy further coverage criteria [29]. In Sect. 7 we report on some experimental results, followed by related and future work in Section 8. Due to space limitations generated test cases and proofs of theorems cannot be reproduced here. On the web page i12www.ira.uka.de/~engelc/testCases/ proofs of theorems as well as full specifications of the examples in JML and generated test cases can be found.

2   Background

Test Coverage Criteria. To make the paper self-contained we define some standard notions of test coverage [29]. Recall that in general an implementation under test (IUT) has an infinite number of execution paths, but only a finite number of branches.

Definition 1. *A formula* φ *is a* path condition *for an execution path* p *through the IUT iff* p *is executed whenever* φ *holds before the execution of the IUT.*

A feasible execution path *is an execution path that has a satisfiable path condition. A branch or statement in the IUT is called* feasible *if it is contained in at least one feasible execution path. We say a branch (a path) is* covered *by a test case iff it is executed when running the test case.*

A test set for a given IUT satisfies the feasible branch (path) *coverage criterion iff each feasible branch (path) is covered by it.*

JAVA CARD.   The JAVA CARD programming language is a dialect of JAVA characterized by the absence of a number of language features (mainly floating point types, multiple threads, dynamic class loading) and the presence of others (persistent vs. transient memory, atomic transactions). Most language features, however, are available in JAVA CARD just like in JAVA. While JAVA CARD achieves unprecedented independence from the hardware platform, one can state that the gap between the behaviour of programs in desktop simulators and after actual deployment on the target hardware is a serious concern for JAVA CARD software developers. In practice, *all* JAVA CARD developer workspaces are equipped not only with emulators, but with various JAVA CARD hardware platforms, and for good reasons: in principle, it is possible to test JAVA CARD applications with the help of a simulator in a standard JAVA environment on a desktop. There are also emulators that mimic the behaviour of smart card hardware. The simulated and the actual behaviour, however, differs considerably. This is due to ambiguities [20] in the JAVA CARD language definition, but also because simulators and emulators do not implement all JAVA CARD aspects or the implementation on the device is faulty. As a consequence, even if JAVA CARD code has been formally verified it is essential to test it, because correct execution cannot be assumed.

Formal verification.   Our approach to automatic test generation is based on a white box analysis of the richest possible program model: the target source code together with a formal programming language semantics. Such representations are realized in formal software verification systems. In these systems a program logic (for example, Hoare logic or dynamic logic—see below) allows to express properties of programs which then can be formally proven from a set of logical inference rules that capture the axiomatic semantics of the target language. State-of-the-art program verification systems are able to prove security and correctness properties of industrial JAVA CARD software [2,21,25]. The implementation described in this paper is based on the verification tool KeY [2].

Dynamic Logic for JAVA CARD. In our method the target program and its specification are both modeled in a version of a dynamic logic (DL) [18] calculus called JAVA DL [2]. Dynamic logic is a program logic that generalizes Hoare logic. It can be seen as a modal logic with modalities $\langle p \rangle \varphi$ and $[p] \varphi$ for every program p with an arbitrary formula φ in its scope (which in turn may contain modalities). JAVA DL formulas are interpreted over first-order Kripke structures $\mathcal{K} = (\mathcal{S}, \rho)$, where $\mathcal{S}$ is a set of first-order structures including interpretations of the identifiers occurring in programs, and ρ is a function that assigns to a program p its operational semantics as a transition relation $\rho(p) \subseteq \mathcal{S} \times \mathcal{S}$: if p is a legal JAVA CARD program and started in state $s \in \mathcal{S}$, then $(s, s') \in \rho(p)$ iff p terminates normally (i.e., not abruptly) in final state s'. The formula $\langle p \rangle \varphi$ holds in $s \in \mathcal{S}$ iff p terminates normally and in the final state after termination φ holds. In other words, p is *totally correct* with respect to postcondition φ. Dually, $[p] \varphi$ expresses *partial correctness*: if p terminates normally, then in the final state φ holds.

State Updates. In JAVA (as in other object-oriented programming languages), different object type variables may refer to the same object. This phenomenon, called aliasing, causes difficulties for the handling of assignments in a calculus for JAVA DL. For example, whether or not the formula o1.f $\doteq$ 1 holds after (symbolic) execution of the assignment o2.f = 2;, depends on whether o1 and o2 refer to the same object. Therefore, JAVA assignments cannot be symbolically executed by syntactic substitution. In the JAVA DL calculus another solution is used, based on the notion of (state) *updates*.

Definition 2. Atomic updates *are of the form* loc := val, *where* val *is a logical term without side effects and* loc *is either a program variable or a simple field access or an array access. Updates may appear in front of any formula or term, where they are surrounded by curly brackets for easy parsing. The semantics of* {loc := val}φ *is the same as that of* $\langle$loc=val;$\rangle$ φ.

The idea with updates $\mathcal{U}$ is that during symbolic execution they represent the current computation state in which a program formula $\mathcal{U}\langle p \rangle \varphi$ is executed. They are continuously simplified during symbolic execution, but their application to modal formulas in their scope is delayed until the program has been completely executed.

Sequent Calculus. As it is usual for program logics, the axiomatization of JAVA DL is based on a sequent calculus. The central notion is that of a sequent, which is an expression of the form $\Gamma \Rightarrow \Delta$, where Γ and Δ are finite sets of formulas. The sequent $\Gamma \Rightarrow \Delta$ is valid, if and only if the conjunction of the formulas in Γ implies the disjunction of the formulas in Δ in all states of any JAVA DL-Kripke structure. The rules of a sequent calculus are denoted with schematic reasoning patterns that characterize validity of formulas occurring in the conclusion of a rule. Their general format is:

$$\frac{\Gamma_1 \Rightarrow \Delta_1 \quad \cdots \quad \Gamma_n \Rightarrow \Delta_n}{\Gamma \Rightarrow \Delta}$$

Soundness of the calculus requires that for each rule the validity of the sequents above the line imply the validity of the sequent below the line. There is a sequent rule for each top-level operator both for left and right sides of the sequent arrow. For example,

$$\frac{\Gamma \Rightarrow \varphi, \Delta \quad \Gamma \Rightarrow \psi, \Delta}{\Gamma \Rightarrow \varphi \wedge \psi, \Delta} \quad \text{AND-RIGHT}$$

is a rule that characterizes conjunction on the right and is named accordingly. Here φ and ψ (Γ and Δ) are schematic variables that can be instantiated with any (set of) formula(s). Rules with an empty set of premisses are admissible. They are called *axioms* and their premiss is labelled with $*$. A typical axiom has the conclusion $\Gamma \Rightarrow t \doteq t, \Delta$.

Rules are read bottom-up: the bottom sequent is the sequent on which the rule is applied. The sequents on top are the results of the rule-application. Thus, when proving validity of a formula φ the proof starts with the sequent $\Rightarrow \varphi$ (the empty set of formulas on the left is omitted). Partial proofs in a sequent calculus take the shape of trees whose nodes are labelled with sequents. In *complete proofs* all leaves are labelled with $*$.

Symbolic Execution. The programs occurring in JAVA DL formulas are executable JAVA code. Rules for program formulas operate on sequents of the form $\Gamma \Rightarrow \mathcal{U}\langle \pi p \omega \rangle \varphi, \Delta$, where $\mathcal{U}$ is an update containing the current state of symbolic execution and p is a single JAVA statement called the *first active statement*. The prefix π consists of an arbitrary number of opening braces, try-blocks and method frames (the stack trace), and ω is the whole rest of the program. Each rule for a program formula specifies how to execute symbolically one particular JAVA expression or statement, possibly with additional restrictions. *Symbolic* execution entails that locations have no concrete but symbolic values and the effect of the execution of a statement is described by logical means with symbolic values. When a loop or a recursive method call is encountered, it is in general necessary to perform induction or supply a suitable invariant.

JAVA DL extends other variants of DL used for theoretical investigations or verification purposes, because it handles such phenomena as side effects, aliasing, object types, exceptions, and finite integer types. Since deduction in the JAVA DL calculus is based on symbolic program execution and simple program transformations, it is close to a programmer's understanding of JAVA.

In a symbolic setting, the code branch that the control flow takes after evaluation of a conditional statement cannot always be determined as it depends on symbolic values. In general, a case distinction has to be introduced in the proof. One may also view this as symbolic execution branching into different execution paths. Each symbolic execution path is governed by a branch condition that is syntactically added to the left side of sequents during evaluation of conditional statements. Thus, the branching conditions accumulate in the sequent during symbolic execution and the current path condition for each execution path (including incomplete execution paths that have not yet terminated) is always contained in the leaves of proof trees during any phase of symbolic evaluation. This is illustrated in Fig. 1.

Example 1 (Rule for the if-statement). When an **if** statement is symbolically executed a case distinction whether the guard is true or not has to be made. This is reflected by a split in the proof tree.

$$\frac{\Gamma, c \doteq TRUE \Rightarrow \langle \pi \{p\} \, \omega \rangle \psi, \Delta \quad \Gamma, c \doteq FALSE \Rightarrow \langle \pi \, \omega \rangle \psi, \Delta}{\Gamma \Rightarrow \langle \pi \, \textbf{if} \, (c) \, \{p\}; \omega \rangle \psi, \Delta} \quad \text{IfThenSplit}$$

The conditional **if** (c) {p} is the first active statement in the modality, where c is a boolean side-effect free expression. The updates before the program formulas are not explicitly written. The left premiss represents the case that the expression c holds, thus we find $c \doteq TRUE$ on the left side which becomes part of the path condition on the corresponding execution path. As c holds, the body of the **if**-statement is executed, therefore, the program formula $\langle \pi \, \textbf{if} \, (c) \, \{p\}; \omega \rangle \psi$ is transformed into $\langle \pi \{p\} \, \omega \rangle \psi$, where symbolic execution continues. The right premiss represents the case that !c holds thus we find $c \doteq FALSE$ on the left side of the sequent. In this case the body of the if statement is not executed and we get the new program formula $\langle \pi \, \omega \rangle \psi$.

3   Overview of Verification-Based Test Generation

Verification-based testing (VBT) is motivated by the insight that a formal analysis of a specification and/or the corresponding code, as performed in a formal proof attempt, yields enough information to produce test cases. In our view a full description of a software system consists of *both, implementation and specification*. In order to detect as many errors as possible, it is essential to analyse and compare two levels of modeling.

Several ideas from other test generation methods are as well found in VBT, for example, to synthesize a test oracle from a formal specification (the postcondition) or to use reasoning technologies such as deduction, constraint solving and symbolic execution to achieve a high automation of the test generation process.

We walk through our test generation method guided by an example. It will demonstrate the automatic creation of self-contained unit tests for an implementation under test (IUT) containing only a finite number of feasible execution paths (the general case is handled in Sect. 4). In this case we obtain a test set satisfying the rather strong feasible execution path coverage criterion (Def. 1). The reason for this can be found in the soundness of the JAVA DL sequent calculus: if a certain path p with path condition φ in a code fragment c would not figure in a complete proof then also a complete proof for the invalid formula $\varphi \rightarrow \langle c \rangle \, false$ could be constructed which would imply that the calculus is unsound.

Example 2. Method conditionalSwap swaps the values of the field value of two objects x and y of type NaturalNumberWrapper provided that x.value >= y.value. Its behaviour is specified using JML [23] as shown below.

```
public class NaturalNumberWrapper{

    private /*@spec_public@*/ int value;

    //@ public invariant value > 0;
```

```
/*@ public normal_behavior
  @   requires x!=null && y!=null;
  @   ensures \old(x.value) >= \old(y.value) ?
  @     (\old(x.value)==y.value && \old(y.value)==x.value) :
  @     (\old(x.value)==x.value && \old(y.value)==y.value);
  @*/
public static void conditionalSwap(NaturalNumberWrapper x,
                                   NaturalNumberWrapper y){
    if(x.value >= y.value){
        swap(x, y);
    }
}

public static void swap(NaturalNumberWrapper x,
                        NaturalNumberWrapper y){
    y.value += x.value;
    x.value = y.value - x.value;
    y.value -= x.value;
}
}
```

Clearly, there are two feasible execution paths characterized by the path condition x.value $\geq$ y.value, resp., by x.value $<$ y.value that are induced by the guard of the conditional occurring in conditionalSwap, see also Fig. 1.

Extraction of the IUT. KeY's JML front end automatically translates [15] JML specifications to JAVA DL formulas that constitute a proof obligation (PO) for the KeY verifier. For the method conditionalSwap and its JML specification the PO is

$$\forall x'.\forall y'.\{x := x', y := y'\}((inv \wedge pre) \rightarrow \langle \text{conditionalSwap(x,y);} \rangle \Phi), \quad (1)$$

where Φ is a first-order formula representing the post condition, *inv* is the formula $\forall z.z.\text{value} > 0$ representing the class invariant for class NaturalNumberWrapper and *pre* := $(x \neq \textbf{null} \wedge y \neq \textbf{null})$ the precondition of conditionalSwap defined by the JML specification. After quantifier elimination by skolemization and pushing in updates (where S abbreviates $\{x := c_{x'}, x := c_{x'}\}$) we obtain:

$$S(inv \wedge pre) \rightarrow S\langle \text{conditionalSwap(x,y);} \rangle \Phi. \quad (2)$$

This formula is the root node in the partial proof tree depicted in Fig. 1 (the left part of the implication is abbreviated with Γ). From this formula we extract the IUT

```
x = c_x'; y = c_y'; conditionalSwap(x,y);
```

and the postcondition Φ. Later we generate a test oracle from Φ. The node in the proof tree used for extracting the IUT (2) is called *code node*.

Extraction of Path Conditions from the Proof Tree.

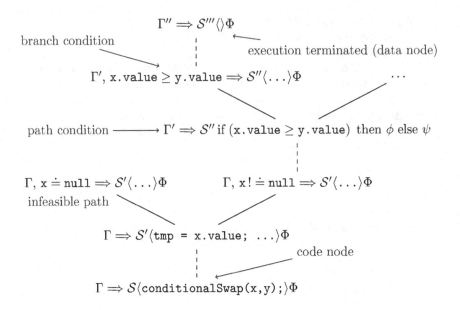

Fig. 1. Partial proof tree for the example in the text

Definition 3. *A proof tree in which each branch is either closed or ends with a leaf that contains no code fragments anymore (indicating termination of symbolic execution on that branch) is called* fully executed.

A fully executed proof tree for the PO (1) is constructed automatically by the KeY system. It is partially shown in Fig. 1. Recall from Sect. 2 that branches in the proof tree can be identified with execution paths through the IUT. Since each node contains a path condition that leads to the current point of symbolic program execution, we are interested in exactly those nodes that contain an empty program (signifying termination of symbolic execution). These nodes are the leaves of open branches in a fully executed proof tree and referred to as *data nodes* from now on. They have the form

$$\Gamma \Rightarrow \mathcal{U}\langle\rangle\,\Phi, \Delta, \qquad (3)$$

where Γ and Δ are sets of first-order formulas and $\mathcal{U}$ is a sequence of updates representing the effect of the symbolic execution of the IUT on the branch of the proof tree whose path condition is, therefore, given by:

$$\bigwedge_{\gamma\in\Gamma}\gamma \wedge \bigwedge_{\delta\in\Delta}\neg\delta. \qquad (4)$$

It is important to realize that closed branches where symbolic execution did not terminate need not be considered, since those branches must have been closed because of an unsatisfiable path condition and, therefore, cannot be reached. In Fig. 1, for example, the node labelled "infeasible path" originates from the null pointer check performed each time when an attribute on an object reference is accessed, here $x \doteq$ **null**. Symbolic execution of this node leads to a new proof goal of the form

$$\Gamma, c_{x'} \doteq \textbf{null} \Rightarrow \mathcal{S}'\langle \pi \, \textbf{throw new} \, \texttt{NullPointerException();} \, \omega \rangle \, \Phi. \quad (5)$$

It represents the case that a null pointer exception is thrown. It can be closed immediately, because the formula $c_{x'} \mathbin{!} \doteq \textbf{null}$ is contained in the precondition Γ (originating from the requires clause of the JML contract). In the fully executed proof tree we find the following data nodes:

$$c_{y'} \doteq c_{x'}, \, inv_1 \Rightarrow \mathcal{U}_1 \langle \rangle \, \Phi, \, pre_1 \quad (6)$$

$$c_{y'}.\texttt{value} \leq c_{x'}.\texttt{value}, \, inv_2 \Rightarrow \mathcal{U}_2 \langle \rangle \, \Phi, \, pre_2, \, c_{y'} \doteq c_{x'} \quad (7)$$

$$c_{y'}.\texttt{value} \geq c_{x'}.\texttt{value} + 1, \, inv_2 \Rightarrow \mathcal{U}_3 \langle \rangle \, \Phi, \, pre_2 \quad (8)$$

Here, inv_1 is $\{inv, c_{x'}.\texttt{value} \geq 1\}$ and inv_2 is $\{inv, c_{x'}.\texttt{value} \geq 1, c_{y'}.value \geq 1\}$. They are derived from the invariant of the JML specification. Formula pre_1 stands for $c_{x'} \doteq$ **null** and pre_2 for $\{c_{x'} \doteq \textbf{null}, c_{y'} \doteq \textbf{null}\}$. They stem from the precondition of the JML method contract. In (4) we defined path conditions in such a way that, in addition to branching conditions, they may contain constraints like $pre_{\{1,2\}}$ and $inv_{\{1,2\}}$ stemming from formulas present in the code node. The formulas $c_{y'}.\texttt{value} \geq c_{x'}.\texttt{value} + 1$ and $c_{y'}.\texttt{value} \leq c_{x'}.\texttt{value}$ are introduced by a case distinction performed when the **if** statement occurring in $\texttt{conditionalSwap}$ is symbolically executed (see Fig. 1). The formula $c_{y'} \doteq c_{x'}$ occurring in data node (6) on the left and in data node (7) on the right side are introduced by another case distinction caused by an alias analysis when the assignments in $\texttt{swap}$ are symbolically executed. This case distinction is needed for distinguishing whether x and y are referencing the same object. From the data nodes the path conditions are obtained via (4).

Generation of Integer Test Data. For creating suitable test data for each execution path we have to find first-order models of the corresponding path condition formulas. For integer types concrete interpretations are currently found by applying *Cogent* [12] or *Simplify* [14] to the formula

$$\bigwedge_{\gamma \in \Gamma} \gamma \to \bigwedge_{\delta \in \Delta} \delta,$$

i.e., the negation of the path condition (4). If the path condition is satisfiable and the decision procedure manages to deliver a counter example for its negation the integer type test data are derived from the returned counter example. While *Simplify's* integer arithmetic is unbounded, Cogent, as a decision procedure for C expressions, uses bounded 32-bit arithmetic. Thus for getting meaningful results one has to restrict the arithmetic operations allowed in the specification to 32-bit Java **int** operations and the permitted **int** literals to values expressible in 32-bit **int** arithmetic (i.e. discrete values in the interval $[-2^{31}, 2^{31} - 1]$). This is possible in KeY.

In contrast to *Cogent*, *Simplify* does not necessarily return a concrete counter example. In general the counter examples provided by *Simplify* have the form $\bigwedge_{\pi \in \Pi} \pi$, where π is an atomic formula of the form $p(t_1, t_2)$ with top level predicate $p \in \{<, \leq, >, \geq, \doteq\}$. If for each $p(t_1, t_2) \in \Pi$ t_1 represents a Java location and t_2 an integer literal we have found a concrete counter example. Otherwise, *Simplify* is applied recursively to the refined formula $\neg(t_1 \doteq t_2 \land \bigwedge_{\pi \in \Pi} \pi)$, where t_1 and t_2 are chosen in such a way that one of the following conditions holds:

- $t_1 \leq t_2 \in \Pi$,
- $t_1 \geq t_2 \in \Pi$,
- $t_3 < t_2 \in \Pi$ with $t_1 := t_3 + 1$,
- $t_1 > t_3 \in \Pi$ with $t_2 := t_3 + 1$ or
- t_1 occurs in Π and t_2 is an arbitrary integer literal iff no inequations occur in Π and thus none of the previous conditions can be met.

The procedure is repeated until Simplify returns a concrete counter example. This relatively naive approach is sufficient in practice, because path conditions are easily satisfiable for non-pathological programs.

Generation of Reference Type Test Data. As a first step the set R of all terms that occur in the path condition and whose type is non-primitive is grouped into equivalence classes $R_{/\sim}$ where $a \sim b$ iff $\bigwedge_{\gamma \in \Gamma} \gamma \land \bigwedge_{\delta \in \Delta} \neg \delta \models a \doteq b$ (In JAVA DL $a \doteq b$ means object identity). For each of these equivalence classes C test data are chosen to be either (i) **null** iff **null** $\in C$ or (ii) an object of type t where t is the minimal static type of the terms $t \in C$ if t is not an array type or (iii) an array of length n otherwise, where n is the concrete value found for a term $a.length$ with $a \in C$ during the integer type test data generation phase. If no such term a exists an arbitrary value n is chosen.

Test Oracle. The test oracle is generated by transforming the postcondition Φ of the IUT into loops iterating over boolean JAVA expressions. Quantified subformulas are only allowed to occur in Φ if they match one of the following patterns

$$\forall x. (a \prec_1 x \land x \prec_2 b \rightarrow \Psi) \qquad \exists x. (a \prec_1 x \land x \prec_2 b \land \Psi),$$

where x has an integer type and $\prec_1, \prec_2 \in \{<, \leq\}$. This restriction essentially confines postconditions within the *guarded fragment* of first-order logic [19]. Guarded quantified formulas can be evaluated by a loop iterating over the range given by the bounded guard predicate $a \prec_1 x \land x \prec_2 b$. The postcondition of Example 2 is quantifier-free and can be trivially turned into boolean JAVA expression.

Example 3 (Sort). The following approximate specification of a sorting algorithm has a post condition containing quantified expressions obeying the above restrictions:

```
/*@ public normal_behavior
  @   ensures a!=null ==>
  @             (\forall int i; 0<=i && i<a.length-1; a[i]<=a[i+1])
  @          &&
  @             (\forall int i; 0<=i && i<a.length;
  @                (\exists int j; 0<=j && j<a.length; \old(a[i])==a[j])
  @             );
  @*/
public static void sort(int[] a) { ... }
```

From the first quantified JML subexpression

>**\forall int** i; 0<=i && i<a.length-1; a[i]<=a[i+1]

the following JAVA oracle is computed:

```
boolean result = true;
for (int _i0 = (0); _i0 <= ((-2) + _old2_a.length); _i0++) {
  result = result && TestBubbleSort0.subformula1(_i0,_old2_a,buffer);
}
buffer.append(...);
return result;
```

Here, `TestBubbleSort0.subformula1` is a wrapper method for the oracle created from the subexpression a[i]<=a[i+1] (a and i are renamed to _old2_a and _i0). It has parameters _i0, _old2_a needed to evaluate a[i]<=a[i+1] and the `StringBuffer` variable `buffer` is used for logging results of the evaluation of subexpressions. This provides valuable information when a test run fails.

In the case of the trivial postcondition *true* the test oracle always succeeds. In this case the resulting unit tests can only fail if the execution hangs or throws an uncaught exception. Even in this case we obtain meaningful and important tests, because uncaught exceptions are the cause of many serious errors.

Generation of Unit Tests. The generated tests are in JUnit (www.junit.org) format. For every feasible execution path found a separate test method is created. In this way erroneous execution paths can easily be identified after failed tests.

For the example above three test methods are created corresponding to the path conditions of data nodes (6)–(8). Each test method contains a different test case for each first-order model obtained from the path condition.

The test case generated from (6) reports a failure when executed. Analysis of the reason why the postcondition is not satisfied exhibits a bug: whenever the arguments x and y of swap point to the same object the result state is x.value $\doteq$ y.value $\doteq$ 0 irrespective of the initial value. The branching condition $c_{y'} \doteq c_{x'}$ in (6) covers exactly this case.

This kind of bug is not easy to discover with model-based test generation, because the case distinction on whether the arguments are identical objects is an implementation issue and does not occur in the specification naturally.

Modification of the Implementation under Test. In contrast to some other white box test generation methods [27,28] the program logic JAVA DL is capable of handling symbolic reference type values. In order to provide a fixture for reference type test data a modified version of the IUT is included in the generated unit test. The modifications consist of supplying default constructors and *get* and *set* methods for **private** and **protected** fields so that the test fixture can create objects with the properties determined by the found models of the path conditions. The new methods are uniquely named and do not change the semantics of the IUT. This means in the case of the example that methods for accessing and modifying the field `value` are added to the class `NaturalNumberWrapper`. In general, also **final** modifiers are removed from final instance fields and from final static fields that are not initialized with a compile time constant.

4   Unbounded Number of Execution Paths and Test Coverage

An IUT containing loops or recursive method calls may give rise to an infinite number
of feasible execution paths if its specification imposes no upper bound on the number
of iterations of the loop or the recursion depth. In this case it is obviously not possible
to find a finite proof tree that covers every feasible execution path. We can see two
approaches to deal with this situation:

1. Unwind the loop (unfold the recursive method call) a fixed number of times. This
   strategy creates only a partial proof. One uses only those execution paths on which
   symbolic execution has terminated.
2. Replace non-linear constructs such as loops and method calls by suitable specifications, i.e., an invariant in the case of loops and a contract in the case of method
   calls. This allows to obtain complete proof trees.

The first approach does not try to produce fully executed proofs. Proof attempts are
simply stopped after a given resource bound has been reached and the information obtained so far is exploited. The second approach formally constructs a fully executed and
possibly even complete proof tree, but this proof tree either has gaps (where a contract
is used) or relies on an invariant supplied by the user. Which of the two approaches is
appropriate depends on the specific IUT and the targeted coverage as pointed out below.

4.1   Partial Proofs

To unwind a loop of the form **while**(b) {p}; means to syntactically replace it with

$$\text{l1: } \textbf{if}(b) \{ \text{ l2: } p'; \textbf{ while}(b) \{p\} \};,$$

where p' is obtained from p by replacing the occurring *break* and *continue* statements
in an appropriate way by local jumps to the fresh labels l1 and l2.

By unwinding we may successively explore the potentially unlimited number of terminating execution paths that lead through the loop statement. Since every feasible
branch contained in the loop body is taken[1] on some finite execution path we can obtain
branch coverage if we only unwind the loop often enough. In practice we can usually
not guarantee this except for the case that for every branch in the IUT a containing
feasible execution path has been found and thus every branch is feasible. However, this
can in general not be assumed since for realistic programs with array or attribute accesses branches containing raised NullPointer- or ArrayIndexOutOfBounds-exceptions
are usually infeasible if the program is correct, and there is no way to determine which
branches are feasible by means of unwinding alone.

The advantage of this approach is that it is highly automatic and requires no additional input such as loop invariants. It also yields high code coverage in most cases,
because it turns out that very often all feasible execution paths through the loop are
already feasible in the first iteration of the loop and, hence, can be discovered by unwinding the loop merely once. Similar considerations as for unwinding of loops can be
made for the symbolic execution of method bodies of recursive method calls.

---

[1] Otherwise the branch would not be feasible by definition. JAVA does not allow infinite loops,
    so each branch must occur on at least one finite execution path.

4.2 Complete Proofs

By supplying suitable loop invariants it is possible to find complete proofs even for code that contains unbounded loops. In this case one obtains branch coverage for the resulting test cases provided that (i) every loop is symbolically executed under its invariant and (ii) symbolic execution terminates on every branch of the proof tree.

In order to understand why this is the case, let us first look at the invariant rule. We do not use the standard invariant rule, but one that has been optimized for usage in imperative programming languages [3]. In the rule below I represents the invariant. The point where the rule deviates from the usual invariant rules is the update set $\mathcal{V}$. It represents all locations that can possibly be changed in the loop body q, the so-called *modifier set*, by assigning fresh constants to all critical locations. The first premiss states as usual that the invariant holds in the current state $\mathcal{U}$. In the standard rule the second premiss (invariance property) must be shown for arbitrary states which often requires to strengthen invariants. It turns out to be sound to show the invariance property in the state $\mathcal{U}\mathcal{V}$ which contains all locations from $\mathcal{U}$ that are not modified in the loop body. This is exploited in the rule below. The guard b is free of side effects.

$$\frac{\Gamma \Rightarrow \mathcal{U}I, \Delta \quad \Gamma, \mathcal{U}\mathcal{V}(I \wedge b) \Rightarrow \mathcal{U}\mathcal{V}[q]I, \Delta \quad \Gamma, \mathcal{U}\mathcal{V}(I \wedge \neg b) \Rightarrow \mathcal{U}\mathcal{V}[\pi\,\omega]\Phi, \Delta}{\Gamma \Rightarrow \mathcal{U}[\pi\,\textbf{while}\,(\textbf{b})\,\{\textbf{q}\}\,\omega]\Phi, \Delta}$$

We will argue that if we apply the loop invariant rule to every subgoal containing the formula $[\pi\,\textbf{while}\,(\textbf{b})\,\{\textbf{q}\}\,\omega]\Phi$ (that is, in every partial execution path reaching the loop statement **while**(b) {q}) we can achieve full feasible branch coverage of both q and of $\pi\omega$, hence of the whole loop.

Let p be the symbolic execution path corresponding to the proof branch from the root to node $\Gamma \Rightarrow \mathcal{U}[\pi\,\textbf{while}\,(\textbf{b})\,\{\textbf{q}\}\,\omega]\Phi, \Delta$ with path condition φ_p obtained with (4). The subgoal from the leftmost premiss in the invariant rule is irrelevant for finding execution paths since no further symbolic execution takes place. Let *inv* be the second subgoal obtained from the middle premiss. It is valid if the invariant is preserved by the execution of the loop body. All code branches occurring in the body q that are occurring on any feasible execution path, of which p is a prefix and whose path condition implies φ_p are also feasible when the symbolic execution of q starts in the state defined by the node *inv* and are thus contained in the proof subtree starting with *inv*. This is owed to the soundness of the applied loop invariant rule [3]. If there were a feasible branch br in q that is not explored by symbolic execution of q, then the loop invariant rule would not be sound, because the invariant is possibly not preserved by some feasible execution path through q that contains br. Thus the proof subtree starting with node *inv* covers all branches in q that are feasible under the precondition φ_p. The subgoal *post* from the rightmost premiss in the invariant rule represents the situation after the loop has been executed and it contains the code $\pi\,\omega$. It can be argued in a similar way.

The usage of loop invariants in symbolic execution not only ensures branch coverage, but it is also more efficient than finite unwinding, because typically less code is symbolically executed. Nevertheless, even a symbolic execution tree covering all feasible branches is not always sufficient to generate tests that satisfy the feasible branch coverage criterion. The problem are the fresh constants introduced in updates $\mathcal{V}$ of the invariant rule representing the new values of the locations in the modifier set of the loop. These constants might become part of branching conditions and, hence, path conditions. If branching conditions containing these new constants cannot be expressed with the help of terms whose values were already known in the prestate of the IUT, that is with the help of terms occurring in the code node, it becomes impossible to tell how such conditions evaluate during a run with the chosen test data and which of the associated branches is therefore covered by the test case.

Example 4. To illustrate the effect of loop unwinding during exploration of execution paths by symbolic execution we look at an implementation of the bubble sort algorithm that was specified in Example 3.

```
1   public static void sort(int[] a) {
2       if (a == null) { return; }
3       boolean sorted = false;
4       int help;
5       while (!sorted) {
6           sorted = true;
7           for (int i = 0; i < (a.length - 1); i++) {
8               if (a[i] > a[i + 1]) {
9                   help = a[i];
10                  a[i] = a[i + 1];
11                  a[i + 1] = help;
12                  sorted = false;
13  }}}}
```

We list the case distinctions that occur and the path conditions that are obtained during the symbolic execution of this code. The evaluation of the conditional statement in line 2 leads to the first case distinction.

$a \doteq null$: Symbolic execution terminates after the execution of the **return** statement leading to path condition $a \doteq null$.

$a\,!\doteq null$: Symbolic execution continues in line 3 and $a\,!\doteq null$ is added to the left-hand side of the sequent, i.e., to the current path condition. The next case distinction is encountered when the **while** loop is reached whose symbolic execution by unwinding needs to distinguish whether $sorted \doteq TRUE$ holds.

   $sorted \doteq TRUE$: Since sorted has been initialized with **false** this branch leads to an infeasible path condition and it can be closed immediately.

   $sorted \doteq FALSE$: Since sorted has the value **false** at this point of the program execution this branch condition is equivalent to *true* and thus does not change the current path condition (still being $a\,!\doteq null$). When executing the first iteration of the **for** loop, which is unwound in the same manner as the **while** loop, a case distinction on the expression i < (a.length - 1) is made. Whether this expression can be evaluated without raising an exception depends on whether $a \doteq null$ holds.

     $a \doteq null$: The path condition is $a\,!\doteq null$. This code branch is infeasible and the corresponding branch in the proof tree closable.

     $a\,!\doteq null$: This branch condition is implied by the path condition. The evaluation of the guard 0 < (a.length - 1) terminates without raising an exception, but gives rise to a further case distinction:

$0 \geq (a.length - 1)$: The for loop is not executed. Since the guard of the **while** loop does not hold in its next iteration, symbolic execution terminates on this proof branch without introducing a new branch condition. The path condition obtained is $a\,! \doteq null \wedge 0 \geq (a.length - 1)$ from which $a\,! \doteq null \wedge (0 \doteq a.length \vee 1 \doteq a.length)$ can be derived, because the length of an array cannot be negative (this knowledge is provided by JAVA DL calculus rules).

$0 < (a.length - 1)$: The path condition is now $a\,! \doteq null \wedge 1 < a.length$. The execution of the first iteration of the **for** loop starts which makes a case distinction on the guard of the conditional in line 8 necessary.

The exploration of execution paths through the outer and inner loop can be continued for arbitrarily many loop iterations depending on the desired coverage or the number of desired test cases. Path conditions are continuously simplified during this process, enabling us to avoid symbolic execution of infeasible paths by closing the corresponding proof branch. This is all done fully automatically.

Approximating Method Calls. For the purpose of generating unit tests it is often not desirable to take into account the implementation of all methods called in the IUT. Using modifier sets (and the method's postcondition) one can approximate symbolic execution of a method call. The idea is the same as for invariants and the above arguments apply. Of course, branch coverage is not obtained for the method body then.

5 Increasing Automation

Pruning of the Proof Tree. The subtrees below data nodes in proofs have no significance for the creation of unit tests, because they contain no symbolic execution steps. Thus, when the verification system is run with the purpose of test case generation, we prune any proof steps below data nodes. This prevents proof trees from becoming closed, but increases efficiency. The same applies to other nodes containing no code fragments such as the subgoal from the leftmost premiss of the invariant rule.

Obviously, the pruned part of a proof tree might not have been closable. It is easy, for example, to specify a too strong invariant that is preserved by the loop body, but simply does not hold at the beginning of the loop. This is checked in the first premiss of the invariant rule and if that part of the proof is not explored, then the application of the invariant rule simply becomes unsound. For test case generation this means that we might lose coverage of those branches that are feasible under the given precondition but not under the assumed invariant. We found that in practice this happens rarely and it is outweighed by the advantage of improved automation and speed. If branch coverage is important, the user can enforce full exploration of trees.

Automatic Instantiation of Quantifiers. In order to prove subgoals that contain quantified formulas it is in general necessary to provide suitable terms for instantiation of quantifiers. Owing to the undecidability of first-order logic, it is not possible to restrict these instances in a finite way. First-order quantifiers with variables ranging over the integers are instantiated during proof search by external theorem provers such as Simplify [14]. This leaves first-order quantifiers over object reference types. It would do to ask the user to instantiate them interactively, but we found that the following brute force method works well in practice: object type quantifiers occurring in open proof goals are automatically instantiated with all symbolic object references that occurred so far during symbolic execution of the IUT and that are known to be not **null**.

6 Additional Coverage Criteria

As pointed out in Section 4, complete proof trees satisfy the feasible path coverage criterion if they are constructed by finite unwinding of all feasible execution paths and neither loop invariant rules nor approximation of methods are used. This holds even for incomplete proof trees constructed in this manner, where each open branch contains a data node indicating complete symbolic evaluation of every feasible execution path. In addition, such proof trees meet a variant of the multiple condition coverage (MCC) criterion [29] of the precondition.

Definition 4 (Minimal Partial Interpretation). *A partial interpretation is a mapping s from first-order formulas that contain no unbound variables into* $\{true, false, \perp\}$ *satisfying* $s(a \wedge b) = \min(s(a), s(b))$ *and* $s(a \vee b) = \max(s(a), s(b))$ *under the total order* $false < \perp < true$ *as well as* $s(\neg \perp) = \perp$.

Let $\Phi[a_1, \ldots, a_n]$ *be a first-order formula, where* $a_1, \ldots, a_n$ *are exactly those atomic or quantified subformulas in* Φ *that contain no unbound variables. We call a partial interpretation s minimal relatively to* $\Phi[a_1, \ldots, a_n]$ *if the following conditions hold:*

– $s(\Phi[a_1, \ldots, a_n]) = true$ *or* $s(\Phi[a_1, \ldots, a_n]) = false$
– $s_i(\Phi[a_1, \ldots, a_n]) = \perp$ *for all* $1 \leq i \leq n$ *such that* $s(a_i) \neq \perp$, *where*

$$s_i(q) = \begin{cases} s(q), & \text{if } q \neq a_i \\ \perp, & \text{if } q = a_i \end{cases}.$$

The idea behind minimal partial interpretations is that they fix the interpretation of just enough subformulas of Φ in order to determine its truth value. In order to cover all possible interpretations of a first-order formula it is, therefore, sufficient to cover merely those combinations of subformulas that are fixed by at least one of its minimal partial interpretations. Since we base our variant of multiple condition coverage on minimal partial interpretations (instead of complete interpretations) it results in less test cases while still ensuring full logical coverage of a condition.

Definition 5 (MCC). *Let* $\Phi[a_1, \ldots, a_n]$ *be the precondition of the IUT in a proof tree T. We say T meets the* MCC_p (MCC_b) *criterion iff it contains for every minimal interpretation s such that* $s(\Phi[a_1, \ldots, a_n]) = true$ *every execution path (branch) that is feasible under the precondition*

$$\bigwedge_{a:\, s(a)=true \text{ and } a \in \{a_1, \ldots, a_n\}} a \;\wedge\; \bigwedge_{b:\, s(b)=false \text{ and } b \in \{a_1, \ldots, a_n\}} \neg b.$$

Theorem 1. *Test cases generated from complete proofs satisfy the MCC_b criterion implying full feasible branch coverage. If, in addition, proofs have been constructed without using loop invariant rules then test cases satisfy MCC_p which implies full feasible path coverage.*

The proof is by a straightforward induction over the syntactic structure of the precondition of the IUT. It is contained in the long version of this paper.

As explained in Sect. 4.2, whether a test with the same coverage as the proof tree actually can be constructed depends on the concrete form of invariants and contracts which may introduce fresh constants from modifier sets in the path conditions.

7   Evaluation

In order to evaluate our approach we first injected a number of typical errors into some standard algorithms: the `median` of three integers, the `insert` method of binary search trees (BST), a shift-add multiplier, and bubblesort. In each case we were able to detect the bugs with our automatically generated test cases. The specifications of `insert` and `sort` were incomplete and would be easy to create for a non-expert. The results are summarized in the table below (BC/PC = branch/path coverage obtained):

Method	Specification	Proof	BC	PC	covered paths
`conditionalSwap`	precise	no	yes	yes	3
`median`	precise	yes	yes	yes	6
BST, `insert`	lightweight	no	yes	∞	65
Shift-add multiplier	lightweight	no	yes	no	16
Bubblesort, `sort`	approximate	no	yes	∞	42
dto., fixed length (4)	approximate	yes	yes	yes	24

We also briefly compared our results with two model-based test generation tools (unfortunately, no code-based test generation tools were made available): ESC/Java2 [11] and UTJML [9]. None of the two tools is able to detect all bugs. This is not surprising, because none of them satisfies code-based coverage criteria. ESC/Java2 produces occasional spurious warnings and UTJML, which is in an early development stage, cannot cope with more complex methods such as `sort`. Details on the comparison are in [16].

Finally, we started to evaluate our method with an industrial application. The smart cart vendor association GlobalPlatform (www.globalplatform.org) provides a hardware-, operating system-, and vendor-neutral card specification [17] for JAVA CARD applications. An implementation for this specification is currently being made by IBM Deutschland Entwicklung GmbH. In order to validate vendor-specific implementations against a reference it is necessary to provide test cases with good code coverage. Based on the card specification [17] we wrote a lightweight JML specification for a part of the card life cycle management and used our tool to automatically create test cases for the `process` method of the applet and for `setAppletLifeCycle`. The method calls to the JAVA CARD API were approximated with a JML-based specification provided by W. Mostowski at www.cs.ru.nl/~woj/software/software.html.

The methods do not contain loops or recursive calls, so we could achieve execution path coverage (modulo JAVA CARD API calls). We produced several dozen test cases which are able to detect a number of typical coding and specification errors.

8   Conclusion, Related and Future Work

We presented a new method for automatic test case generation based on possibly incomplete, but automated attempts at formal verification of the IUT. We are able to generate self-contained unit tests in JUnit format. The implementation is based on the verification system KeY [2] and supports the JAVA CARD programming language. The approach exploits the full information available in the IUT and it is adaptable to the formal methods skill of users. In particular, a detailed formal specification of the IUT is not required. Depending on the completeness of the underlying proof attempts the method guarantees strong hybrid coverage criteria.

Related Work. The most common ATCG methodolology is specification- or model-based test generation [1,4,5,9,10,11]. Here, test cases are generated from a formal specification or model of the IUT which itself is not required or taken into account. Consistency of the test oracle with the specification is guaranteed. The drawback is that the information contained in the IUT is not analysed, therefore, no code coverage guarantees can be given. Test cases such as the one that exhibited an implementation error at the end of Section 3 are easy to miss in model-based approaches. Another problem is that a detailed formal model of the underlying system is required in order to create relevant test cases. Such models often do not exist or are too expensive to create.

More recently, white box ATCG approaches appeared [8,26,27,28] that are based on code-driven state exploration by symbolic execution. Often, they support only a limited subset of the target language features. Symbolic execution performed by the relatively advanced system Symstra [28], for instance, does not yet feature symbolic values that have a reference type. Closest among this family of ATCG approaches to ours regarding scope and performance is [26] where, however, verification cannot be combined with testing and the target language is restricted to CIL bytecode.

A different starting point is used in the systems TestEra and Korat [6,22], where systematically all non-isomorhpic inputs up to a fixed bound are generated that pass a feasibility filter based on method preconditions. A uniform framework for verification and testing has been formalised in HOL/Isabelle for a toy target language in [7], but the test generation process is not automatic. Independently of the present work, a very similar method than ours has been developed [24] based on the Bogor verification tool. This is very recent work and yet unpublished, so a detailed comparison has to wait.

Future Work. We obtained promising results on non-trivial programs but a more thorough evaluation and comparison to other automatic test generation methods is required, in particular, to model-based [1,10] and state exploration-based [27,28] approaches. We also plan to generate comprehensive test cases for a GlobalPlatform reference implementation (Section 7) in collaboration with IBM and the GlobalPlatform Association.

The syntactic form of postconditions is currently restricted to first-order formulas with finite guards in order to achieve full automation when computing test oracles. Using advanced first-order theorem proving technology, this can probably be generalized.

Incomplete proofs constructed by finite unwinding of unbounded loops to a fixed bound are not guaranteed to satisfy feasible branch coverage, however, as stated in Sect. 4.2, the obtained path conditions are easier to turn into test cases as in complete proofs that involve loop invariants, due to the absence of fresh constants related to modifier sets. It would be interesting to combine the information from both approaches.

As stated in Section 4.1, by *sufficient* finite unwinding it is always possible to obtain feasible code branch coverage of the generated test data, because each feasible code branch is executed after a finite number of execution steps. Even though it is not possible to compute the number of unwinding steps uniformly for each program, one could implement an incomplete check whether a *given* proof tree enjoys branch coverage by relating the statements in feasible paths of the proof tree to code branches. As argued in Section 4.1, branch coverage tends to happen early, so this would be a useful test.

In order to approximate execution path coverage, arguably a data-driven approach to unwinding is more useful than the naive code-driven one we are currently using. Data-driven unwinding has been realized in Kiasan [13], where it is called k-bounding.

Acknowledgments. We thank Klaus Peter Gungl from IBM Deutschland Entwicklung GmbH for letting us have the source code of their GP Card Spec implementation.

References

1. Ambert, F., Bouquet, F., Chemin, S., Guenaud, S., Legeard, B., Peureux, F., Vacelet, N., Utting, M.: BZ-TT: A tool-set for test generation from Z and B using constraint logic programming. In: Hierons, R., Jerron, T. (eds.) Formal Approaches to Testing of Software, FATES 2002 workshop of CONCUR'02, August 2002, pp. 105–120. INRIA Report (2002)
2. Beckert, B., Hähnle, R., Schmitt, P.H. (eds.): Verification of Object-Oriented Software: The KeY Approach. LNCS (LNAI), vol. 4334. Springer, Heidelberg (2007)
3. Beckert, B., Schlager, S., Schmitt, P.H.: An improved rule for while loops in deductive program verification. In: Lau, K.-K., Banach, R. (eds.) ICFEM 2005. LNCS, vol. 3785, pp. 315–329. Springer, Heidelberg (2005)
4. Bouquet, F., Dadeau, F., Legeard, B., Utting, M.: JML-Testing-Tools: a Symbolic Animator for JML Specifications using CLP. In: Halbwachs, N., Zuck, L. (eds.) TACAS 2005. LNCS, vol. 3440, pp. 551–556. Springer, Heidelberg (2005)
5. Bourdonov, I.B., Kossatchev, A., Kuliamin, V.V., Petrenko, A.: UnitesK test suite architecture. In: Eriksson, L.-H., Lindsay, P.A. (eds.) FME 2002. LNCS, vol. 2391, pp. 77–88. Springer, Heidelberg (2002)
6. Boyapati, C., Khurshid, S., Marinov, D.: Korat: Automated testing based on Java predicates. In: Frankl, P.G. (ed.) Proc. ACM Intl. Symp. Software Testing and Analysis, July 2002. Software Engineering Notes, vol. 27, 4, pp. 123–133. ACM Press, New York (2002)
7. Brucker, A.D., Wolff, B.: Interactive testing with HOL-TestGen. In: Grieskamp, W., Weise, C. (eds.) FATES 2005. LNCS, vol. 3997, pp. 87–102. Springer, Heidelberg (2006)
8. Campbell, C., Grieskamp, W., Nachmanson, L., Schulte, W., Tillmann, N., Veanes, M.: Testing concurrent object-oriented systems with Spec Explorer. In: Fitzgerald, J., Hayes, I.J., Tarlecki, A. (eds.) FM 2005. LNCS, vol. 3582, pp. 542–547. Springer, Heidelberg (2005)
9. Cheon, Y., Kim, M., Perumandla, A.: A complete automation of unit testing for Java programs. In: Arabnia, H.R., Reza, H. (eds.) Proc. Intl. Conf. on Software Engineering Research and Practice, Las Vegas, USA, vol. 1, pp. 290–295. CSREA Press (2005)
10. Cheon, Y., Leavens, G.T.: A simple and practical approach to unit testing: The JML and JUnit way. In: Magnusson, B. (ed.) ECOOP 2002. LNCS, vol. 2374, pp. 231–255. Springer, Heidelberg (2002)

11. Cok, D.R., Kiniry, J.: ESC/Java2: Uniting ESC/Java and JML. In: Barthe, G., Burdy, L., Huisman, M., Lanet, J.-L., Muntean, T. (eds.) CASSIS 2004. LNCS, vol. 3362, pp. 108–128. Springer, Heidelberg (2005)
12. Cook, B., Kroening, D., Sharygina, N.: Cogent: Accurate theorem proving for program verification. In: Etessami, K., Rajamani, S.K. (eds.) CAV 2005. LNCS, vol. 3576, pp. 296–300. Springer, Heidelberg (2005)
13. Deng, X., Lee, J., Robby,: Bogor/Kiasan: a k-bounded symbolic execution for checking strong heap properties of open systems. In: Proc. 21st IEEE/ASM Intl. Conference on Automated Software Engineering, Tokyo, Japan, pp. 157–166. IEEE Computer Society Press, Los Alamitos (2006)
14. Detlefs, D., Nelson, G., Saxe, J.B.: Simplify: a theorem prover for program checking. J. ACM 52(3), 365–473 (2005)
15. Engel, C.: A Translation from JML to JavaDL. Studienarbeit, University of Karlsruhe (2005)
16. Engel, C.: Verification based test case generation. Master's thesis, Department of Computer Science, University of Karlsruhe (August 2006)
17. GlobalPlatform, Foster City, USA. GlobalPlatform Card Specification, version 2.2 edn. (March 2006)
18. Harel, D., Kozen, D., Tiuryn, J.: Dynamic Logic. MIT Press, Cambridge (2000)
19. Hladik, J.: Implementation and optimization of a tableau algorithm for the guarded fragment. In: Egly, U., Fermüller, C.G. (eds.) TABLEAUX 2002. LNCS (LNAI), vol. 2381, pp. 145–159. Springer, Heidelberg (2002)
20. Hubbers, E., Poll, E.: Transactions and non-atomic API calls in Java Card: specification ambiguity and strange implementation behaviours. Dept. of Computer Science NIII-R0438, Radboud University Nijmegen (2004)
21. Jacobs, B., Marché, C., Rauch, N.: Formal verification of a commercial smart card applet with multiple tools. In: Rattray, C., Maharaj, S., Shankland, C. (eds.) AMAST 2004. LNCS, vol. 3116, pp. 241–257. Springer, Heidelberg (2004)
22. Khurshid, S., Marinov, D.: TestEra: Specification-based testing of Java programs using SAT. Automated Software Engineering 11(4), 403–434 (2004)
23. Leavens, G.T., Poll, E., Clifton, C., Cheon, Y., Ruby, C., Cok, D., Müller, P., Kiniry, J., Chalin, P.: JML Reference Manual, Draft revision 1.193 (May 2006)
24. Robby: Bogor/Kiasan: Combining symbolic execution, model checking, and theorem proving. Presentation at European Science Foundation Exploratory Workshop on Challenges in Program Verification, University of Nijmegen (October 2006)
25. Stenzel, K.: Verification of Java Card Programs. PhD thesis, Fakultät für angewandte Informatik, University of Augsburg (2005)
26. Tillmann, N., Schulte, W.: Parameterized unit tests. In: Wermelinger, M., Gall, H. (eds.) Proc. 10th European Software Engineering Conference/13th ACM Intl. Symp. on Found. of Software Engineering, Lisbon, Portugal, pp. 253–262. ACM Press, New York (2005)
27. Visser, W., Pasareanu, C.S., Khurshid, S.: Test input generation with Java PathFinder. In: ISSTA '04: Proceedings of the 2004 ACM SIGSOFT international symposium on Software testing and analysis, pp. 97–107. ACM Press, New York, USA (2004)
28. Xie, T., Marinov, D., Schulte, W., Notkin, D.: Symstra: A framework for generating object-oriented unit tests using symbolic execution. In: Halbwachs, N., Zuck, L.D. (eds.) TACAS 2005. LNCS, vol. 3440, pp. 365–381. Springer, Heidelberg (2005)
29. Zhu, H., Hall, P.A.V., May, J.H.R.: Software unit test coverage and adequacy. ACM Comput. Surv. 29(4), 366–427 (1997)

Using Model Checking to Generate
Fault Detecting Tests

Angelo Gargantini

Department of Management and Information Technology
Università di Bergamo
angelo.gargantini@unibg.it

Abstract. We present a technique which generates from Abstract State Machines specifications a set of test sequences capable to uncover specific fault classes. The notion of *test goal* is introduced as a state predicate denoting the detection condition for a particular fault. Tests are generated by forcing a model checker to produce counter examples which cover the test goals. We introduce a technique for the evaluation of the fault detection capability of a test set. We report some experimental results which validate the method, compare the fault adequacy criteria with some classical structural coverage criteria and show an empirical cross coverage among faults.

Keywords: model based testing, fault based testing, Abstract State Machines, test.

1   Introduction

Specification-based testing aims to reduce the cost of testing and to increase the reliability of safety critical systems. One benefit of a formal method is that the high-quality specification it produces can play a valuable role in software testing. For example, the specification may be used to automatically construct a suite of test sequences. These test sequences can then be used to automatically check the implementation software for faults. However, specification-based testing is not widely adopted [35], while white box or program based testing is well known and used in practice: many tools support it and software developers and testers are familiar with it. In the wake of the success of program based testing, specification-based testing criteria that mimic the coverage criteria for programs have been proposed. They are generally called structural criteria because they analyse the structure of the specification and require the coverage of particular elements (like states, rules, conditions, and so on). Examples are the Modified Condition Decision Coverage (MCDC), one of the most powerful criteria used in practice, applied to Abstract State Machines [19] or the coverage of properties and assertions for a program given by using the Assertion Definition Language (ADL) as proposed by [10].

Since the aim of software testing is to demonstrate the existence of errors, selecting tests that can reveal faults is of paramount importance. The fault detection capability of structural criteria is not definitely assessed though. Recent works

B. Meyer and Y. Gurevich (Eds.): TAP 2007, LNCS 4454, pp. 189–206, 2007.

hypothesize some classes of faults and analyze the fault detection capability of most used criteria with respect to these classes of faults. The analysis can be formal [29,31,32,34] and/or empirical [39]. The main result is that many coverage criteria cannot assure the detection of several fault classes. For instance, MCDC is unable to detect faults due to missing brackets in boolean expressions. Stronger coverage criteria have been introduced (as in [29]) with the aim to detect more faults, but still the relationship between coverage criteria and faults is not well established and it is infeasible to evaluate the effectiveness of a test criterion in general [23]. For example, it can be shown "that the fact that criterion C_1 subsumes criterion C_2 does not guarantee that C_1 is better at detecting faults [17]".

Other papers define testing criteria focusing on certain classes of faults, which model commonly committed mistakes. For instance, Weyuker et al. [39] introduce the meaningful impact strategies for boolean expressions to target specifically the variable negation fault that occurs when a boolean variable is erroneously substituted by its negation. Chen and Lau develop three more powerful testing strategies capable to detect several fault classes [11]. These criteria specify also the algorithms (with some possible non determinism) which can be used for test generation. Within this framework, assessing the fault detection capability of a criterion with respect to other criteria is important, since one should choose one criterion and generate the tests from it in accordance with the expected faults, although experimental data show that resulting tests are generally effective for detecting faults in other classes. The introduction of a new fault class would require the definition of new criteria capable to detect it or the investigation (formal or empirical) of the capability of existing criteria to detect it.

In this paper we introduce a novel approach which specifically aims at detecting faults in an implementation given its specification. Specifications are Abstract State Machines which are explained briefly in Section 2. We assume (as [14]) that implementations contain only relatively simple faults (*competent programmer hypothesis*) of the kinds introduced in Section 3 and that a test set which detects all simple faults will detect more complex faults (*fault coupling effect*). Our approach could appear similar to the *mutation analysis* [8], but it does not require any mutation at all. Instead, we introduce in Section 4 the detection condition for a fault and define adequacy criteria in terms of these detection conditions. In Section 5 we present a method which uses the detection conditions to generate and to evaluate fault detecting tests. This method is based on the counter example generation of the model checker SPIN [24]. Our approach makes the introduction of a new fault class, the generation of tests detecting these faults, and the evaluation of other tests easy to realize. In Section 6 we discuss experimental results, some of which were unexpected. Related work is presented in Section 7.

2   Preliminaries

2.1   Abstract State Machines

Even if the Abstract State Machines (ASM) method comes with a rigorous scientific foundation [9], the practitioner needs no special training to use the ASM method since Abstract State Machines are a simple extension of Finite State Machines, obtained by replacing unstructured "internal" control states by states comprising arbitrarily complex data, and can be understood correctly as pseudo-code or Virtual Machines working over abstract data structures. A complete introduction on the ASM method can be found in [9], together with a presentation of the great variety of its successful application in different fields as: definition of industrial standards for programming and modelling languages, design and re-engineering of industrial control systems, modelling e-commerce and web services, design and analysis of protocols, architectural design, language design, verification of compilation schemes and compiler back-ends, etc. ASM theory is the basis of several languages and tools including the Abstract State Machine Language by Microsoft [6] and the AsmGofer [37].

An ASM *state* models a machine state, i.e. the collection of elements and objects the machine "knows", and the functions and predicates it uses to manipulate them. Mathematically, a *state* is defined as an algebraic structure, where data come as abstract objects, i.e. as elements of sets (also called *domains* or *universes*, one for each category of data) which are equipped with basic operations (partial *functions*) and *predicates* (attributes or relations).

In this paper we consider only *single agent basic ASMs*, whose behavior is specified by a finite sets of so-called *transition rules* of the form

$$R = \textbf{if } \varphi \textbf{ then } \textit{updates} \tag{1}$$

which model the actions performed by the machine to manipulate elements of its domains and which result in a new state. The guard φ under which a rule is applied is an arbitrary predicate logic formula without free variables, whose interpretation evaluates to true or false. *updates* is a finite set of assignments of the form $f(t_1, t_2, \ldots, t_n) := t$, whose execution is to be understood as changing (or defining, if there was none) in parallel the value of the occurring functions f at the indicated arguments $t_1, t_2, \ldots, t_n$ to the indicated value t. A update is not *trivial* if the value of $f(t_1, t_2, \ldots, t_n)$ had a value different from the value of t before the update.

A more general schema is the conditional rule of the form:

$$\textbf{if } \varphi \textbf{ then par } R1,..,Rn \textbf{ endpar else par } Q1,..,Qn \textbf{ endpar endif} \tag{2}$$

The meaning is: if φ is true then execute $R1,\ldots, Rn$ in parallel, otherwise execute $Q1 \ldots, Qn$. If $Q1,\ldots, Qn$ are omitted (since they are optional), from a semantic view it is assumed that the else part is equal to *skip*, which is the empty rule whose meaning is: do nothing.

2.2   Test Sequence

Adapting to ASMs some definitions common in literature for state transition systems [3,33], we define a *test sequence* or *test* as follows.

Definition 1. *A **test sequence** or **test** for an ASM $\mathcal{M}$ is a finite sequence of states (i) whose first element belongs to a set of initial states, (ii) each state follows the previous one by applying the transition rules of $\mathcal{M}$.*

A test sequence ends with a state, which might be not final, where the test goal is achieved. Informally, a test sequence is a partial ASM run and represents an expected system behavior.

Definition 1 assumes the use of ASM specification as test oracle, since states supply expected values of outputs. The importance of test oracles is well known, since the generation of the sole inputs (often called *test data*) does rise the problem of how to evaluate the correctness of the observed system behavior.

We define a collection of test sequences as follows.

Definition 2. *A* **test set** *or* **test suite** *is a finite set of test sequences.*

Given a predicate P over an ASM state we say that a test sequence t covers P, if t contains a state such that P is true in that state.

2.3   Structural Coverage Criteria for ASMs

We summarize the following coverage criteria, originally presented in [19]. They are compared in Section 3 with the new fault based coverage criteria.

Basic rule (BR). coverage requires that for every guard (decision) there exists a test which covers the case when the decision is taken (the guard is evaluated true at least in one state belonging to a test sequence) and when the decision is not taken (the guard is evaluated false).

MCDC. requires the classical modified condition decision coverage in the masking form [12] to every guard in the ASM.

Complete rule (CR). coverage requires that for every rule, its guard is evaluated true at least once and at least one update in the rules is not trivial.

Update. coverage (UC) requires that for every update (in every rule) there exist a test sequence in which the update is applied and is not trivial.

BR and MCDC can be classified as (model-based) *control oriented* coverage criteria [40] as they consider only the control flow of the model, while CR and UC can be classified as data flow coverage criteria, since they consider the value of variable before its assignment to a possibly new value (this kind of an update can be considered a new *definition*). Note that MCDC implies BR and UC implies CR.

3   Fault Classes

While test coverage criteria like the CR and UC, presented in Section 2.3, aim to detect faults in updates, in this paper we focus only on faults which may occur in the guards of the ASM specification under test. Note that a *fault* in a implementation is a cause that results in a failure [27], which is an erroneous evaluation of a guard in the implementation in our approach. We consider only faults originated by typical programmer mistakes like use of incorrect control predicates, missing conditions, and the incorrect use or order of boolean and relational operators in rule guards. These types of mistakes result in faults that regard the conditions and their operators, where with *condition* we intend atomic boolean expressions which cannot be further decomposed in simpler boolean expressions. A condition can be a boolean variable, like `overridden`, or a relational expression like `pressure > TooLow`. We exclude faults inside conditions except the incorrect use of relational operators (for instance the use of $>$ instead of $<$). We follow the notation proposed in [32]: a *literal*[1] is an occurrence of a condition inside a guard (note that a condition or a boolean variable may occur several times in the same guard). While many papers [31,38,32] assume that the boolean expressions are given in disjunctive normal form (DNF), we remove such restriction (as in [34]). We study the following fault classes:

– Operand faults (i.e. regarding the literals or sub expressions):

LNF. *Literal negation fault* An occurrence of a condition (i.e. one literals) is replaced by its negation. For example, from $a \wedge b \wedge (a \vee b)$ we obtain the following four faulty expressions: $\neg a \wedge b \wedge (a \vee b)$, $a \wedge \neg b \wedge (a \vee b)$, $a \wedge b \wedge (\neg a \vee b)$, and $a \wedge b \wedge (a \vee \neg b)$

ENF. *Expression negation fault* It consists of replacing a sub expression (but not a condition or literal) with its negation. For example, from $a \wedge b \wedge (a \vee b)^2$ we obtain the following three faulty expressions: $\neg (a \wedge b \wedge (a \vee b))$, $\neg (a \wedge b) \wedge (a \vee b)$, and $a \wedge b \wedge \neg (a \vee b)$

MLF. *Missing literal fault* It causes the absence of one literal or condition in the formula. If the same condition occurs several times in the formula, we introduce several faults and not just one. For example, from $a \wedge b \wedge (a \vee b)$, we obtain the following four faulty expressions: $b \wedge (a \vee b)$, $a \wedge (a \vee b)$, $a \wedge b \wedge b$, and $a \wedge b \wedge a$.

ST0/1. *Stuck at 0/at 1 fault* This is a classical hardware fault, which consists in replacing an input with 0 or with 1. In our case, it causes a replacement of a literal by *false* (ST0) or *true* (ST1). For example, from $a \wedge b \wedge (a \vee b)$, we obtain for the ST0 the following four faulty expressions: *false* $\wedge b \wedge (a \vee b)$, $a \wedge$ *false* $\wedge (a \vee b)$, $a \wedge b \wedge ($*false* $\vee b)$, and $a \wedge b \wedge (a \vee$ *false*$)$. ST0U1 denotes the union of ST0 and ST1, i.e. the replacement of a literal by false and true.

– Boolean Operator faults:

ASF. *Associative Shift fault* This fault is due to the misunderstanding about operator evaluation priorities and missing brackets. For example from $a \wedge b \wedge (a \vee b)$ we would obtain by deleting the brackets $(a \wedge b \wedge a) \vee b$.

ORF. *Operator Reference fault* $'\wedge'$ is replaced by $'\vee'$ and vice-versa. $a \wedge b \wedge (a \vee b)$ would be implemented as $a \wedge b \vee (a \vee b)$, $(a \vee b) \wedge (a \vee b)$, and $a \wedge b \wedge (a \wedge b)$.

---

[1] A literal is sometimes called *clause* as in [34], a condition is often called *variable* especially in papers dealing with boolean specifications [32,31,38].

[2] We assume that logical binary operators are left associative, hence $a \wedge b \wedge (a \vee b)$ must be read as $(a \wedge b) \wedge (a \vee b)$.

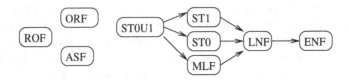

Fig. 1. Boolean fault hierarchy

Furthermore we add the following fault class, which introduces faults in relational expressions with pattern $E\ op\ F$, where E and F are either arithmetic expressions or expressions of enumerative type and op is one of $<$, $\leq$, $=$, $>$, $\geq$, and $\neq$.

ROF. *Relational Operator Fault* Replace a relational operator by any other relational operator (note that replacing an operator with its opposite is equal to LNF). If the expression is an enumeration, then replace only $=$ with $\neq$ and vice-versa (we allow only "equals" and "differs" comparison between two enumerative values). For example, from $x \leq c$ one would obtain the following faulty expressions: $x > c$, $x \geq c$, $x = c$, $x \neq c$, and $x < c$.

We have chosen LNF, ENF, MLF, ASF, and ORF because they are the most studied faults in the literature [31,38,32]. ST0/1 faults are commonly considered a realistic model of manufacturing faults in hardware circuit testing. ROF is introduced and studied in [34] (called Relational Operator Reference Fault) and models a typical software fault. Faults of omission (modeled by the MLF class) are known to be very common, constituting approximately half of the bug reports posted on Usenet [31]. In a recent realistic case, Dupuy and Leveson examined an attitude control software for the HETE-2 (High Energy Transient Explorer) scientific satellite and uncovered an important operator reference fault (ORF) which replaced an AND operator by an OR [15].

The hierarchy among fault classes for boolean expressions have been intensively studied. For instance, empirical work [39] showed that tests generated to detect variable negation fault (our LNF) always detected expression negation faults. Kuhn proposed a rigorous approach to formally prove the existence of a hierarchy among faults in boolean specifications given in normal form [31]. The initial hierarchy proposed by Kuhn was first enriched by [38] and then by [32]. Okun et alt. [34] developed a novel analytic technique to find the hierarchy among faults of arbitrary boolean expressions, not just those in disjunctive normal form. According to the results presented in the literature, the hierarchy among the fault classes used in this paper is presented in Figure 1, where $C_1 \rightarrow C_2$ means that every test suite able to detect C_1 detects C_2 as well. In this case, we say that C_1 is *stronger* than C_2.

Note that a pair of fault classes C_1 and C_2 is proved to be independent in the hierarchy when there exists a test suite which guarantees to detect faults of C_1 but not those of C_2 and vice-versa. In our case, ORF, ROF, and ASF are independent of each other and with all the other fault classes, and MLF, ST0, and ST1 are independent of each other. This fact has practical consequences:

since a test set T_1 which detects a fault C_1 does not guarantee to detect C_2 and vice-versa, one should generate a test suite for C_1 and a test suite for C_2. Therefore, one should generate a test suite for every independent fault class. However, T_1 may detect C_2 as well for the particular specification under test and the generation for C_2 may be skipped. To assess the actual fault detection capability of a test suite, we introduce in Section 5.1 a method to evaluate tests with respect to possible faults in the specification under test and regardless of the way such tests have been generated.

4   Discovering Faults

The erroneous implementation of a boolean expression φ as φ' can be discovered only when the expression $\varphi \oplus \varphi'$, called *detection condition*, evaluates to true, where $\oplus$ denotes the logical *exclusive or* operator. Indeed, $\varphi \oplus \varphi'$ is true only if φ' evaluates to a different value than the correct predicate φ. The detection condition is also called *boolean difference* or *derivative* [1].

Consider a simple rule R of an ASM specification $\mathcal{M}$:

R = **if** φ **then** *updates*

Let $\mathcal{M}'$ be the faulty implementation of $\mathcal{M}$. Assume that the guard φ of R in $\mathcal{M}$ is erroneously implemented as φ' in $\mathcal{M}'$ due to the fault F, and that rule *updates* are not all trivial. F can be detected during testing only if there exists a test sequence t containing a state s in which $\varphi \oplus \varphi'$ is evaluated to true, i.e. φ and φ' have different values in s for $\mathcal{M}$ and $\mathcal{M}'$. In this case, when we apply t, the rule R fires in $\mathcal{M}$ and performs its updates but it does not fire in $\mathcal{M}'$ or vice-versa. The predicate $\varphi \oplus \varphi'$ is the detection condition of F and it is called *test predicate* or test goal. For example, if the guard $x \leq c$ in the specification is implemented as $x < c$, then the test goal is $x \leq c \oplus x < c$ which is equivalent to $x = c$. Only a test sequence containing a state s in which $x = c$ can uncover the fault.

Let φ be a guard and C be a fault class. We denote with $F_C(\varphi)$ the set of all the possible faulty implementations of φ according to the fault class C (as explained in Section 3). The test predicates to discover the fault C in φ are the expressions $\varphi \oplus \varphi'$ with φ' in $F_C(\varphi)$. For example, if the guard is $a \wedge b$ and C is the MLF, then $F_{MLF}(a \wedge b) = \{a, b\}$ and the test predicates are the following two expressions: $(a \wedge b) \oplus a$ (which is $a \wedge \neg b$) and $(a \wedge b) \oplus b$ (which is $\neg a \wedge b$).

In case of a nested rule of kind (2), test predicates must include the guards of outer rules. Let φ be the guard of an inner rule R and $g_1, \ldots, g_n$ be the guards of the outer rules or their negation (in case of else) such that if $g_1 \wedge \ldots \wedge g_n$ holds, then R is executed (and its updates fired if φ is true). We call $g_1, \ldots, g_n$ *outer guards* of R. The test predicates to discover the fault C in φ are the expressions $g_1 \wedge \ldots \wedge g_n \wedge (\varphi \oplus \varphi')$ with φ' in $F_C(\varphi)$.

Definition 3. *Test Predicates.* *Let R be a rule in an ASM $\mathcal{M}$, φ be its guard, $g_1, \ldots, g_n$ be the outer guards of R, and C be a fault class. The set $\Gamma_C(R)$ of test predicates is given by the expressions $g_1 \wedge \ldots \wedge g_n \wedge (\varphi \oplus \varphi')$ with φ' in $F_C(\varphi)$.*

A test suite is adequate to test the guard φ of a rule R with respect to a fault class C if it covers every test predicate generated for R and C:

Definition 4. *Fault Detecting Adequacy Criteria.* *A test suite T is adequate with respect to the fault class C and the ASM M, if for every rule R of M and for every test predicate tp in $\Gamma_C(R)$ there exists a state s in a test sequence of T such that the test predicate tp evaluates to true in s.*

5   Generation of Tests

To automatically generate the test sequences which cover a set of test predicates, we exploit the capability of the model checker Spin [24] to produce counter examples. Model checkers have been successfully applied to formal verification of properties, normally given in temporal logic, for systems modeled by means of automata. They automatically perform the proof of a desired property p by analyzing every possible system behavior, checking that p is true, and producing a counter example in case the property p does not hold in the model. The counter example is a possible system behavior that shows a case where the property p is falsified.

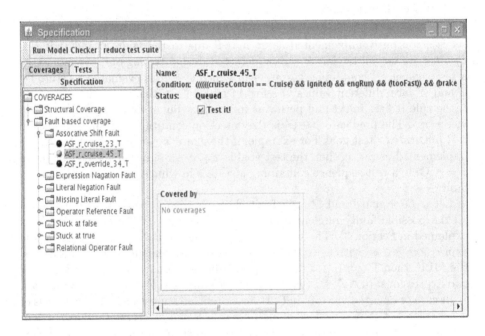

Fig. 2. An ATGT screen-shot

The method presented in this section has been implemented in a prototype tool ATGT[3] - a screen-shot is reported in Fig. 2 - and consists in the following steps as illustrated in Figure 3.

---

[3] Available at http://cs.unibg.it/gargantini/projects/atgt/

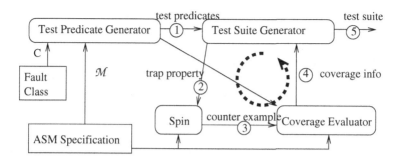

Fig. 3. Steps in the proposed generation method

- First, denoted by ①, a *Test Predicate Generator* computes the test predicate set $\Gamma_C = \{tp_i\}$ for the desired fault classes C introduced in Section 3 and for all the rule guards in the ASM specification under test given in the syntax of the AsmGofer [37].

- Second ②, the *Test Suite Generator* selects a test predicate tp_i, either randomly or according to the user request, and computes the *trap property* stating that tp_i is never true, i.e. p = **never**(tp_i) which is translated in PROMELA, the language of Spin, as the statement `assert(!tp_i)`. The trap property p is not a desired property of the system; on the contrary, we look for a system behavior which falsifies p, i.e. where tp_i becomes true. This method has been introduced in [18,20].

- Third ③, the model checker is used to find the test sequence, by encoding the ASM specification in PROMELA, following the algorithms described in [20] and trying to prove the trap property p. If the model checker finds that p is false, i.e. a state where the tp_i is true, it stops and prints as counter example the state sequence leading to that state (plus the updates generated by the last update). This sequence represents the test that covers tp_i.

- Fourth ④, the *Coverage Evaluator* reads the counter example to produce the actual test sequence and to evaluate its coverage as explained in the following section against all the test predicates generated in the first step and provides the coverage information back to the Test Suite Generator.

- The process is iterated starting from the second step for each test predicate that has not been already covered. In the end, ⑤, a complete test suite is generated, except for the cases where the model checker fails to find a counter example as explained in Section 5.2.

5.1   Evaluating the Fault Coverage

A test sequence that is generated to cover a particular test predicate likely covers also many other test predicates, i.e. it contains a state where other test predicates are true and it can, therefore, discover other faults as well. Finding which predicates are covered can reduce the time and the resources to obtain a complete test suite - because we can decide to skip the generation of tests for test predicates already covered - and it can reduce the size of the test suite - because we could decide to discard a test if the test predicates that it covers are covered also by other tests -.

To evaluate the coverage for a test, we give an unique identification (ID) to each test predicate and we add in the PROMELA file an instruction which prints a particular message if the test predicate is covered. For example, we introduce for the test predicate $(a \wedge b) \oplus a$ with identification tc_*ID* the following statement:

```
printf("_Covered: tc_ID %d \n",((a || b ) ^ a));
```

This instruction will print the ID for the test predicate followed by 1 or 0 whether the test predicate has been covered or not. The printf instruction is actually computed only during the last phase (④) and it does not complicate the model nor introduces new state variables since it is ignored during phase ③.

The proposed method for test evaluation can be used to evaluate any test sequence, regardless the way it has been generated. As we show in Section 6, we use this technique to get valuable insights over the fault detection capability of the structural coverage criteria presented in Section 2.3.

5.2   Undetectable Faults

When the model checker terminates, one of the following three situations occurs. The best case occurs when the model checker stops finding that the trap property is false, and, therefore, the counter example that covers the test predicate is generated.

The second case happens when the model checker checks every possible behavior without finding any state where the trap property is false, and, therefore, it actually proves the trap property $\mathbf{never}(tp_i)$. A test predicate, in our case, has always the pattern $A \wedge \varphi \oplus \varphi'$ (where A is a conjunction of outer guards), and $\mathbf{never}(A \wedge \varphi \oplus \varphi')$ is equivalent to $\mathbf{always}(A \to \neg(\varphi \oplus \varphi'))$, i.e. $\mathbf{always}(A \to (\varphi \leftrightarrow \varphi'))$. Therefore, SPIN proves that when A holds, φ is always equivalent to its mutation φ' and that the fault does not introduce an actual change in the behavior of the system. In this case we say that such a fault is undetectable and we can safely ignore tp_i and simply warn the user that its model is insensitive in that rule guard to that fault.

In the third case, the model checker terminates because it finishes the maximum time or memory allocated for the search (set by the user or decided by model checker itself) but without completing the state space search and without finding a violation of the trap property, and, therefore, without producing any counter example (generally because of the state explosion problem). In this case, we do not know if either the trap property is true (i.e., the fault cannot be discovered) but too difficult to prove, or it is false but a counter example is too hard to find (i.e. the fault could be discovered if an appropriate test sequence could be found). When this case happens, our method simply warns the tester that the test predicate has not been covered, but it might be feasible.

Model Checking Limits. Model checking applies only to finite models. Therefore, our method works for ASM specifications having variables and functions with finite domains. The problem of abstracting models with finite domains from models with infinite domains such that some behaviors are preserved, is under investigation. Moreover, since model checkers perform an exhaustive state space (possibly symbolic) exploration, they fail when the state space becomes too big and intractable. This problem is known as *state explosion problem* and represents the major limitation in using model checkers. Note, however, that we use the model checker not as a prover of properties we expect to be true, but to find counter examples for trap properties we expect to be false. Therefore, our method does generally require a limited search in the state space and not an exhaustive state exploration. However, undetectable faults require a complete state search.

Model Checking Benefits. Besides its limits, model checking offers several benefits. For instance, SPIN adopts sophisticated techniques to compute and explore the state space, and to find property violations. It represents a state and the state space in a very efficient way using state enumeration, hashing techniques, and state compression methods. Moreover, SPIN explores the state space using practical heuristics and other techniques like partial order reduction methods and on-the-fly state exploration based on a nested depth first search. For these reasons, we have preferred existing model checkers instead of developing our own tools and algorithms for state space exploration. Moreover, the complete automaticity of model checkers allows to compute test sequences from ASM specifications without any human interaction.

6   Experiments

We report the result of applying our method to two case studies, the Cruise Control (CC) specification [32,5] and a simple model for a Safety Injection System (SIS) of a nuclear plant [13,19,18]. The CC has one monitored (i.e. modified only by the environment) enumerative variable, 4 monitored boolean variables and one controlled (i.e. modified only by the system) variable. It has 9 rules with rather complex boolean expressions as guards, which admit numerous boolean operator faults. The SIS includes three monitored variables (one integer in the interval [0,2000] and two switches), two internal variables (a boolean and an enumerative) and an output (boolean). It has 7 transition rules with guards which contain several relational operators and hence admit numerous ROFs. The number of test predicates is shown in Table 1. Note that 20 test predicates in the CC for the ROF were proved unfeasible by the model checker, which completed the search without finding any violation of the trap property, therefore actually proving that the faults are undetectable as explained in the second case of Section 5.2.

6.1   Generation of Tests

We have applied three strategies for test generation. In strategy 1 and 2 we use the breath first search (BFS) algorithm of Spin, which normally requires more time and memory than the default nested depth first search (nDFS) algorithm, but it guarantees that the shortest counter example is found. In strategy 3 we use

Table 1. Test Predicates and Tests for SIS and CC

#tp	ENF	LNF	MLF	ASF	ORF	ST0	ST1	ROF	/unfeasible
for SIS	9	16	16	1	9	23	24	32	0
for CC	24	33	33	3	24	54	54	33	20

Table 2. Runs for test generation

strategy	#runs	time (sec)	#test	#states
1 - BFS, weak to strong	59	116	22	635
2 - BFS, strong to weak	59	102	22	637
3 - DFS, strong to weak	42	258	8	11760

the nDFS which is faster but finds long counter examples. Furthermore, in the first strategy we start from weaker fault classes and then we increase the fault detection capability of the tests by choosing stronger faults, while in the second and third strategy we start from strong coverage classes. Results are shown in Table 2, in which we report the number of runs, the total time required[4], the number of tests (some tests are discarded because they cover only test predicates covered by other test sequences in the test suite), and the total number of states in the test sequences.

Although several papers [31,32,28] suggest that hierarchical information about fault classes can be useful during test generation and that starting the test generation from the strongest coverage would require less time and fewer test cases than starting from the weakest coverage, we found no evidence of this fact. Indeed, strategy 2 (strong to weak) performed as well as strategy 1 (weak to strong). This result can be explained by considering that our method is iterative (it produces a test sequence at a time) and that we perform test evaluation at the end of every cycle. If the criterion S is stronger than the criterion W, any test set T_S adequate according to S includes any set of test T_W adequate according to W. The test generation starting from S produces a test suite T_S, whose evaluation stops the test generation because T_S covers W as well. The test generation starting from W initially produces T_W which still requires the generation of $T_S - T_W$ and not of the complete T_S. In both cases the number of test cases is the same (except for some non determinism in the generation and in the optimization of the test suites). However, our examples are too small to draw the definitive conclusion that hierarchical information about fault classes are useless during test generation.

Another unexpected result was that the test generation with the DFS algorithm performed worse than the others, although the DFS proved to be more efficient per visited state than the others: it explored around 11760 states (18 times more then the others) but it took only about twice as much time. By analyzing the runs, we found that the sole model checker execution (step ③ in Fig. 3) actually took

---

[4] We have used a PC with an AMD Athlon 3400+ and 1 GB of RAM.

Table 3. Structural vs fault coverage (in %)

	BR	MCDC	CR	UC
ENF	66	41	0	26
LNF	91	67	50	63
MLF	94	82	50	74
ASF	59	20	0	11
ORF	78	52	0	42
ST0	100	76	100	84
ST1	94	73	50	68
ST0U1	100	84	100	84
ROF	78	53	50	42

	#tp	ENF	LNF	MLF	ASF	ORF	ST0	ST1	ROF
BR	32	100	96	63	0	88	90	79	58
MCDC	98	100	100	100	75	100	100	100	65
CR	2	27	29	20	0	27	19	24	37
UC	19	100	96	67	25	88	91	81	58

↑(b) Fault detection capability of structural coverage

←(a) Structural coverage of fault criteria

less time than the same step in other strategies, but the other steps which analyze the results to evaluate the coverage took much more time, since the DFS produces very long counter examples. We believe that strategy 3 may perform better than the others for complex specifications, since in complex cases the model checker execution is the most critical step in the proposed test generation method. Moreover, strategy 3 is useful when one prefers very few test cases (for example if resetting the system is expensive) and because long test sequences may discover more faults (like extra states) [33,22].

6.2   Comparison with Structural Coverage Criteria

We have compared our new fault based adequacy criteria and the structural criteria presented in Section 2.3. Tests for structural criteria are generated following the technique introduced in [19,20]. Table 3 (a) reports the structural coverage of tests generated to cover faults. The ST0U1 has covered most structural parts in our specification, but not all. No fault based test set has been able to achieve the complete MCDC and Update Rule Coverage. Table 3 (b) reports the fault detection capability of tests generated by using the structural criteria. MCDC performed better then the others, but no structural coverage has been able to achieve the ASF and ROF criteria. These data suggest that fault based criteria and structural criteria are complementary to each other.

6.3   Cross Coverage Among Fault Classes

We have also analyzed the *cross coverage* among the fault based criteria and results are reported in Table 4, which must be read as follows. The tests generated for a fault class in a row (cross) covers also the shown percentage of the test predicates for other fault classes displayed in the columns. Besides the confirmation of the theory (continuous arrows in the figure of Table 4), we have found some empirical relationships among fault classes (dotted arrows in the figure). For instance, ROF covered all the ENFs, ORF covered all the ENFs, and LNF covered all ORFs. MLF seems stronger than ST1 and ST0 individually, and ROF

Table 4. Cross Coverage (%)

	ENF	LNF	MLF	ASF	ORF	ST0	ST1	ROF
ENF	-	78	41	*0*	85	53	63	32
LNF	*100*	-	73	25	*100*	79	94	63
MLF	*100*	*100*	-	75	*100*	94	95	63
ASF	82	33	31	-	67	10	53	34
ORF	*100*	90	57	*0*	-	65	72	49
ST0	*100*	*100*	84	25	*100*	-	87	62
ST1	*100*	*100*	82	50	*100*	82	-	63
ST0U1	*100*	*100*	*100*	75	*100*	-	-	65
ROF	*100*	96	59	25	97	64	81	20

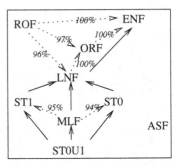

seems stronger than LNF and ORF. Although this empirical extended hierarchy may not hold in general, we believe that for most boolean expressions these relationships are likely to be true. This information may be useful in practice if one has a test suite that targets a specific fault and want to approximately judge the test suite's fault detection capability. We found that ASF is really complementary with respect all other criteria.

7   Related Work

Many papers tackle the problem of tests generation or selection. The subject of using model checkers for test generation starting from models has been studied for many years. For a (not so recent) survey see [2]. In [16] the authors used Spin to generate test sequences for a protocol augmented by a test predicate, called test purpose, written by the designer by hand. Classical control oriented tests generation is presented for SCR in [18] and for ASMs in [19]. Several recent papers apply the same concepts to UML state diagrams [30], to StateCharts [26], and to Stateflow [21] specifications. [36] presents state coverage, decision coverage and MCDC (not masked) for specifications written in RSML^{-e}. They all share the same approach. They introduce some control oriented coverage, derive the test predicate from decision points in the model and then use the model checker to obtain the test sequences.

A first attempt to introduce data flow oriented coverage criteria can be found in [19] where the rule update criterion (presented in Section 2.3) covers the real update of a variable. A novel approach is presented in [25], which shows how the classical data flow coverage criteria can be translated in terms of the Computation Tree Logic (CTL).

The combined use of model checking and mutation testing is presented in [3,8]. Their approach, that we could classify as fault oriented [40], is very similar to ours, but the technique is completely different. Differently from us, they do not use test predicates derived from the specifications by using the boolean difference. Instead, they directly apply mutation techniques to models. The original specification, written for the model checker SMV, is initially augmented by many temporal logic properties (*constraints*) that represent the correct behavior. In the extraction of these properties (also called *expounding*) there are several "subtle issues that require attention [4]" and may reduce the fault detection capability of the tests. Afterwards, the specification or the constraints are repeatedly modified applying mutation operators (more general than our fault classes), that introduce faults in the models or in the constraints. Counter examples are automatically generated by SMV either (*approach 1*) trying to prove the original properties in faulty models to obtain wrong behaviors that implementations must not exhibit or (*approach 2*) proving mutated properties for the correct model to obtain tests sequences that discover particular faults (or *kill* mutants).

We can compare their approach 2 with ours as follows. In the extraction of constraints, they build a set of safety properties which are always true in the original model. Given a safety property **always**(P), they look for a counter example by trying to prove **always**(P') where P' is a possible mutation of P. If a counter example is found, they have found a state where the mutated property is false, i.e. $\neg P'$. They actually find a state where P is true (safety property) while P' is false, i.e. $P \wedge \neg P'$, which is a particular case of $P \oplus P'$, the boolean difference of P. Our approach does not require the extraction of safety properties, since test conditions are defined as boolean differences over guards, which are not always true.

Ammann et alt. tackle also the problem of evaluation of test sequences against specification-based coverage criteria [4]. They show how the model checker SMV can be used to evaluate a test sequence with respect to the capability to discover (or *kill*) mutations of the original specification. The test sequence (regardless the way it has been generated) is transformed in a SMV model to run together with the mutated specification. This requires a run for every test and every mutation, rising the problem how to reduce (*winnow*) the number of mutations really necessary to evaluate the coverage of a test. Tests which kill a subset of mutations of other tests, can be discarded. In our approach, we can evaluate the capability of a test sequence to detect all faults in one run by using test conditions. Furthermore we are able not only to discard duplicated test cases, but also to avoid the generation of tests for test predicates already covered.

Model checkers can be used to generate tests in program based testing too: the model checker BLAST is used in [7] to generate test suites and to detect dead code in C programs.

8   Conclusions and Future Work

Although we have shown how to generate tests to detect several fault classes, we plan to introduce other fault classes, possibly involving not only boolean expressions but also integers (like off-by 1 fault or at the boundaries faults). Moreover, while this paper focuses on faults in the rule guards, we plan to define other fault classes involving the rule updates. Our method has been applied to the generation and evaluation of tests for several case studies, but more experiments with real specifications are needed to assess its real applicability. Abstract State

Machines are chosen as formal method, but our approach can be easily adapted to any formalism based on guarded state transitions. We have discovered that the hierarchy among faults is useless in the prioritization during test generation, but further experiments and theoretical research is needed to definitely prove that.

References

1. Akers, S.B.: On a theory of boolean functions. Journal Society Industrial Applied Mathematics 7(4), 487–498 (1959)
2. Ammann, P., Black, P.E., Ding, W.: Model checkers in software testing. Technical Report NIST-IR 6777, National Institute of Standards and Technology (2002)
3. Ammann, P., Black, P.E., Majurski, W.: Using model checking to generate tests from specifications. In: ICFEM'98. 2nd IEEE International Conference on Formal Engineering Methods, Brisbane, Australia, December 1998, p. 46. IEEE Computer Society Press, Los Alamitos (1998)
4. Ammann, P.E., Black, P.E.: A specification-based coverage metric to evaluate test sets. International Journal of Reliability, Quality and Safety Engineering 8(4), 275–300 (2001)
5. Atlee, J.M., Buckley, M.A.: A logic-model semantics for SCR software requirements. In: ISSTA '96. Proceedings of the 1996 ACM SIGSOFT international symposium on Software testing and analysis, pp. 280–292. ACM Press, New York, USA (1996)
6. Barnett, M., Schulte, W.: The ABCs of specification: AsmL, behavior, and components. Informatica 25(4), 517–526 (2001)
7. Beyer, D., Chlipala, A.J., Henzinger, T., Jhala, R., Majumdar, R.: Generating tests from counterexamples. In: Proc. International Conference on Software Engineering (ICSE), Edinburgh, May 2004, pp. 326–335. IEEE CS Press, Los Alamitos (2004)
8. Black, P.E., Okun, V., Yesha, Y.: Mutation of model checker specifications for test generation and evaluation. In: Wong, W.E. (ed.) Mutation Testing for the New Century, proc. of Mutation 2000, October 2000, pp. 14–20. Kluwer Academic Publishers, Dordrecht (2000)
9. Börger, E., Stärk, R.: Abstract State Machines: A Method for High-Level System Design and Analysis. Springer, Heidelberg (2003)
10. Chang, J., Richardson, D.J.: Structural specification-based testing: Automated support and experimental evaluation. In: Nierstrasz, O., Lemoine, M. (eds.) Software Engineering - ESEC/FSE '99. LNCS, vol. 1687, pp. 285–302. Springer, Heidelberg (1999)
11. Chen, T.Y., Lau, M.F.: Test case selection strategies based on boolean specifications. Softw. Test., Verif. Reliab. 11(3), 165–180 (2001)
12. Chilenski, J., Richey, L.A.: Definition for a masking form of modified condition decision coverage (mcdc). Technical report, Boeing, Seattle WA (1997)
13. Courtois, P.-J., Parnas, D.L.: Documentation for safety critical software. In: Proc. 15th Int'l Conf. on Softw. Eng. (ICSE '93), Baltimore, MD, pp. 315–323 (1993)
14. DeMillo, R.A., Guindi, D.S., King, K.N., McCracken, W.M., Offutt, A.J.: An extended overview of the Mothra software testing environment. In: Proceedings of the Second Workshop on Testing, Analysis, and Verification, pp. 142–151. IEEE Computer Society Press, Los Alamitos (1988)

15. Dupuy, A., Leveson, N.: An empirical evaluation of the mc/dc coverage criterion on the hete-2 satellite software. In: The 19th Digital Avionics Systems Conferences. Proceedings DASC (2000)
16. Engels, A., Feijs, L., Mauw, S.: Test generation for intelligent networks using model checking. In: Brinksma, E. (ed.) TACAS 1997. LNCS, vol. 1217, pp. 384–398. Springer, Heidelberg (1997)
17. Frankl, P.G., Weyuker, E.J.: A formal analysis of the fault-detecting ability of testing methods. IEEE Transactions on Software Engineering 19(3), 202–213 (1993)
18. Gargantini, A., Heitmeyer, C.: Using model checking to generate tests from requirements specifications. In: Nierstrasz, O., Lemoine, M. (eds.) Software Engineering - ESEC/FSE '99. LNCS, vol. 1687, pp. 6–10. Springer, Heidelberg (1999)
19. Gargantini, A., Riccobene, E.: ASM-based testing: Coverage criteria and automatic test sequence generation. Journal of Universal Computer Science 7(11), 1050–1067 (2001)
20. Gargantini, A., Riccobene, E., Rinzivillo, S.: Using Spin to generate tests from ASM specifications. In: Börger, E., Gargantini, A., Riccobene, E. (eds.) ASM 2003. LNCS, vol. 2589, pp. 263–277. Springer, Heidelberg (2003)
21. Hamon, G., de Moura, L.M., Rushby, J.M.: Generating efficient test sets with a model checker. In: SEFM 2004. 2nd International Conference on Software Engineering and Formal Methods, Beijing, China, September 28-30, 2004, pp. 261–270 (2004)
22. Heimdahl, M.P., George, D.: Test-suite reduction for model based tests: Effects on test quality and implications for testing. In: Automated Software Engineering, Linz, Austria (September 2004)
23. Hierons, R.M.: Comparing test sets and criteria in the presence of test hypotheses and fault domains. ACM Trans. Softw. Eng. Methodol. 11(4), 427–448 (2002)
24. Holzmann, G.J.: The model checker SPIN. IEEE Transactions on Software Engineering 23(5), 279–295 (1997)
25. Hong, H.S., Cha, S.D., Lee, I., Sokolsky, O., Ural, H.: Data flow testing as model checking. In: ICSE'03, Portland, Oregon, (May 3-10, 2003)
26. Hong, H.S., Lee, I., Sokolsky, O., Cha, S.D.: Automatic test generation from statecharts using model checking. In: Proceedings of FATES'01, Workshop on Formal Approaches to Testing of Software, August 2001. BRICS Notes Series, vol. NS-01-4, pp. 15–30 (2001)
27. IEEE: IEEE Standard Glossary of Software Engineering Terminology. Institute of Electrical and Electronics Engineers, 610.12
28. Kapoor, K., Bowen, J.P.: Ordering mutants to minimise test effort in mutation testing. In: Grabowski, J., Nielsen, B. (eds.) FATES 2004. LNCS, vol. 3395, pp. 195–209. Springer, Heidelberg (2005)
29. Kapoor, K., Bowen, J.P.: A formal analysis of MCDC and RCDC test criteria. Softw. Test. Verif. Reliab. 15(1), 21–40 (2005)
30. Kim, Y.G., Hong, H.S., Cho, S.M., Bae, D.H., Cha, S.D.: Test cases generation from UML state diagrams. IEE Proceedings - Software 146(4), 187–192 (1999)
31. Kuhn, D.R.: Fault classes and error detection capability of specification-based testing. ACM Transactions on Software Engineering and Methodology 8(4), 411–424 (1999)
32. Lau, M.F., Yu, Y.-T.: An extended fault class hierarchy for specification-based testing. ACM Trans. Softw. Eng. Methodol. 14(3), 247–276 (2005)
33. Lee, D., Yannakakis, M.: Principles and methods of testing finite state machines - A survey (Published as Proceedings of The IEEE 84(8)). In: Proceedings of The

IEEE, August 1996, pp. 1090–1123. IEEE Computer Society Press, Los Alamitos (1996)

34. Okun, V., Black, P.E., Yesha, Y.: Comparison of fault classes in specification-based testing. Information and Software Technology 46, 525–533 (2004)

35. Pretschner, A.: Model-based testing in practice. In: Fitzgerald, J.A., Hayes, I.J., Tarlecki, A. (eds.) FM 2005. LNCS, vol. 3582, pp. 537–541. Springer, Heidelberg (2005)

36. Rayadurgam, S., Heimdahl, M.P.: Generating MC/DC adequate test sequences through model checking. In: 28th Annual NASA Goddard Software Engineering Workshop (SEW 03) (2003)

37. Schimd, J.: Executing ASM specifications with AsmGofer, http://www.tydo.de/AsmGofer

38. Tsuchiya, T., Kikuno, T.: On fault classes and error detection capability of specification-based testing. ACM Trans. Softw. Eng. Methodol. 11(1), 58–62 (2002)

39. Weyuker, E., Goradia, T., Singh, A.: Automatically generating test data from a Boolean specification. IEEE Transactions on Software Engineering 20(5), 353–363 (1994)

40. Zhu, H., Hall, P., May, J.: Software unit test coverage and adequacy. ACM Computing Surveys 29(4), 366–427 (1997)

White-Box Testing by Combining Deduction-Based Specification Extraction and Black-Box Testing

Bernhard Beckert and Christoph Gladisch

University of Koblenz-Landau, Dept. of Computer Science
beckert@uni-koblenz.de, gladisch@uni-koblenz.de

Abstract. We propose to use deductive program verification systems to generate specifications for given programs and to then use these specifications as input for black-box testing tools. In this way, (1) the black-box testing method can make use of information about the program's structure that is contained in the specification, and (2) we get a separation of concerns and a clear interface between program analysis on the one hand and test-case generation and execution on the other hand, which allows the combination of a wide range of tools.

The method for specification extraction using a program verification calculus described in this paper has been successfully implemented in the KeY program verification system.

1 Introduction

Overview. We propose to use deductive program verification systems to generate specifications for given programs and to then use these specifications as input for black-box testing tools (e.g. [17,13,14]). Thus, (1) the black-box testing method can make use of information about the program's structure that is contained in the specification, and (2) we separate concerns and get a clear interface between program analysis on the one hand and test-case generation and execution on the other hand, which allows the combination of a wide range of tools.

To achieve goal (1), the structure of the extracted specification must reflect the structure of the analysed program. That is easy to achieve using the symbolic execution rules that are an inherit part of verification calculi while excluding simplification rules that would replace parts of the resulting specification by (simpler) logically equivalent formulae with less structural information.

Using deductive techniques, it is easy to fine-tune the specification generation process, yielding different levels of testing coverage. More scalability of quality assurance in the software development process can be achieved.

Background. The work reported in this paper has been carried out as part of the KeY project [1,3] (www.key-project.org). The goal of this project is to develop a tool supporting formal specification and verification of JAVA CARD programs within a commercial platform for UML-based software development.

B. Meyer and Y. Gurevich (Eds.): TAP 2007, LNCS 4454, pp. 207–216, 2007.

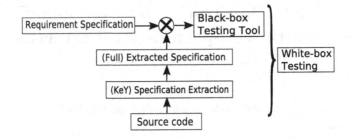

Fig. 1. Overview of our approach

The method for specification extraction using a program verification calculus described in this paper has been successfully implemented in KeY. In the following, we use the KeY verification system, its verification calculus (dynamic logic), and target language (JAVA CARD) to describe our approach. However, the ideas we present in this paper are independent of particular programming languages and verification calculi, and are easily adapted to other tools.

Another method combining testing and verification has been implemented in KeY that uses similar techniques but is different from our method in that it does not use specification generation as an intermediate step [8].

2   The General Approach

A symbiosis of software testing and verification techniques is a highly desired goal, but at the current state of the art most available tools are dedicated to only either one of the two tasks: verification and testing. They do not offer interfaces providing information that could be used for the other task.

The solution that we propose (see Figure 1), is to use *specifications* that are extracted from programs for interfacing. Generated specifications are in the middle between program analysis and deductive verification (using symbolic execution) on one side and test-case generation on the other side. On both sides, there are tools that can produce specifications resp. take them as input for test-case generation (tools that do not immediately offer required interface can be extended with little effort).

As explained in detail in the following section, deductive verification mechanism that use rules for symbolically executing programs can be used for specification generation. These derived specifications can be weak (i.e., partial) or strong (i.e., complete) depending on the methods used and the complexity of the program. Derivation of a strong—or even the strongest—specification can be done automatically in some cases but may require user interaction (if a complicated invariant has to be provided). For testing purposes, the strongest specification is usually not required, so that automatic specification generation is sufficient.

The extracted specification consists of pre- and post-conditions expressed in classical first-order or higher-order logic. Since that is the basis for virtually all specification languages—such as the Object Constraint Language (OCL), Z, the Java Modeling Language (JML), or Spec#—simple syntactic changes are sufficient to generate the appropriate input for a particular testing tool.

When the structure-preserving extraction of a specification is combined with a black-box testing tool that analyses the specification's structure, the result is effectively a white-box testing method (as illustrated by Figure 1). The black-box testing tool generates test cases for every pair of pre- and post-conditions in the specification and, thus, generates tests for every execution path that has been obtained by symbolically executing the program. Depending on the methods used for its extraction, the specification may not cover iterations of loops above a certain limit. However, by combining the extracted specification with a given requirement specification, black-box testing methods can generate tests that exercise random amounts of loop iterations including those not covered by the extracted specification alone. In this way, it is also possible to achieve a combination of code coverage and data coverage criteria from both techniques.

3   A Deductive Program Verification Calculus

Dynamic Logic. The program logic we consider in this paper is an instance of dynamic logic [11]. This instance, called JAVA CARD DL, is the logical basis of the KeY system's software verification component [2]. Dynamic logic is a multi-modal logic with a modality $[p]$ for every program p of the considered programming language. The formula $[p]\phi$ expresses that, if the program p terminates in a state s, then ϕ holds in s. A formula $\psi \rightarrow [p]\phi$ expresses that, for every state s_1 satisfying pre-condition ψ, if a run of the program p starting in s_1 terminates in s_2, then the post-condition ϕ holds in s_2. For deterministic programs, there is exactly one such world s_2 (if p terminates) or there is no such world (if p does not terminate). The formula $\psi \rightarrow \langle p \rangle \phi$ is thus equivalent to the Hoare triple $\{\psi\}p\{\phi\}$. In contrast to Hoare logic, the set of formulas of DL is closed under the usual logical operators.

State Updates. We allow *updates* of the form $\{x := t\}$ resp. $\{o.a := t\}$ to be attached to formulas, where x is a program variable, o is a term denoting an object with attribute a, and t is a term. The semantics of an update is that the formula that it is attached to is to be evaluated after changing the state accordingly, i.e., $\{x := t\}\phi$ has the same semantics as $\langle \texttt{x = t;} \rangle \phi$. We also allow parallel updates of the form $\{u_1 \,\|\, u_2\}$. Updates can be seen as a language for describing program transitions. The KeY system has a powerful update simplification mechanism that transforms sequences of updates into a single parallel update.

Program Verification by Symbolic Execution. The JAVA CARD DL calculus used for program verification in the KeY system is a sequent calculus that works by reducing the question of a formula's validity to the question of the validity of several simpler formulae. Since JAVA CARD DL formulae contain programs, the JAVA CARD DL calculus has rules that reduce the meaning of programs to the meaning of simpler programs, which corresponds to a *symbolic execution* [12]. For example, to find out whether the sequent ("$\Longrightarrow$" is the sequent symbol)

$$\Longrightarrow \langle \texttt{o.next.prev=o;} \rangle \texttt{o.next.prev} \doteq \texttt{o}$$

is valid, we symbolically execute the JAVA code in the diamond modality. At first, the calculus rules transform it into an equivalent but longer (albeit in a sense simpler) sequence of statements:

$$\Longrightarrow \langle \texttt{ListEl v; v=o.next; v.prev=o;} \rangle \texttt{o.next.prev} \doteq \texttt{o} \ .$$

This way, we have reduced the reasoning about a complex expression to reasoning about several simpler expressions (unfolding).

Now, when analysing the first of the simpler assignments (after removing the variable declaration), one has to consider the possibility that evaluating the expression o.next may produce a side effect if o is null (in that case an exception is thrown). However, it is not possible to unfold o.next any further. Something else has to be done, namely a case distinction. This results in the following two new goals:

$$\neg(\texttt{o} \doteq \texttt{null}) \Longrightarrow \{\texttt{v} := \texttt{o.next}\} \langle \texttt{v.prev=o;} \rangle \texttt{o.next.prev} \doteq \texttt{o}$$
$$\texttt{o} \doteq \texttt{null} \Longrightarrow \langle \texttt{throw new NullPointerException();} \rangle \texttt{o.next.prev} \doteq \texttt{o}$$

Thus, we can state the essence of symbolic execution: the JAVA code in the formulae is step-wise unfolded and replaced by case distinctions and syntactic updates. Loops and recursion are handled using invariants and induction.

4   Specifications Extraction in the Simple Case

In the following, we describe the automatic specification extraction that has been implemented in the KeY system. The main idea is: (1) We use symbolic execution to construct an update and a path condition for every execution path of the program (as described in the previous section). Consider, for example, the simple program x=x+2;x=x+3; that has only one path (and no condition). The resulting update is $\{\texttt{x} := \texttt{x+5}\}$. (2) To construct a specification, the updates are then applied to a (trivial) post-condition Φ consisting of equalities of the form $x' \doteq x$ (for every location x that may be changed by the program). The new variable x' represents the post-value of x. In the example, applying the update results in the equality $x' \doteq \texttt{x+5}$, which specifies the program.

We demonstrate this idea in more detail using the following program that switches the values of the variables x and y:

—— JAVA ——————————————————————————————

```
1    d=myMath.abs(x-y);
2    if (x<y) { x=x+d; y=y-d; }
3    else       { x=x-d; y=y+d; }
```

——————————————————————————————— JAVA ——

The specification extraction is realised by the construction of a proof tree for the proof obligation $\Gamma \Longrightarrow \langle\alpha\rangle\Phi$, where α is the above JAVA program and Φ is the (trivial) post-condition $x' \doteq x \wedge y' \doteq y$ (where x', y' represent the post-values of x resp. y). In general, Φ contains an equation for every location that the program may change (these locations may be given by the user or found automatically by analysing the program). If an approximation is used and not all locations occur in Φ that are actually changed, the constructed specification lacks information about locations not mentioned in Φ but is correct.

The premiss Γ may contain lemmas and specifications of library functions. In our example, it consists of the method contract for the method abs:

$$(x \geq 0 \rightarrow \langle\text{res=abs(x)}\rangle\text{res} \doteq x) \wedge (x < 0 \rightarrow \langle\text{res=abs(x)}\rangle\text{res} \doteq -x) .$$

Using this contract and applying some simplification steps to perform the case distinction between $x \geq 0$ and $x < 0$, we obtain the following partial proof tree:

$$\cfrac{\cfrac{(B_1) \qquad (B_2)}{\begin{array}{c}\Gamma', x \geq y \Longrightarrow \\ \{d := x - y\}\langle\text{if } ...\rangle\Phi\end{array}} \qquad \cfrac{(B_3) \qquad (B_4)}{\begin{array}{c}\Gamma', x < y \Longrightarrow \\ \{d := -(x - y)\}\langle\text{if } ...\rangle\Phi\end{array}} \qquad (B_5)}{\Gamma \Longrightarrow \langle\text{d=myMath.abs(x-y); if } ...\rangle\Phi}$$

where Γ' contains the additional condition $\neg(\text{myMath} \doteq \text{null})$ and the subtree (B_5) considers the case of a null pointer dereferencing in line 2 of the source code. The subtrees (B_1) and (B_2) examine the case $x \geq y$. Moreover, (B_1) analyses the execution path where the condition in the if-statement is true. Thus, (B_1) is the following closed proof branch:

$$\cfrac{\cfrac{*}{..., x \geq y, x < y \Longrightarrow ...}}{..., x \geq y, \{d := x - y\}(x < y) \Longrightarrow \{d := x - y\}\langle\text{x=x+d; y=y-d}\rangle\Phi} \quad (B_1)$$

(B_1) and (B_4) are closed by a contradiction on the left side of the sequent as they corresponds to execution paths that, in fact, are infeasible.

The specification parts corresponding to feasible execution paths are contained in open proof branches such as (B_2), which considers the case where the condition of the if-statement is false:

$$\cfrac{\cfrac{\cfrac{\cfrac{..., x \geq y \Longrightarrow x' = y \wedge y' = x}{..., x \geq y \Longrightarrow \{x := y \,||\, y := x\}\Phi}}{..., x \geq y \Longrightarrow \{d := x - y \,||\, x := y \,||\, y := y - (x - y)\}\Phi}}{..., x \geq y, \neg(x < y) \Longrightarrow \{d := x - y \,||\, x := x + (x - y)\}\langle\text{y=y-d}\rangle\Phi}}{..., x \geq y, \{d := x - y\}\neg(x < y) \Longrightarrow \{d := x - y\}\langle\text{x=x+d; y=y-d}\rangle\Phi} \quad (B_2)$$

The open goal in (B_2) yields the pre-/post-conditions $\neg(\text{myMath} \doteq \text{null}) \wedge x \geq y$ and $x' = y \wedge y' = x$. The branche (B_3) is similar and yields the pre-/post-condition pair $\neg(\text{myMath} \doteq \text{null}) \wedge x < y$ and $x' = y \wedge y' = x$.

These two pairs could be simplified into one but that would remove structure from the specification. If the intended coverage criterion is path coverage, the black-box technique must be provided a distinct specification for each path.

Branch (B_5) handles the case that a `NullPointerException` is thrown at line 2 of the source code. We obtain the open goal

$$\texttt{myMath} \doteq \texttt{null} \Longrightarrow \langle\texttt{throw e;}\rangle\Phi$$

which expresses that an exception is thrown if `myMath` $\doteq$ `null`.

The generated specification can now be translated into input languages for testing tools. In the example, we use the Java Modeling Language (JML):

—— JAVA + JML ——————————————————————————

```
1  /*@        requires REQ;
2  @          ensures  ENS;
3  @ also requires x>=y && myMath != null && REQ;
4  @          ensures  y=\old(x) && x=\old(y) && ENS;
5  @ also requires x<y  && myMath != null && REQ;
6  @          ensures  y=\old(x) && x=\old(y) && ENS;
7  @ also requires myMath == null        && REQ;
8  @          signals  (NullPointerException e) true && ENS; @*/
9  public swap() throws NullPointerException  { d=myMath... }
```
—————————————————————————————— JAVA + JML ——

`REQ/ENS` are the `requires`/`ensures` pairs from the original requirement specificaiton. A conjunctive cross-product has to be made from both specifications.

The generation of the test cases, the computation of the preamble, and the execution of the test suite is then performed by a black-box testing tool like UTJML [7] or JMLTT [4]. Using the structure of the specification, the test data $\{1, 0, M\}$, $\{0, 1, M\}$, $\{1, 0, null\}$ may be generated for the program variables $\{\texttt{x}, \texttt{y}, \texttt{myMath}\}$ (where M refers to an appropriate object). In this way all execution paths are excercised.

If the symbolically executed source code does not contain loops or recursive methods, then the set of the extracted pre-/post-conditions *can* ensure path coverage and even stronger coverage criteria. Which criterion is satisfied by the extracted specification depends on properties of the used method contracts and in particular on the subset of calculus rules that are actually used in the construction of a proof tree. Certain rules could simplify the program or the formulas too much with the effect that structural properties of the program are lost. The relation between the used verification calculus rules and coverage criteria is one of our current research topics.

Integer overflow checks and the creation and initialization of objects and classes, which has been ignored here due to space limitations, are covered by the KeY JAVA CARD DL calculus.

5 Handling Loops and Recursion

The automatic extraction of a (partial) specification from a program that contains loops is implemented in the KeY tool by unwinding or unfolding. Invariant generation in general requires user interaction but in simple cases invariants can be automatically generated.

Since loops can create arbitrarily long execution paths, it is impossible to create a test set that satisfies a criterion like full path coverage in this case. However, by loop unwinding, a set of partial specifications can be generated that satisfies the path coverage criterion for a bounded amount of total loop iterations. Our experiences show that most loops behave similarly on loop iterations with different bounds. We will refere to the bound by K.

We describe the specification extraction by loop unwinding using the following program P as an example:

```Java
k=0; j=0; n=a.length; line.prev=null;
while (k<n) {
  if (j=23) {
    j = 0; oldline = line;
    line = new Line(23);
    oldline.next = line; line.prev = oldline;
  }
  if (j>23 || k>n) throw new Exception();
  line.setCharAt(j,a[k]);  k++; j++;
}
```

This program copies values from the array a into dynamically created Line objects, where only 23 values can be saved in any one line (we assume that the first Line object is created and the array is initialised before P is started). Again due to space restrictions, we cannot present all details in program execution that are considered by the KeY tool.

By unwinding a loop, an if-cascade is created (for nested loops this has to be done recursively). From the program P, we obtain the following if-cascade:

```Java
if (k<n){if(j=23){..};if(j>23||k>n)..setCharAt(j,a[k]);k++;j++;
  if(k<n){if(j=23){..};if(j>23||k>n)..setCharAt(j,a[k]);k++;j++;
    ...
    while(k<n){...}
  }
}
```

The specification extraction process results in a proof tree with K sequents of the following form as its leaves, where body represents the loop body:

$$\Gamma, \neg(k < n) \implies \langle\rangle\Phi$$
$$\Gamma, k < n, \neg(k+1 < n) \implies \langle body;\rangle\Phi$$
$$\Gamma, k < n, k+1 < n, \neg(k+2 < n) \implies \langle body; body;\rangle\Phi$$
$$\dots$$

These sequents already show the desired pre-conditions; post-conditions are extracted as follows. From the formula $\langle\rangle\Phi$ we get the post-condition for the case that the loop iterates zero times, which is:

$$k' \doteq 0 \land j' \doteq 0 \land n' \doteq \texttt{a.length} \land a' \doteq \texttt{a} \land line' \doteq \texttt{line} \tag{1}$$

Simplification of the formula $\langle body\rangle\Phi$ results in the post-condition that holds for all execution paths where the loop iterates exactly once. We assume that the following contract is given for the method `setCharAt`:

$$\neg(\texttt{line} \doteq \texttt{null}) \land \langle\texttt{ret=line.getLength()}\rangle(0 < \texttt{x} \land \texttt{x} < \texttt{ret}) \rightarrow$$
$$\langle\texttt{line.setCharAt(x,c); res=line.getCharAt(x)}\rangle(\texttt{res} \doteq a[\texttt{x}]) \tag{2}$$

Then, the post-condition that is extracted for the case where the loop executes exactly once is the following conjunction:

$$k' \doteq 1 \land j' \doteq 1 \land n' \doteq \texttt{a.length} \land a' \doteq \texttt{a} \land line' \doteq \texttt{line} \land \tag{3}$$
$$\langle\texttt{ret=line.getCharAt(0)}\rangle(\texttt{ret} \doteq a[0]) \tag{4}$$

Conjunction (3) is an updated version of the post-condition (1), and (4) it the result of applying the method contract (2).

An invariant inference tool that generates inequalities is able to infere the invariant

$$0 \le k \le n \land 0 \le j \le n \land j \le 23$$

automatically. This invariant is not the strongest and therefore it is less accurate on the first K iterations than the specification we have obtained by unrolling. But in contrast to unrolling it contains information about *all* possible iterations of the loop. Using this invariant allows to generate different test cases that exercise the if-statements in the loop body. In order to execute the then-case of the if-statement, the condition $\texttt{j} \doteq 23$ must be true. Applying an invariant rule results in a proof obligation that the invariant is in fact preserved by the loop body. Applying calculus rules to that obligation corresponds to a symbolic execution of the loop body (including the if-statement). Leaves of that part of the proof then result in pre-/post-condition pairs from which test cases with array length 23 can be generated.

The purpose of this example was to show that loop unwinding and the invariant rule are complementary concepts by which different kinds of test sets can be produced that execute different parts of code. The automatic generation of loop invariants will be implemented in the KeY tool and an integration of the dynamic invariants inference tool Daikon is considered (similar to the integration of Daikon into ESC/Java [15]). Relevant work on automatic invariant inference can also be found in [9,10,6,16].

6 Related Work

In the Echo approach [18], a requirement specification is manually refined until an implementation is obtained. The correctness of the manual refinement process is then verified by extracting a specification from the implementation and comparing it to the requirement specification (this does not involve testing).

Synergies between using specifications and testing are also explored in [20]. This approach is similar to our's, because it coincides with the second step in our approach. The difference is, however, in the first step as the extracted specification is obtained by *dynamic* analysis and, therefore, the result is a black-box testing method.

Another related approach is described by Nimmer [15]. It involves, however, dynamic analysis (where we use static analysis) and, in the second step, theorem proving (where we use testing). The Korat system [5] uses symbolic execution to generate test cases (without generating a specification).

Deduction-based specification extraction is similar to test-case generation by symbolic execution (like in Symstra [19])—except that our approach allows to also derive post-conditions.

Our approach is complementary to these methods, and there is no work that more clearly separates static program analysis from test case generation (like it is done in our approach), in order to combine test coverage criteria from the two complementary techniques.

7 Conclusion

We have described how deductive program verification systems can be used to generate specifications, which then can be used as input for black-box testing tools, turning them into white-box testing methods. This approach can be adapted to other symbolic execution methods (e.g., weakest precondition calculi) that allow to extract specifications from programs, provided that the structure of the extracted specification reflects the structure of the program. Since the pre- and post-conditions are extracted a reference implementation can be used as a requirement specification. Furthermore this allows to establish a connection between variables before and after the program execution.

Future work is to investigate the precise relation between test coverage and different simplification rules used for specification extraction.

References

1. Ahrendt, W., Baar, T., Beckert, B., Bubel, R., Giese, M., Hähnle, R., Menzel, W., Mostowski, W., Roth, A., Schlager, S., Schmitt, P.H.: The KeY tool. Software and System Modeling 4, 32–54 (2005)
2. Beckert, B.: A dynamic logic for the formal verification of Java Card programs. In: Attali, I., Jensen, T. (eds.) JavaCard 2000(revised papers). LNCS, vol. 2041, pp. 6–24. Springer, Heidelberg (2001)

3. Beckert, B., Hähnle, R., Schmitt, P.H. (eds.): Verification of Object-Oriented Software: The KeY Approach. LNCS (LNAI), vol. 4334. Springer, Heidelberg (2007)
4. Bouquet, F., Dadeau, F., Legeard, B., Utting, M.: JML-testing-tools: a symbolic animator for JML specifications using CLP. In: Halbwachs, N., Zuck, L. (eds.) TACAS 2005. LNCS, vol. 3440, pp. 551–556. Springer, Heidelberg (2005)
5. Boyapati, C., Khurshid, S., Marinov, D.: Korat: automated testing based on java predicates. In: Proceedings, International Symposium on Software Testing and Analysis, Roma, Italy, pp. 123–133. ACM Press, New York (2002)
6. Bundy, A., Lombart, V.: Relational rippling: A general approach. In: Proceedings, International Joint Conference on Artificial Intelligence, Montréal, Canada, pp. 175–181. Morgan Kaufmann, San Francisco (1995)
7. Cheon, Y., Kim, M., Perumandla, A.: A complete automation of unit testing for java programs. In: Proceedings, Software Engineering Research and Practice (SERP), Las Vegas, USA, pp. 290–295. CSREA Press (2005)
8. Engel, C., Hähnle, R.: Generating unit tests from formal proofs. In: Gurevich, Y. (ed.) Proceedings, Testing and Proofs, Zürich, Switzerland. LNCS, Springer, Heidelberg, 2007 (to appear)
9. Ernst, M.D., Cockrell, J., Griswold, W.G., Notkin, D.: Dynamically discovering likely program invariants to support program evolution. IEEE Trans. Software Eng. 27(2), 99–123 (2001)
10. Flanagan, C., Qadeer, S.: Predicate abstraction for software verification. In: Proceedings, Principles of Programming Languages (POPL), Portland, USA, pp. 191–202. ACM Press, New York (2002)
11. Harel, D., Kozen, D., Tiuryn, J.: Dynamic Logic. MIT Press, Cambridge (2000)
12. King, J.C.: Symbolic execution and program testing. Communications of the ACM 19(7), 385–394 (1976)
13. Kosmatov, N., Legeard, B., Peureux, F., Utting, M.: Boundary coverage criteria for test generation from formal models. In: Proceedings, Software Reliability Engineering, Saint-Melo, France, pp. 139–150. IEEE CS Press, Los Alamitos (2004)
14. Legeard, B., Peureux, F., Utting, M.: Automated boundary testing from Z and B. In: Eriksson, L.-H., Lindsay, P.A. (eds.) FME 2002. LNCS, vol. 2391, Springer, Heidelberg (2002)
15. Nimmer, J.W., Ernst, M.D.: Static verification of dynamically detected program invariants: Integrating Daikon and ESC/Java. Electr. Notes Theor. Comput. Sci. 55(2) (2001)
16. Nimmer, J.W., Ernst, M.D.: Automatic generation of program specifications. In: ISSTA, pp. 229–239 (2002)
17. Parasoft: JTest manual (2004), http://www.parasoft.com/jtest
18. Strunk, E.A., Yin, X., Knight, J.C.: Echo: a practical approach to formal verification. In: Proceedings, Formal Methods for Industrial Critical Systems (FMICS), Lisbon, Portugal, pp. 44–53. ACM Press, New York (2005)
19. Xie, T., Marinov, D., Schulte, W., Notkin, D.: Symstra: A framework for generating object-oriented unit tests using symbolic execution. In: Halbwachs, N., Zuck, L.D. (eds.) TACAS 2005. LNCS, vol. 3440, pp. 365–381. Springer, Heidelberg (2005)
20. Xie, T., Notkin, D.: Exploiting synergy between testing and inferred partial specifications. In: Proceedings, ICSE Workshop on Dynamic Analysis (WODA), Portland, USA, pp. 17–20 (2003)

Lecture Notes in Computer Science

For information about Vols. 1–4542

please contact your bookseller or Springer

Vol. 4587: R. Cooper, J. Kennedy (Eds.), Data Management. XIII, 259 pages. 2007.

Vol. 4586: J. Pieprzyk, H. Ghodosi, E. Dawson (Eds.), Information Security and Privacy. XIV, 476 pages. 2007.

Vol. 4585: M. Kryszkiewicz, J.F. Peters, H. Rybinski, A. Skowron (Eds.), Rough Sets and Intelligent Systems Paradigms. XIX, 836 pages. 2007. (Sublibrary LNAI).

Vol. 4584: N. Karssemeijer, B. Lelieveldt (Eds.), Information Processing in Medical Imaging. XX, 777 pages. 2007.

Vol. 4583: S.R. Della Rocca (Ed.), Typed Lambda Calculi and Applications. X, 397 pages. 2007.

Vol. 4582: J. Lopez, P. Samarati, J.L. Ferrer (Eds.), Public Key Infrastructure. XI, 375 pages. 2007.

Vol. 4581: A. Petrenko, M. Veanes, J. Tretmans, W. Grieskamp (Eds.), Testing of Software and Communicating Systems. XII, 379 pages. 2007.

Vol. 4580: B. Ma, K. Zhang (Eds.), Combinatorial Pattern Matching. XII, 366 pages. 2007.

Vol. 4579: B. M. Hämmerli, R. Sommer (Eds.), Detection of Intrusions and Malware, and Vulnerability Assessment. X, 251 pages. 2007.

Vol. 4578: F. Masulli, S. Mitra, G. Pasi (Eds.), Applications of Fuzzy Sets Theory. XVIII, 693 pages. 2007. (Sublibrary LNAI).

Vol. 4577: N. Sebe, Y. Liu, Y.-t. Zhuang (Eds.), Multimedia Content Analysis and Mining. XIII, 513 pages. 2007.

Vol. 4576: D. Leivant, R. de Queiroz (Eds.), Logic, Language, Information and Computation. X, 363 pages. 2007.

Vol. 4575: T. Takagi, T. Okamoto, E. Okamoto, T. Okamoto (Eds.), Pairing-Based Cryptography – Pairing 2007. XI, 408 pages. 2007.

Vol. 4574: J. Derrick, J. Vain (Eds.), Formal Techniques for Networked and Distributed Systems – FORTE 2007. XI, 375 pages. 2007.

Vol. 4573: M. Kauers, M. Kerber, R. Miner, W. Windsteiger (Eds.), Towards Mechanized Mathematical Assistants. XIII, 407 pages. 2007. (Sublibrary LNAI).

Vol. 4572: F. Stajano, C. Meadows, S. Capkun, T. Moore (Eds.), Security and Privacy in Ad-hoc and Sensor Networks. X, 247 pages. 2007.

Vol. 4571: P. Perner (Ed.), Machine Learning and Data Mining in Pattern Recognition. XIV, 913 pages. 2007. (Sublibrary LNAI).

Vol. 4570: H.G. Okuno, M. Ali (Eds.), New Trends in Applied Artificial Intelligence. XXI, 1194 pages. 2007. (Sublibrary LNAI).

Vol. 4569: A. Butz, B. Fisher, A. Krüger, P. Olivier, S. Owada (Eds.), Smart Graphics. IX, 237 pages. 2007.

Vol. 4568: T. Ishida, S. R. Fussell, P. T. J. M. Vossen (Eds.), Intercultural Collaboration. XIII, 395 pages. 2007.

Vol. 4566: M.J. Dainoff (Ed.), Ergonomics and Health Aspects of Work with Computers. XVIII, 390 pages. 2007.

Vol. 4565: D.D. Schmorrow, L.M. Reeves (Eds.), Foundations of Augmented Cognition. XIX, 450 pages. 2007. (Sublibrary LNAI).

Vol. 4564: D. Schuler (Ed.), Online Communities and Social Computing. XVII, 520 pages. 2007.

Vol. 4563: R. Shumaker (Ed.), Virtual Reality. XXII, 762 pages. 2007.

Vol. 4562: D. Harris (Ed.), Engineering Psychology and Cognitive Ergonomics. XXIII, 879 pages. 2007. (Sublibrary LNAI).

Vol. 4561: V.G. Duffy (Ed.), Digital Human Modeling. XXIII, 1068 pages. 2007.

Vol. 4560: N. Aykin (Ed.), Usability and Internationalization, Part II. XVIII, 576 pages. 2007.

Vol. 4559: N. Aykin (Ed.), Usability and Internationalization, Part I. XVIII, 661 pages. 2007.

Vol. 4558: M.J. Smith, G. Salvendy (Eds.), Human Interface and the Management of Information, Part II. XXIII, 1162 pages. 2007.

Vol. 4557: M.J. Smith, G. Salvendy (Eds.), Human Interface and the Management of Information, Part I. XXII, 1030 pages. 2007.

Vol. 4556: C. Stephanidis (Ed.), Universal Access in Human-Computer Interaction, Part III. XXII, 1020 pages. 2007.

Vol. 4555: C. Stephanidis (Ed.), Universal Access in Human-Computer Interaction, Part II. XXII, 1066 pages. 2007.

Vol. 4554: C. Stephanidis (Ed.), Universal Acess in Human Computer Interaction, Part I. XXII, 1054 pages. 2007.

Vol. 4553: J.A. Jacko (Ed.), Human-Computer Interaction, Part IV. XXIV, 1225 pages. 2007.

Vol. 4552: J.A. Jacko (Ed.), Human-Computer Interaction, Part III. XXI, 1038 pages. 2007.

Vol. 4551: J.A. Jacko (Ed.), Human-Computer Interaction, Part II. XXIII, 1253 pages. 2007.

Vol. 4550: J.A. Jacko (Ed.), Human-Computer Interaction, Part I. XXIII, 1240 pages. 2007.

Vol. 4549: J. Aspnes, C. Scheideler, A. Arora, S. Madden (Eds.), Distributed Computing in Sensor Systems. XIII, 417 pages. 2007.

Vol. 4548: N. Olivetti (Ed.), Automated Reasoning with Analytic Tableaux and Related Methods. X, 245 pages. 2007. (Sublibrary LNAI).

Vol. 4547: C. Carlet, B. Sunar (Eds.), Arithmetic of Finite Fields. XI, 355 pages. 2007.

Vol. 4546: J. Kleijn, A. Yakovlev (Eds.), Petri Nets and Other Models of Concurrency – ICATPN 2007. XI, 515 pages. 2007.

Vol. 4545: H. Anai, K. Horimoto, T. Kutsia (Eds.), Algebraic Biology. XIII, 379 pages. 2007.

Vol. 4544: S. Cohen-Boulakia, V. Tannen (Eds.), Data Integration in the Life Sciences. XI, 282 pages. 2007. (Sublibrary LNBI).

Vol. 4543: A.K. Bandara, M. Burgess (Eds.), Inter-Domain Management. XII, 237 pages. 2007.